THE MALE COUPLE
How Relationships Develop

THE MALE COUPLE
How Relationships Develop

David P. McWhirter, M.D.
Andrew M. Mattison, M.S.W., Ph.D.

Prentice-Hall, Inc.
Englewood Cliffs, NJ

©1984 by

David P. McWhirter, M.D.
and
Andrew M. Mattison, M.S.W., Ph.D.

Prentice-Hall International, Inc., *London*
Prentice-Hall of Australia, Pty. Ltd., *Sydney*
Prentice-Hall Canada, Inc., *Toronto*
Prentice-Hall of India Private Ltd., *New Delhi*
Prentice-Hall of Japan, Inc., *Tokyo*
Prentice-Hall of Southeast Asia Pte. Ltd., *Singapore*
Whitehall Books, Ltd., *Wellington, New Zealand*
Editora Prentice-Hall do Brasil, Ltda. *Rio de Janeiro*
Prentice-Hall Hispanoamericana, S.A., *Mexico*

Fifth Printing . . . . . December 1987

Library of Congress Cataloging in Publication Data
McWhirter, David P.
  The male couple.
  Bibliography: p.
  Includes index.
  1. Homosexuals, Male—United States—Longitudinal
studies. I. Mattison, Andrew M. II. Title.
HQ76.2.U5M38   1984   306.7'66   83-15944

ISBN 0-13-547563-5

Printed in the United States of America

For our growing family

CONTENTS

INTRODUCTION

Many of the old myths about gay men and their relationships have been proven wrong by the findings of the study that forms the basis of *The Male Couple*. There are many male couples who have been together for years, living out their lives quietly and productively in the mainstream of American life. They work, socialize, love and care as the couples they are. This is a study of 156 such male couples in loving relationships lasting from one to thirty-seven years. Over the course of five years we personally interviewed these couples in their homes to get answers to the questions other male couples were asking in psychotherapy. Many of the couples were seen several times over the five-year period, adding a longitudinal element to our research. At the outset we were interested in how they lived. We wanted to know how they handled work, chores, money, and their sexuality. We were interested in how they dealt with lovers, families, former wives, children, parents, and friends.

Aside from these questions, more complex issues began to emerge during the course of the study. How do two men, with similar social scripting, get along together? Does their homosexuality work for or against them? Does male bonding help their relationships? How can they resolve their competitiveness and angers? What keeps them together over time? What kinds of problems do they have? How are they like heterosexual couples, and how are they different?

We have been traveling around the United States giving lectures and leading discussions about our findings for several years. We always have been careful to explain that the very nature of our research sample, its size (156 couples), its narrow geographic location, and the natural selectiveness of the participants prevent the findings from being applicable and generalizable to the entire gay male community. Strictly speaking, the sample is neither large enough, randomly selected nor geographically dispersed enough to represent necessarily the majority of male couples. As behavioral scientists we cannot report our conclusions as being derived from a representative sample. However, as clinicians working with a variety of male couples, we have found daily applicability to every couple we have seen in the past three years. As lecturers and discussion leaders with scientific and clinical groups as well as with audiences of single gay men and couples, we have found agreement with our findings everywhere we have gone.

One of the major new discoveries of the study was that, regardless of the differences among the men, the relationships themselves form separate entities and pass through a series of developmental stages in much the same way that a person grows and develops. We have been able to identify six stages, each possessing a unique set of characteristics with both positive and negative features. Couples move through these stages as the relationship grows. They may find it necessary at times to revert to some characteristic of an earlier stage, but even with these excursions, the movement from the first stage to the sixth stage follows an orderly development that is essential for growth. The importance of this discovery lies in the fact that, prior to this time, many persons believed that they had personality flaws when the problems that arose really were nothing more than some of the unpleasant manifestations of the various stages of the relationship, like the "terrible twos" or the "feisty fives" of the developing child.

Regardless of the setting in which we have presented our findings, opposite-sex and female couples invariably are quick to agree to the presence of stages in their relationships that are similar or identical to those we found in male relationships. Although it is not supported by an exacting research at this time, we firmly believe that this new theory of relationship stages is equally applicable to all relationships. There may be differences in the time intervals, and even the characteristics may be different, but the general principle of developmental stages still applies.

Audiences have given us rapt attention for long periods as we introduced and explained this theory of relationship stages. They often jump to their feet applauding and surround us afterwards to ask questions and offer supportive anecdotes and comments. We receive letters from couples and individuals seeking advice and referral. Couples have come to us for evaluation and treatment from as far away as Hawaii and St. Louis. A brief summary of our relationship staging theory appeared in *The Advocate*[1] and more recently as an article in the *Journal of Homosexuality*.[2] Inquiries have come from Europe and even from Iron Curtain countries, Latin America, and the Orient for further information and reprints.

All of us, male and female, gay and nongay, live in a world hungering for more knowledge and insight into how our relationships function and how we can gain the greatest satisfaction and fulfillment together. The findings in this book will change people's thinking about all relationships, shedding new light on old problems. We, and most others familiar with our research, believe that what we have discovered about the coupled relationships of gay men are valuable insights directly applicable or adaptable to any couple.

As strong as these statements may sound, we still want to offer a few caveats about this work. Although we believe that the general principles of relationship staging will continue to be applicable, we offer our findings tentatively as hypotheses for future study, replication, and correction. We clearly recognize the risks of having our findings etched in stone as *the* way male couples should and must be, setting new standards, as it were, against which others will measure themselves. Once again, the limitation of a nonrandom, geographically limited, moderately sized sample must be recognized. Also, we anticipate the development of a still young gay culture to influence male couples in the future. We did not intend or want a new typology for male couples to emerge from these hypotheses. The dangers of creating new myths about male relationships through studies such as this clearly are to be avoided. We are treading on new territory in the application of staging theory to dyadic relationships. There are some in the behavioral science community who would take strong issue with our methods and with the application of staging to something other than individuals. Descriptive research usually generates hypotheses such as our applications of staging theory to these couples. Such applications derive from the research data and from our knowledge as investigators. The discovery of the hypothesis of staging was a dramatic and serendipitous moment as we walked along a magnificent Hawaiian beach in deep discussion about how to examine our huge accumulation of data. It was Andrew who actually suggested, in a startling statement of clarity, "These couples are only going through stages." David's quick pickup on the concept led us to many solid hours of reviewing our data in the light of this new idea. With that review came the clear emergence of characteristics described similarly by the participants. Of course, the initial outlines have passed through many developmental stages themselves, and we hope that these changes will continue as other researchers follow in our footsteps.

One more caveat about the stages themselves is necessary here. The movement from one stage to the next may appear to the reader to occur in an even, step-by-step forward motion. In fact, most individuals and couples move a few steps backward in the process of moving ahead. Also, an individual may not traverse stages at the same speed at which his partner is traveling. And, further, individuals can be dealing with issues of more than one stage at the same time. Most importantly, each characteristic in every stage is a process, not an event. Dealing with stage-related issues happens over time, sometimes again and then again, and sometimes the process does not stop. Therefore, if your relationship does not fit the stages, we caution you not to try to make them fit. Instead, pick out those characteristics that seem to apply and discover how they assist or interfere with the relationship.

Not many years ago, the very fact that we are a male couple ourselves would have been an issue used by some to discredit our study. Fortunately, as the times and attitudes have changed, most people recognize that our status as a male couple actually gives the research a more firm footing in truth. The ability to obtain data that would accurately describe the participants' relationships was enhanced because they were aware that, like themselves, we too were a male couple. Knowing this, they could describe themselves more openly and honestly, with their strengths, and most especially their weaknesses and problems, assured of our nonjudgmental attitude. We knew many of the questions to ask and how to ask them. It would have been more difficult for nongay researchers to obtain the same degree of accuracy we achieved.

Although we are a male couple, we did bring some negative biases to the research. For instance, our psychiatric and psychological training had imbued us with a certain suspicion about the psychopathology of homosexual persons, even though our own lives and relationship belied the old assumptions. In our earliest days together, like other Stage One couples, we considered ourselves unique and the exceptions to all that we had been taught. Finally it dawned on us that the old assumptions were just dead wrong, biased by unexamined theory and faulty research with homosexual participants in psychiatric treatment who were by definition disturbed persons. No one in our sample was in psychotherapy or counseling at the time we interviewed them.

The idea of gay men forming couples may be new to many people. The word *couple* usually refers to a male–female relationship. For many readers, the novelty of the concept of the male couple will be intriguing or shocking. For male couples themselves, this book offers validation of aspects of their own lives together that they already know. It offers information about how other male couples are similar to or different from them. For every reader, gay or nongay, single or coupled, it provides a new way of looking at the development and life of a very old phenomenon—a couple.

We have enriched our own lives enormously by getting to know other male couples. Our participants welcomed us into their homes and lives with generosity and enthusiasm. They all were interested in and supportive of the project. Many were eager to have their stories told, wishing to share their experiences with younger couples—like the men who built a house on the adjoining lot, successfully searching for a younger male couple to occupy it. Throughout the text we pass along to the reader the actual comments our participants made as a way for them to tell you their stories as they told them to us. Although we have a variety of participants, we have used quotations from the most articulate to convey the generally enthusiastic responses to our questions. To assure privacy and to prevent participants from being recognized, we have changed names, mixed up jobs, and modified events in the illustrations.

Long-term, even life-long relationships, especially in marriage, have been endowed culturally with high value. Heterosexual and homosexual people alike have been taught by religion and society that the inability to maintain a lasting relationship is indicative of personal failure. For heterosexual persons these failures generally are believed to result from interpersonal relationship problems. For homosexual persons the failure to maintain an ongoing relationship was ascribed, more often than not, to their homosexuality.

As cultural values begin to shift, we have witnessed a general decline in negative attitudes toward divorce. The statistical evidence of the widespread increase in the rate of divorce and the ubiquitous presence of divorced and remarried persons is contributing to the gradual softening of the stigma of divorce. The arguments supporting the naturalness of lifetime commitments in marriage are being weakened by the very fact that they are less frequent. Having a primary relationship with several different partners over a lifetime is gradually becoming more usual than the single lifetime partnership.

Longevity in and of itself tells us little or nothing about relationships. To really understand them, it is necessary to assess the complexity of relationships in some depth.

Millions of human beings live, work, and play in our society as single, fulfilled individuals—whether they are heterosexual or homosexual. Many people are not seeking relationships that have the characteristics of those in this study. Their needs for companionship, love, and growth are met without a primary relationship. We do not assume that being coupled is better than being single. We are examining the phenomenon of male coupling simply because it exists, without endorsing or denying the time-honored belief that maturity is accompanied by the establishment of an intimate primary relationship.

We stopped conducting new interviews in late 1979. At that time we had been invited to join the Gender Identity Group at UCLA. This group has been meeting intermittently for about twenty years. It is composed of well-known clinicians and researchers in the area of gender identity and homosexuality. Members of the group included Robert Stoller, M.D., Judd Marmor, M.D., Evelyn Hooker, Ph.D., Laud Humphreys, Ph.D., Brian Miller, Ph.D., the late Martin Hoffman, M.D., Martha Kirkpatrick, M.D., Joseph Carrier, Ph.D. and others. After we had presented our preliminary findings, it was Dr. Evelyn Hooker who stopped us in our tracks: "Stop the interviews. You have plenty of data. Write the book. Your public awaits."

We followed that sound advice, and since then we have been contacted by dozens of others who were willing to be interviewed. Many of these are couples who have been together for forty or fifty years. In a few instances we have included their insights and even a few examples. Perhaps our next investigation will be with male couples who have been together longer than thirty years.

In retrospect, we have seen our own relationship move through two of the stages since we began this work. At first, we were affected by every interview, examining our own relationship anew each time. That process rapidly exhausted itself, and our observations seemed to become more objective. Still, the most exciting part was conducting the interviews. We became experts at it. As indicated above, we stopped the data collection in 1979 shortly after the discovery of stages. For the reader who is interested in the data base for the theory of staging, we suggest reading chapters 9 through 14 before reading the six chapters on stages.

Writing this manuscript has been by far the most difficult task. It has passed through many formats and revisions. We have had the editorial support of a sparkling array of friends. The outstanding ones include Dr. Bruce Voeller, Dr. C. A. Tripp, Scott Anderson, and Dr. Don Clark. Each gave us editorial suggestions at the right moments, adding leaven and spice. Dr. Don Clark generously spent dozens of hours helping us rewrite and clarify our thinking. Tom Tighe laboriously checked the references and compiled the bibliography. Dr. John Gonsiorek read the completed manuscript and gave us valuable commentary.

Many others have provided moral, spiritual, and physical support. Dr. Karol Parham and Dr. Fred Klein were very early supporters, even before the research began. Our two children, Paul and Monica McWhirter, have waited, cooked, talked, typed, and written new computer programs, putting up with our grumpiness and seeing us off on yet another trip to Hawaii "to finish the book." Paul Koprowski, Paul Stravinsky, and Vince Huntington have lived with us through the stages of these many years, always available and willing to satisfy our needs. It was David B. Goodstein who recommended us and our work to his own publisher, Prentice-Hall, and his own literary agent, Mr. Mitch Douglas at International Creative Management.

The chapters that follow are about relationships between men who happened to be gay. It is our hope that what we have discovered about these lovers will be useful to all lovers everywhere.

D. P. McW. and A. M. M.

Sunset Beach, Oahu, Hawaii
St. Valentine's Day
February 14, 1983

CHAPTER 1

OUR INTEREST IN MALE COUPLES

The joining of two individuals is a phenomenon that has captured human attention in all places and at all times. Scientists are intrigued. Poets are awed. We, too, have been unable to escape the need to learn more about the nature of human relationships.

The scope of the research presented in this book would have been impossible without the social changes of the last two decades. The 1980s appear to comprise a decade during which many taboos will be reassessed less passionately than was possible when discussion was too breathtaking or shocking for reasoned and scientific inquiry.

This study offers information that is of value to all persons interested in relationships or pairing. It suggests the probable evolution of durable human coupled relationships, heterosexual and homosexual, as we speed into the unstructured future.

Sexual pairing is a biological imperative among animals. There is, however, a distinction to be made between sexual pairing and the formation of a relationship. Sexual pairing, in the biological sense, results in the reproduction of the species. Only one of the natural bases for sexual pairing is survival of the species.

There are a number of species, however, who pair and become couples for their entire lives, and not merely for the purpose of reproduction. For these species, pairing becomes more than a simple requirement for reproduction. The pair becomes a couple; in these instances far more than procreation and care of the young is involved. Scientists have described coupling among a wide range of birds and animals. Their behaviors have been interpreted as indications of the animals' needs for companionship and mutual protection. This sort of relationship occurs in some species long before the pair is capable of reproduction and is sustained long after reproduction ceases (Lorenz).[1]

It takes the right moment in history for people to want to examine a human situation that has been with us since ancient times, often shrouded by fear and superstition. But the world seems ready, finally,

1

to look with less anxiety and more objectivity at male couples. There is genuine interest in how they live and share their lives together.

In our clinical practice as psychotherapists, we work with gay and nongay persons, individuals and couples. Male couples, however, offer a special challenge. They ask us repeatedly about the relationships of other male couples. Who are these men, and what are their backgrounds? What are their jobs and professions? What are their daily lives like? What keeps them together as couples? Who are their relatives and friends? What are their social lives and their sexuality like? What about their homosexuality and its impact on them? There are also the complex questions about relationship problems. What about the problems they are having? Do other couples have those same problems too? How do they handle those problems? Are we like the others or is each couple different? How do two men find the best way to handle money? How do they handle visits from parents? Do gay couples stay together? And if they do, for how long?

These male couples who were our patients needed and deserved answers. Our training, while complete by the usual standards, was of little help in meeting the challenge posed by male couples. The available professional literature offered even less help. Before this study, our limited experience and knowledge about male couples was tainted with some of the same unsubstantiated assumptions our patients held. We were familiar with writing by professionals who spoke of the non-existence or brevity of male–male relationships and postulated unhelpful reasons. On the other hand, we discovered that no research had sufficiently examined the anatomy of male relationships to justify scientifically the acceptance of various assumptions about personality defects in homosexual men that might impair their ability to establish an intimate, loving relationship.

One of the explanations for the lack of research that might have provided helpful answers may be the general lack of research about male couples and female couples. This, of course, was due to the pervasiveness of an illness theory of homosexuality. With the strongly held belief that homosexuality was an illness, investigations focused on incidence, etiology, and treatment methods following the medical model of disease. Although there were a few beacons in the early darkness questioning the illness theory, it was not until 1973 that homosexuality was eliminated from the list of mental illnesses of the American Psychiatric Association.[2] With this change in focus from what went wrong and how to cure it, research about homosexuality has turned to the descriptive and phenomenological approach to examine homosexual persons as they are and as they live. The development of new theories about sexuality and relationships depends upon such work.

Patients, heterosexual and homosexual, suffer with depression and self-esteem problems, anxiety and phobias, and individual background and personality differences. From our clinical work we knew that there were many areas of similarity between homosexual and heterosexual persons. However, male couples were asking different questions about relationships than heterosexual couples were asking.

Heterosexual couples do not grapple with issues about roles, finances, ownerships, and social obligations in the same way as gay men do. The heterosexual couple that was concerned about acceptance by their mutual families was exceptional, whereas this was the rule for homosexual couples.

The expectation of outside sexual activity was the rule for male couples and the exception for heterosexuals. Heterosexual couples lived with some expectation that their relationships were to last "until death do us part," whereas gay couples wondered if their relationships could survive.

Heterosexual couples have a wide variety of models for their partnerships—Adam and Eve, Romeo and Juliet, Ozzie and Harriet, Kramer and Kramer. Gay men have only the same heterosexual models, including their own families, which they may try to emulate but find unsuitable.

Heterosexual individuals or couples rarely grapple with issues of self-disclosure to parents, friends, employers, and others, while gay persons must always deal with them. Nongay people rarely question the rightness or wrongness of their sexual orientation, but at some point gay persons do. Decisions about birth control and conception frequently arise for heterosexual couples but never for gay men.

Although there is a deep sense of negativity toward sexuality pervading all of society, there is an even deeper set of antihomosexual attitudes affecting everyone in general and gay persons in particular. Individual or mutually shared sex negativity and antihomosexual attitudes can be compounded in male couples, setting the scene for serious relationship problems. Analogously, heterosexual couples often deal with the blatant or subtle manifestations of individual or mutually shared sexism that can be powerfully damaging. Heterosexual couples are often encumbered by societal norms and expectations. Paradoxically, gay couples, lacking such norms and expectations, have the freedom to explore new and alternative pathways.

Since we could not respond to the questions asked by male couples with the information and answers available from the world of heterosexual couples, in 1974 we decided a study must be done. We knew we must go into the nonpatient male couple population and look for answers to the questions asked by our patients and ourselves. We would locate these couples and interview them. The study we undertook is a descriptive investigation of male couples, approached with the belief that homosexuality is not a mental illness but a different expression of erotic object attraction.

Three hundred and twelve gay men (156 couples), who were not patients and who mainly lived in San Diego, California, voluntarily participated in this study. Besides information about their backgrounds, occupations, daily lives, families, social activities, and sexuality, there were additional questions to ask. What keeps them together? What obstacles or benefits come from being a male couple? Are there unique characteristics of male–male relationships? Lacking societal approval, how do these men manage their social and personal lives? How do they see themselves and their relationships? How do they compare and contrast with opposite-sex couples?

These were some of the more obvious questions in the beginning, but as time passed other questions arose. What makes relationships work is much more than first meets the eye. Although love and erotic attraction are powerful ingredients at the start, the subsequent sequence of events in partners' lives together is far more complex. Questions about such issues as the effects of male bonding, the importance of early rearing and developmental social scripting, and the methods of mate selection are but a few that arose from the study.

We examined the men's problems and their joys and became interested in how they saw themselves and their relationships. For five years we personally conducted in-depth interviews with these 156 couples in an attempt to answer that one question: How do other male couples live their lives together?

Our own enlightenment about the phenomena associated with male couples gradually dawned during the process of interviewing. In addition to collecting data, we experienced a richness in these men's lives that did not fit prevailing beliefs that homosexual men did not have satisfying, enduring relationships. Although we found sadness and distress, as we do among heterosexual couples, we also witnessed a wealth of joy and happiness. Gay men can and do establish long-term, committed relationships, which are characterized by stability, mutual caring, generosity, creativity, love, support, and nurturing. Before completing this research we could not have made that statement with any degree of certainty. Our findings require a reevaluation of the long-held notions about relationships between men who love men.

There were interesting discoveries such as the necessary alternative ways male couples maintain intimacy and relationship longevity. Gay men have lacked models for their relationships other than the traditional heterosexual ones. And yet, many of the values and practices that are cornerstones of heterosexual relationships are absent in male couples. Indeed, it was startling to find that some of the qualities identified with stability and intimacy between opposite-sex partners can be detrimental to homosexual relationships. As an example, although most gay couples begin their relationships with implicit or explicit commitment to sexual exclusivity, only seven couples in this study considered themselves to have been consistently sexually monogamous throughout the years of their relationship. Sexual exclusivity is not an ongoing expectation among most male couples. In fact, some couples report that outside sexual contacts have contributed to the stability and longevity of their relationships.

Another outstanding finding is the assumption of equality between two men in a relationship, which is very difficult for opposite-sex partners. Whether because of biology, tradition, religion, or oppression, in most heterosexual relationships the woman has been expected to be dependent upon the man. Usually, he has been expected to make more money and support her. He has greater earning power. While the rise of modern feminism has called attention to this inequity, only a small percentage of male–female couples have succeeded in establishing relationships of complete equality. Lacking the difference in gender, there is equality between gay partners that is expressed in attitudes toward each other and is exemplified in their maintenance of financial separateness during the early years of their relationship.

In addition to answering many of our original questions about male couples, a number of theoretical constructs began to emerge. For instance, when we asked questions about family, friends, social lives, sexuality, how problems developed in the relationship and how those problems worked out, we got different answers from different couples. At first we simply assumed that every individual and couple is indeed different. As we reviewed our findings more carefully, however, we began to notice a pattern.

Couples who had been together for only a few years appeared to have similar responses. Couples together approximately ten years also had responses similar to one another. The responses of couples together ten years were different from the responses of couples together only a few years. And couples together approximately twenty years differed from those together ten years.

At this point we saw the obvious. Factors that keep a couple together in the first year are very different from factors that keep them together in the fifth year. Problems in the fifth year are very different from problems in the tenth year. Issues about family, friends, and social lives in their second year are very different from those in the twentieth year.

We recognized the simple and the obvious. There is, of course, something unique in every relationship, and each couple moves through a characteristic series of *stages in the relationship* mainly related to the length of time they have been together.

The following are sketches of three couples in the study. They do not represent a type of couple; it was not possible to categorize the sample in that fashion. Nor do they represent a "typical couple," but rather are sketched here to illustrate the variety found within the sample.

Ted and Phil

Ted tells how he first met Phil: "It was the blistering cold November of 1944. Being a soldier and fighting another 'war to end all wars' in the dugouts of Alsace-Lorraine wasn't exactly how I had planned my life. After two years of college and then a call to arms, to find myself almost half frozen to death in a bunker on the old Maginot Line was really depressing. The Germans were on the run, yet that didn't make Thanksgiving anything to look forward to. But it turned out to be one of the best Thanksgivings of my life."

Phil takes up the story from there: "Yeah, we met in an old church hall in Strasbourg on November 23, 1944. We haven't been separated for more than a few weeks ever since! But that was thirty-three years ago. Don't think we've forgotten the details, because we haven't."

Ted and Phil have been teachers for twenty-six years. They finished college together on the GI bill, and both got jobs in the same city in 1949. They have seen a lot of changes in each other and in the world around them. Each has kept pace with the times. We perceive them as still fairly much "in the closet" about their homosexuality. Yet within their relationship they are real romantics. Ten years ago they went back to Strasbourg to find the place where they had met twenty-five years earlier.

Joe and Steve

Joe tells a very different kind of story about how he and Steve met: "Well, it was like this. I went to his apartment one day to install a new garbage disposal. Before I knew it he had my clothes off and we were making it on the kitchen floor. Not that I hadn't done it before, but in this case I'm not sure who seduced whom. At any rate, that started the whole thing, and we were living together before that first month was out."

Steve says, "That's not exactly how I remember our meeting, but there was sex involved before the garbage disposal got installed that day. I not only liked his body, but I found out the guy had a brain, too."

Joe and Steve have been inseparable for the past three years. Joe works as a plumber part-time to earn his way through school, and Steve has a small business.

This couple experienced major ups and downs in their first three years. Joe was from a lower-middle-class Italian Catholic family in Boston, where fierce dedication to the right and the wrong way to do things kept the household lively. Steve had come from a genteel, solid Protestant family that had no room for arguments or displays of affection. Their two families differed in how they talked as well as how they lived. Steve's high regard for possessions of "quality" clashed with Joe's interest in rock music, plastic dishes, and double-knits.

Bob and Jack

Bob and Jack had been lovers since their mid-teens. Living in the same neighborhood and going to the same school, they were constant companions. For two years their parents assumed they were just close buddies, until they discovered they had a sexual relationship. The pair moved away from home after high school, and both took menial jobs. One at a time, they attended trade schools and upgraded their employment. Eventually, when they were in their early twenties, they bought a small condominium.

They had lived together as lovers for eight years when we interviewed them. By now, both sets of parents had recognized and accepted their sons' relationship to some degree. At age twenty-three, Jack had a nearly fatal auto accident. He recovered only after many months in the hospital and subsequent months of physical therapy.

Bob says, "We learned a lot about each other in a pretty short time. I really wasn't sure whether he'd make it or not."

Jack says, "I got so depressed for a while there that I really thought suicide was the answer. Bob pulled me through."

Creating the Relationship

Two men meet. Something happens between them. They want to know more of each other and to capture more of the sense of well-being that develops as they learn about each other. Much of the pull toward the other is not conscious. The mating dance has begun.

If their interaction continues, the two men move to a point of recognition and awareness. Somehow, against all of the odds described earlier in this chapter, they become a couple. The relationship has been conceived. There follows a period of gestation during which they protect this precious embryo.

Usually, it is recognized and blessed at a particular point of birth. Friends offer congratulations, and the growth and development of the newly emerged relationship is under way. That moment of emergence or birth is elusive. It is commonly the moment when the male couple chooses to live together under the same roof, in their first home. This is the moment we chose for this study as the operational definition of the beginning or birth of a relationship.

We selected an admittedly narrow definition of a male couple—two gay men living together under the same roof for at least one year and identifying themselves as a couple. We wanted to make sure we were studying a kind of relationship that could be compared with relationships in other studies. Had we included couples with some of the different styles described here, we may have been looking at different relationships. It would have been like comparing apples to oranges. We also wanted to study male couples that could be compared with heterosexual couples in other studies.

As mentioned previously in this chapter, as a consequence of their invisible minority status outside the mainstream of society, lacking norms and expectations, homosexual persons have been forced to experiment with a variety of relationship styles. Here are four examples that do not fit our research population.

1. Two Men Living Apart Who Describe Themselves as a Couple

Such individuals may spend the majority of their free time together. They may sleep in one partner's home, the other's, or sometimes each staying in his own. Reasons for this arrangement include such considerations as the occupation of each man, concern for family sensibilities, and the need for mutual independence.

Both Tom and Jeremy are teachers. They live in their home town, as do both of their families. Although each man is out of the closet to himself and other gay people, neither is out to his family. The potential threat to their jobs and family loyalty necessitates keeping up the two-residence front. These two men consider themselves to be in a primary relationship and look to each other for emotional support, affection, companionship, and sexual gratification.

Howard and John present a somewhat similar living arrangement and give very different reasons for it. They have been together for fifteen years, but for most of that time they have been living in adjoining houses. Both are professionals with active lives. One is a political activist, the other a quiet homebody. John disapproves somewhat of

Howard's gay political activism and has always felt invaded by visits from Howard's friends and fellow activists. In brief periods when the two were living in the same house, the amount of disagreement between them was intolerable. The more comfortable solution of adjoining homes has assured them of their own individual lifestyles while at the same time maintaining the primacy of their relationship. They have continued to spend their free time together, eating meals in one house or the other and sleeping together most nights.

The creative solution Howard and John have reached assures each of them of their independence without either man's surrendering his convictions. At the same time they have maintained their emotional bonding, which both agree provides them with much of the support they need to carry on their busy individual lives.

2. Two Men Who Describe Themselves as a Couple Although Each Lives in a Different City, Sometimes Across the Continent from Each Other

Sometimes these couples live as they do because of their jobs or perhaps one is attending school in a distant city. They see each other on a regular basis, as often as every weekend or as infrequently as three or four times a year. Others live in this fashion because they describe their separation as one important ingredient that helps them to enjoy the relationship. These couples exchange letters and telephone calls and may have sexual and affectionate relationships with others, while considering their lover as the primary partner.

James and Michael had met three years earlier at a business convention in a Midwestern city. They fell in love and spent a considerable amount of time together, even though they lived several hundred miles apart. Each recognized a commitment to his own work and an inability to relocate. They determined that they would try being lovers at a distance, spending as many weekends and vacations together as possible. The arrangement has worked for three years, but they plan to live together as soon as possible.

James and Michael are a couple who want to live together. Their current circumstances have prevented it so far. However, other couples live on opposite coasts of the United States by choice. They refer to each other as lovers and see each other a few times a year. Each has his own lifestyle, friends, and independence, and at the same time enjoys this special relationship with his primary emotional partner.

3. A Male Couple, One Member of Which
Is in a Heterosexual Marriage

One partner maintains his own home while the married partner lives with his wife and children. Sometimes the wife is fully aware of the homosexual relationship and accepts it, while in other instances the relationship is clandestine. Married men in love relationships with other men appear to be more numerous than previously believed.

Fred and Tom are both engineers and have been working together in the same company for 12 years. Prior to that time they had been working in separate companies, but decided that being together at work was important to their thirteen-year relationship, so they changed their jobs. Tom has been married for 20 years and has four children. His wife Joan has been accepting of the situation for many years. In fact, an affectionate bond has formed between Fred and Joan. The four children are now well into adolescence and always have seen Fred as an uncle. Although both Fred and Joan admit to jealousies and hurts over the years, each has grown accustomed to the relationship. Such couples are not always as comfortable as Tom and Fred. Wives often respond less acceptingly than Joan does.

4. Brief Relationships Lasting Less Than One Year

Brief relationships occur with the greatest frequency. For some people, moving from one brief relationship to the next becomes a style of life. For many, there is a series of brief relationships used for learning, as stepping stones leading to a more enduring partnership. And for others, a longer relationship is followed by a few brief ones before another longer-lasting one is formed. We have not studied these relationships or their usefulness in learning how to satisfy relationship needs.

Conclusion

We are excited about the process and results of this study. It is an adventure story for us. We went in search of answers and found more than we had hoped for. With some couples we shared the touching recollection of a funny moment from their past, reported with the punch line obscured by laughter. There were somber moments too, some sad and some poignant. And there were times when we were relieved to finish and leave because of the couple's tension or unrest. We had emotional highs when the interview brought us to mutual understanding that words cannot describe, captured only by the catch in our throats and the tears in our eyes.

Had we discovered only the stages of relationship for male couples, it would have made these years worth all the effort. This concept has added new depth to our therapeutic work with gay men, making formerly misunderstood relationship issues the manageable stage symptoms they are. It already has helped countless couples and other psychotherapists. Most importantly, it has helped us understand ourselves with each other, and has given us the courage to try to help other couples find greater understanding.

CHAPTER 2

A WAY TO VIEW CHANGE— STAGES OF RELATIONSHIPS

A relationship is the product of a union of two individuals. Like a child, it develops its own unique identity as it grows, and is cared for and watched over by parents who live with it. But, unlike a child, the relationship, as it grows, becomes a third partner, the living container in which the two individuals face each other through the flow of life.

At times the relationship offers shelter and solace. At times it is a trap and a drain of individual resources. Always it changes as it develops. Sometimes, when it does not function well, it troubles its parents. Like their anxious counterparts consulting a pediatrician, each man may feel he has failed, is inadequate, or is flawed in some way. Often the answer is that the relationship is going through an uncomfortable growth phase, or it may have developed a "normal," common malady from which it can be helped to recover more quickly.

There are three beings in a male couple: The two men and their offspring, which they shape and which, in turn, shapes them. Its birth, more often than not, is a joy. Its development through the lifetime may cause the couple unnecessary anxiety. Like all growth in nature, its development can be observed and assisted. Understanding helps.

Often the obvious is the easiest to overlook simply because it is right there. We become so accustomed to seeing and talking about it that it is taken for granted. Stages of relationships are obvious but completely overlooked. The concept of developmental stages is certainly not new, but its application to a better understanding of primary partnerships has not been researched. Most of the work on stages has been applied to child development. Continuing the analogy between the relationship and a child, understanding relationship stages is simplified. In 1946, when Dr. Benjamin Spock popularized the developmental psychologists' discoveries of the stages of childhood,[1] suddenly millions of rebellious, difficult two-year-olds became acceptable and even cute because they were passing through a developmental stage labeled the "terrible twos." Spock introduced a new sanity and calmness into childrearing by assigning characteristics, behaviors, and physical growth patterns to specific time periods or stages. These observations were not new to most of Spock's audience, but the common-sense, easy-to-understand way he packaged the information normalized many of the changes of infancy that previously had provoked so much anxiety in parents.

Couple relationships also move through a series of developmental stages, each with its own characteristics, problems, and associated tasks. Although not as clearcut as the stages of childhood and adult experience, relationship stages are nonetheless identifiable. This chapter and the next six will tell the story of stages.

Before beginning, however, remember the warnings in the introduction. This presentation is a tentative formulation, derived from data collected from 156 couples, mostly white, middle-class, and from the same geographic area. What we are offering is a way to view the male couples in this study that may be applicable to others. Certainly, we have found this to be true as we have presented our data to others around the nation over the past three years. It is not our intention to create a new typology for male couples that becomes the norm against which all such relationships are measured. To us that seems more destructive than useful. These stages are not real, but rather are conceptualizations intended to aid in the description and understanding of male partnerships. This is the first systematic, longitudinal look at the male couple. It is a pioneering study. The maps we are offering should be looked upon as similar to the crude maps of the early explorers, filled with inaccuracies and guesses but often enough catching the general shape of things. Much more research is needed. We leave that discussion to the end.

Stage Theory

Studies of individuals have produced an increasingly impressive body of knowledge and literature about stages. The list of contributors includes the early work of Gessell about the growth of the child,[2] Piaget[3] and Freud[4] about the psychological growth of the child with developmental tasks in each stage. More recently Levinson showed that men have seasons in their lives that are related to age.[5] Gould's work[6] was popularized by Sheehy[7] in *Passages*, and Vaillant has added to our ideas about adult staging.[8] Most of the theoretical formulations arising from these studies propose linear, step-by-step stages, one preceding the other, one necessarily building on the other. Stein and Etzkowitz have proposed a spiral theory of individual stage development, postulating that movement through stages does not progress linearly but rather in a back-and-forth, up-and-down fashion, with characteristics of stages overlapping and recurring in different ways as the person grows.[9] If the proposed spiral is visualized as a horizontal rather than vertical spiral, like a big spring lying on its side, this idea is applicable to our understanding of relationship stages.

In the sociologial literature the idea of stages of development of the family has been explored. Family staging usually is seen as dependent upon certain life milestones such as the birth of children, beginning of school, children leaving the home, and so forth. Campbell[10] published a theoretical and clinical work on the stages of intimate male–female relationships, and McKusick[11] proposed a model for counseling male couples including three phases of development. Other than these few references we have not found any work that looks at relationships in stages as this study proposes.

Overview of Stages

Serendipity played a great role in our discovery of the obvious relationship stages. We had been working with the accumulated data for many weeks, puzzling over how to integrate them. We were walking along the beach one afternoon talking about a solution when the idea of passing through various stages was mentioned. It was a "Eureka!" experience. We rushed back to spend the next twenty uninterrupted hours reevaluating the interviews and extracting the theme words from each. By listing the often-repeated themes and then clustering them according to time periods, we arrived at our first crude list of characteristics and stages. Since that first insight, the stages have gone through many refinements, and we recognize that there will be more to come. The time intervals selected for each stage are rough guidelines. Every couple is unique. Most couples, however, do share some characteristics of each stage.

There are six stages, each with a time frame and a name that describes what happens in that stage. The four characteristics listed for each stage describe the major components of that stage. Each relationship stage has many more characteristics than the four listed, but these were the ones reported most frequently by our participants. There are no "good" or "bad" characteristics, and often those from one stage become the building blocks for those in other stages. Remember that the stages are not necessarily linear or flat but rather spiral and multidimensional. Characteristics from one stage also are present in other stages, and they overlap. Remember, too, that not all male couples fit this model. Some have different experiences with few similarities to these formulations. We again caution against attempting to conform to these ideas. This model is a *beginning* in the understanding of the complex phenomenon of male couples.

Stage One—Blending (Year One)

Characteristics

1. Merging
2. Limerence
3. Equalizing of partnership
4. High sexual activity

Stage Two-Nesting (Years Two and Three)

Characteristics

1. Homemaking
2. Finding compatibility
3. Decline of limerence
4. Ambivalence

Stage Three—Maintaining (Years Four and Five)

Characteristics

1. Reappearance of the individual
2. Risk taking

3. Dealing with conflict

4. Establishing traditions

Stage Four—Building (Years Six Through Ten)

Characteristics

1. Collaborating

2. Increasing productivity

3. Establishing independence

4. Dependability of partners

Stage Five—Releasing (Years Eleven Through Twenty)

Characteristics

1. Trusting

2. Merging of money and possessions

3. Constricting

4. Taking each other for granted

Stage Six—Renewing (Beyond Twenty Years)

Characteristics

1. Achieving security

2. Shifting perspectives

3. Restoring the partnership

4. Remembering

There are no Stage One couples in our sample. Data for Stage One were collected in retrospect. The distribution of the sample by stages of the relationship is as follows: Stage Two, thirty-seven couples (24.0 percent); Stage Three, twenty-four couples (15.4 percent); Stage Four, forty-six couples (29.5 percent); Stage Five, twenty-nine couples (18.6 percent); Stage Six, twenty couples (12.8 percent). Table 1 displays these figures. The average length of the relationships is 8.9 years. The median, however, is just over five years; this means

TABLE 1
LENGTH OF TIME IN RELATIONSHIP

Years	Number of Couples
1–2	21
2–3	16
3–4	12
4–5	12
5–10	46
10–15	17
15–20	12
20–25	6
25–30	6
30–35	5
35–37	3

Number of Couples = 156
Mean = 8.9 years
Median = 5.0 years

Stage

Stage		
Two—37	23.7%	
Three—24	15.4%	
Four—46	29.5%	
Five—29	18.6%	
Six—20	12.8%	

*No Stage One couples in the sample.

that half of the couples in the sample have been together less than five years, and the other half have been together more than five years.

Some Factors Affecting Staging

As with any developing entity, a relationship can be influenced and altered by many factors. Each partner brings a unique set of past experiences. These can alter the way in which stages and characteristics form. For instance, couples with a wide disparity in ages from a few years up to twenty years or more may experience stages differently. Some of these couples pass through the early stages more quickly and smoothly, probably as a result of the older partner providing some stability and guidance to the younger man.

Diversity of previous relationship experiences can have positive and negative effects. Three or four previous painful experiences can slow down relationship stages, while past good experiences can provide useful lessons for facilitating stages in the new pairing. Past marriages can have ramifications for staging, especially if the formerly married partner expects to pattern his new male–male relationship after heterosexual couples.

Couples with widely different backgrounds, whether religious, ethnic, or socioeconomic, can bring very different values and expectations to the new relationship. Again, the effects can be positive or negative. Individual personality differences can also affect stage change by influencing the responses each man makes as his feelings change. This is especially true of how each individual deals with growing intimacy. Too much anxiety about it can retard the movement, while a great freedom to establish intimacy may move it onward more rapidly.

Stage discrepancy between partners is one of the most common influences on stage movement. When one partner moves more rapidly or more slowly through a stage than the other, stage development becomes discrepant. This is a problem we see so frequently in the clinic that the concept alone has been very useful in psychotherapy with gay couples. For instance, one man may be individualizing as in Stage Three, while his partner is still deeply committed to the blending of Stage One.

The influence of antihomosexual attitudes, discussed in chapter 9, can have deep influence on stages. The degree of individual homophobia can determine how quickly couples give themselves to the relationship or withhold from it. How much and how equally partners are out of the closet can assist or impede stage changes. (See chapter 9.)

These are but a few of the influences affecting stages. This is not intended to be an exhaustive list but rather an indication of how complex the concept really is.

Summary

Recognizing that these relationships have a life and history of their own was the key to finding the patterns of relationship stages. We took the findings and developed a model that would explain them to others in a useful way. We believe that stages of relationship is a new and helpful way to view changes. Difficulties experienced in relationships sometimes have been misunderstood and thought to be flaws within the individuals or defects in the relationships. In reality they are often nothing more than the "terrible twos" or the "feisty fives. "

CHAPTER 3

STAGE ONE—BLENDING
(First Year)

___

Characteristics

1. Merging
2. Limerence
3. Equalizing of partnership
4. High sexual activity

"It was love at first sex," sighs Wayne as he looks toward Paul, his lover, and describes their first meeting.

"Yeah, we met at the baths. We saw each other in the steam room and hot-footed it to Wayne's room." Paul, a twenty-six-year-old when they met, is a punster. He laughs uproariously at his own puns. "We made love for over an hour and never said a word. Then we lighted a cigarette and talked for three hours."

Within three weeks they were living together.

"I saw him as everything I ever wanted in a lover," says Wayne.

Paul agrees. "We did everything together. In fact, we even started using the same toothbrush during those first few months! People said we even sounded alike on the phone. It was the happiest time of my whole life," Paul says with enthusiasm as Wayne nods his agreement.

"I was so crazy about him I could forget what I was doing right in the middle of getting dressed—I'd be thinking about the sound of his voice."

"We were considered such social bores," Wayne says. "We were so involved with each other that we went to parties and spent most of our time sitting together holding hands and wishing we were alone."

"We spent most of our free time alone together," Paul agrees. "We never argued about anything. It was so great to never be alone. I would have fought World War III to keep the feeling of that first

21

year," he continues. "I really wanted a relationship. I guess we were both ripe for the picking."

Wayne has a Bachelor's degree in history and is currently employed as a real estate salesman. Paul is a landscaper. Both men have had previous male lovers, but each feels this new relationship is the best and is forever. They have a very comfortable apartment in a local beach community.

"Sorry about the way our place looks. When Paul moved in we just set his stuff around and didn't do much for a while." Wayne apologized for the clutter of boxes in a corner of the living room.

"We're more interested in the apartment now. Those first few months it was mainly the bedroom where we spent most of our time at home," Paul continues. "We haven't had much company since we've been together; in fact I am just beginning to see my old friends. I didn't used to let Wayne out of my sight in his free time, so he's just getting back to seeing his old friends, too. It felt almost like our lives just started when we met each other. The clouds are clearing now."

"Was it all that smooth?" we asked.

"Ugh." Paul makes a face. Then he smiles again. "Only good times if you don't look back at the pain," he says. Wayne kissed him and they both laugh.

The two men exchange a glance and a smile. "Well there were *those* times, too," Wayne says, grimacing.

"You mean when you took such good care of me I wanted to kill you?" Paul asks, laughing. "God save us. I loved the orange juice in bed, and I could tolerate the pills when I sneezed, but I had to use a sledge hammer to his head before he saw I could keep a checkbook without his doing my addition."

"You know," Wayne says, "being head over heels in love really hurts sometimes. It's hard to say how it happens, but there is that moment when even a day feels like eternity when you just adore him down to his toenails and you notice he's not looking at you with that melting look in his eyes. You can't help but wonder if it's all over; the rug seems pulled out from under."

"Yeah, I'd think 'Where are the razor blades?' " Paul adds, laughing. "It's funnier now, but it sure as hell seemed like the end of the world then."

The two men move closer together on the couch. Touching increases between them as they reminisce. At one moment we feel al-

most invisible as the couple is carried back to the romance and difficulty of those early months.

None of the couples in our study were currently in Stage One.
All had been together for a year or more. However, every couple had
experienced the special unbalanced jumble of emotions found in that
first year together. Our information about Stage One was gathered
from their memories of those months.

Merging

Merging means two forces joining together to create a new one. No
single word reports the experience of this first stage better. Before the
couple moves in together, similarities and differences have begun to
merge in the newly developing relationship. The two become like
one. In setting aside their former separateness, they describe a feeling
of well-being and satisfaction.

"It was as if we became one person," Joe says, his eyes misting. "It
was so peaceful. We talked with our eyes. We moved with the same
motions. Even when I was at work it felt like Patrick was inside me.
The experience was like walking on air—calm, reassuring. I felt
whole."

The intensity of the merger allows each to take on the new partner's qualities, as if those qualities were his own. Each person, sometimes without conscious awareness, now feels able to own qualities of
the beloved which he heretofore lacked.

"When I walked down the street wearing Patrick's gold chain, I
felt like my English improved and I could stay at the Ritz," Joe says.

"And when I wore Joe's work boots, I swear my biceps grew two
inches," Patrick laughs. "I was him."

"No, I was you!" Joe says.

Another man, Alex, admits, "I couldn't drive around the block
without getting lost. In the beginning Ray either drove the car or nav-
igated me when I drove. I had a new radar inside of me all of a sudden.
I thought I was like Ray! I surprised myself a few months later when he
wasn't in the car and I got lost."

Another striking feature is the sameness these men find in each
other. This sameness provides a seemingly natural harmony. This discovery of multiple similarities—even to the minutest details, like the

kinds of foods they prefer or the brands of soap they use—increases the intimacy, even for couples with wide differences in age or social background. It is like finding the self in the other and liking what is found there.

Joe, a twenty-seven-year-old construction worker, had met Patrick, a thirty-nine-year-old Episcopalian priest, three years earlier at a church social. Joe had a high-school education. He grew up in a large Methodist family in a small town. His parents both worked in the family hardware store. Joe remembered his home life as close-knit, religious, and hardworking.

Patrick was the only child of a well-to-do family from a suburb of a large city. His father already was a busy executive, and his mother was very active in social and civic community organizations. Patrick, a prep-school product, felt like he grew up in the house alone. His family was "special-occasion churchgoers only," according to Patrick. He was showered with gifts and material possessions.

After their first introduction, Joe pursued Patrick—lunches together on Saturday, movies at midweek, then a long holiday weekend together. Because of the apparent differences, some of their friends teasingly nicknamed them the "odd couple." Joe and Patrick, however, experienced each other as mirror images. They liked and disliked the same things, thought in the same ways, and had similar goals.

"We didn't look like each other, but inside we were so much alike that we could finish each other's sentences. I could look at him and know what he was thinking about. It was uncanny how much we were in sync."

Couples avoid conflict at any price. Irritants and differences of opinion or behavior are minimized, side-stepped, or overlooked altogether.

Another couple exemplifies this.

"I loved him like crazy—and, I must admit, he was a slob. But somehow his clothes on the bedroom floor, shaving cream and whiskers in the bathroom sink, didn't bother me at all *then*. I even thought his squeezing the toothpaste in the middle was cute."

Couples make compromises without ever recognizing that they are doing so. Paul says, "I remember saying, 'You probably don't want the roast again tonight do you, dear? We just had it for lunch.' And he'd say, 'Oh, but it was so good! Let's have it cold for sandwiches.' "

At the smallest sign of discord, the two move quickly to squelch it. For example, finding the usual sinkful of last night's dirty dinner dishes waiting in the kitchen, Jim remembers saying, "Oh, you're so lucky that I enjoy doing dishes. Let's see if the neighbors will bring theirs in, too." They both laugh.

"That evening we were both in the kitchen washing everything including the walls!" Ed laughs.

The intensity of the togetherness helps each person believe he understands his partner fully. For example, "I was a gung-ho football fan and wouldn't consider missing a home game of the San Diego Chargers. Billy hadn't so much as picked up a football in his life, but he began going to all the games with me. I loved his enthusiasm and his eagerness to get into the spirit of football. He learned the game fast—from names and positions of players to opposing teams' strengths and weaknesses. He could have written a column. He knew so much. We could talk this same language and look forward to sharing the games together—marital bliss! It wasn't until two years later that he admitted how much he actually hated football. He said he loved *me* and wanted to be with me and like the things that I like. But he never liked the game."

They agree to agree. They also agree not to disagree. "You don't like that blue plaid, do you? Which shirt does go best with these pants?"

Merger provides relief from former loneliness. As Jack says half-jokingly, "My prince had come at last. I could tell him to trade in his Mustang for a white charger and know that's what he really wants to do. He can suggest popcorn at the movies and suddenly I think I have wanted popcorn all my life. But the bottom line is that the porch light is on when I come home at night and either of us would do anything for that hug at the top of the stairs."

Not all couples merge with the same degree of intensity or at the same pace. Sometimes one partner is highly intense in merging while the other is not. Some couples are similar in the lack of intensity each feels in merging.

"Looking back, I slipped right under his skin and it hurt that he didn't do the same with me. It was different, but it was OK, I guess. I did need something more, though. I felt funny asking all the time, but I needed his words of reassurance that he *did* love me."

Ned and Jerry represent another variation. "We were each our own person from the start. We were separate and different. I liked that. We both did," Ned comments.

Jerry adds, "I guess both of us are sort of independent and don't like to get smothered or carried away. We enjoyed doing lots of things together, but each of us also needed to have some time alone with our buddies, whom we knew before Ned and I got together."

"I knew right away when I met Joel that something special was happening. But it was like a roller coaster ride. I loved it when the phone rang at work and he was on the other end, but when I didn't hear his voice for two days my crazy imagination took over. I wondered what he was doing on his lunch hour. Right before I met him, I knew what was in the freezer for dinner, what time I'd be getting up for work, and which busy work to choose to fill time. Suddenly what this one person did or didn't do was so central to my life."

Every variation appears. Usually the merger is not a smooth path. Not only may one partner be more intense than the other, but their difference of intensity also may throw the other off-course. "I'd be up to my nostrils in the 'love swamp' and he'd say something dumb like 'Well, we're getting to see if we like each other. Sooner or later we'll know.' All my circuits would blow, and I'd think, 'Who needs this creep?' "

The most frequent problems that couples experience with merging is resisting it. When merging, one is vulnerable to one's partner. He fears getting hurt, accidentally or otherwise.

Also, he may feel frightened if he is losing his identity to his partner. "I would so easily slip into doing what he liked and thinking just like him. It was scary at times to think that my own personality was slipping away."

A man who has gotten hurt in a previous relationship is likely to be very cautious. Without intending to subvert what is happening, he may block the merging. He fears getting hurt again. He is likely to allow closeness, draw back, try again, stall, and so on.

A couple who skips the merging characteristic may well feel that something is missing in the relationship. "That wonderful feeling of being one together just isn't there. It makes me wonder if something is wrong. Is this what love is supposed to feel like?"

Finally, the partner who manages the merging easily and who values it as a necessary aspect of a good relationship is apt to express dismay or find fault in the partner who does not, although his partner may love as deeply and as well.

Limerence

In *Love and Limerence* Dorothy Tennov coined a new word, *limerence*, to describe the state of falling in love or being romantically in love.[1] Included components are (1) intrusive thinking about the desired person who is a possible sexual partner (referred to as the limerent object), (2) acute longing for reciprocation of feelings and thoughts, (3) buoyancy (a feeling of walking on air) when reciprocation seems evident, (4) a general intensity of feeling that leaves other concerns in the background, and (5) emphasizing the other's positive attributes and avoiding the negative, or rendering them, at least emotionally, into positive attributes. Tennov includes sexual attraction as an essential component of limerence but admits exceptions.

Limerence is a respectable stepping stone on the path of relationship building. It is not just an infatuation, mere puppy love, or humorously going through a phase. The persons are not to be dismissed as simply love-sick. They are developing deep feelings that will influence the quality and tone of their relationship for as long as it lasts—and that may be a lifetime.

The high prevalence of limerence insures and adds to the characteristic of blending. It simultaneously decreases the partners' sensitivity to a possible mismatch caused by the inherent blind spots to faults generated by the limerent feelings.

Limerence is a powerful factor in the blending of Stage One. "I was head over heels in love with him. It was wonderful. Nothing else seemed to be as important. My house started to look like a pigpen. Plants died, friends were hurt because they were ignored, and I was only half there when my sister told me she was getting married."

"I loved everything about him, from the way he walked to the way he parted his hair. I thought his interest in country music was scholarly! He could do no wrong."

"His body was perfect, out of this world. We would make love in ways I had never dreamed possible."

"When he didn't look at me with that yearning gaze, I would feel a little crazy. Like I was out in the world alone again. I immediately had to know what terrible thing had gone wrong between us even if I knew it was only because he was counting the change at the checkout counter."

Limerence does not always happen to both partners to the same degree or at the same time. Indeed, some couples do not experience limerence at all at the beginning of their relationship.

One man in our study remembers the limerence this way: "We met in a supermarket in January, and the cold weather and rain vanished. We took trips every weekend. We disappeared at every party. We lived in each other's arms only—other times were to be endured until we could get to each other again."

Another says, "It was the most wonderful and awful year of my life. I wanted to hear that reassuring sound of his voice. I wanted to have him cast the magic spell and turn me into Prince Charming."

"But," his partner adds, "what I noticed was his kindness. I felt like a good person always when I was with him. I liked his social polish and his ability to be comfortable in any setting. Mostly I loved how much faith he seemed to have in me. I couldn't understand why he said it hurt if I forgot to say 'I love you' when we said goodbye on the phone."

Yet another couple found their love developed more quietly: "Well, it was three years of backpacking when we moved in together to cut down on expenses. Of course, we were sleeping together. We were watching a romantic old movie on TV one night, and I turned to look at him, drinking a cola on the sofa alongside of me, and I thought to myself and said out loud, 'I'll be damned, I really love you.' I mean, all of a sudden I realized this guy was more than just a good friend. He almost fell off the sofa, and when he recovered from my comment, he said, 'I love you too.' That was it. We finally recognized that we were a couple."

Couples who rely predominantly on the constancy of their shared feelings of high romance as the sole measure of the quality of their relationship encounter confusion when limerent feelings no longer are as prominent. "What's wrong with him? He doesn't seem to love me in the same way." Or, "I'm worried that something is not right with us now. I don't seem to be so head-over-heels with him any more."

Frequently the men in this study who were experiencing limerence for the first time believed that the wonderful feeling would last forever and be the everyday assurance that "he is the right man for me." However, no one reported limerence lasting forever or with the same intensity of the first few months or the first few years. Limerence may well thread its way through the years of a satisfying relationship for one or both—now intensely visible, now quiet and hidden—but surely it dulls its loud presence as Stage One nears its end.

Some couples came close to splitting up when the glow of limerence faded. "Toward the end of our first year together Tom and I each recognized that we felt differently. No more whistles and bells and all that stuff. We didn't want to stay together if we really didn't love each other. Boy, did we come close to calling it quits. That was five years ago. Maybe we're not crazy in love any more, but so what? I know that I love Tom. He is number one for me."

From our experience in counseling male couples, we find that the end of the first year of the relationship is one of the most common times for couples to split up or seriously consider ending their relationship. The two most misleading beliefs that contribute to a premature split-up at this time are (1) that the quieting of limerence signals the end of love, and (2) that male couples do not last long anyway.

Limerence can smooth the path for two individuals joining in union, merging. However, the two individuals do not always feel limerence at the same time. Limerence is the double-edged sword cutting through the underbrush to clear the path but equally capable of wounding one or both of the travelers.

Merging can occur in the absence of limerence, and limerence can be present when the merger seems not to be working well. Merging and limerence usually happen in the first stage of a love relationship. Frequently one characteristic influences the other. We must keep both in mind as we try to understand the problems so likely to appear in this stage.

When both individuals are feeling limerence, one might expect a happy, Hollywood romance, living happily ever after. Life is not so simple. One of the two may feel more limerence for an hour, a day, or a month. His partner may feel inadequate in the face of this flood of affection. "Do I still love him?" Or one of the men may notice an apparent cooling or disinterest from his beloved. Frequently the words "What have I done wrong?" startle the partner who had been low in limerence relative to his partner's passion of the day. "Wrong? Nothing. Why do you ask that?"

When the relationship begins with one partner happily limerent and one partner low in limerence, the result can be as awkward and painful, like a seesaw that does not function right. One set of feet are endlessly planted on the earth while the other feet seek foundation in the air. The usual problem of lack of synchronism waits in ambush for this couple as for all others. Not everyone has a good day on the same day. But the limerent–nonlimerent couple faces additional hurdles. They are trained by culture to expect romance, and reality seems flawed.

"He damned near drove me crazy. Doubt, doubt, doubt—I never knew if it was fading, if I never had it in the first place, or if I had a piece missing. I just plain did not feel butterflies and go gushy all the time, and he *did*. He asked questions all the time: 'Why don't you need me the way I need you?' or 'When are you going to wake me with a kiss?' or 'Why do I have to ask you to tell me you love me?' I began to feel like the bad guy."

His partner added, "Sure, life was easy for *him!* The more he went his own merry way, the more I felt abandoned. If he wanted me in the same way, I was there faster than Peter Pan. It was embarrassing. I knew he loved me in his own way, but I wasn't sure his way was real love. It sure as hell didn't look like what was going on with me."

The fact that this all-too-real limerent–nonlimerent beginning of a love relationship weathers the storms and grows into sturdy maturity is a reminder that anger and agony are as real for lovers as romance and roses. The rich stew has many ingredients.

The man who got away is too often one of the two men who failed to experience limerence in the early months of a relationship. With luck such a pair will realize that the good feelings they have for each other are enough for them even if they don't match the current primer of "guidelines for the engaged." As one man says, looking back, "Thank God he didn't go off with somebody else while I was craning my damned fool neck looking for my white knight. He wasn't just a port in a storm, he was and is my place of anchor for all time."

Intimacy is a major problem for almost all of us. Intimacy promises relief from the separateness and isolation of the self. Yet the safety of the unopened self is threatened. Each person's capacity for intimacy is different. Differences between partners can lead to withdrawal, arguments over minor points, feeling of loss of self, confusion, and unexplained anxiety. Frightened by and attracted to intimacy, the limerent person may try to get his own feet on the ground again.

As a result of the combined limerence and merging, a fine rapport exists in the Stage One relationship. If any event unbalances this

finely turned rapport, distress is experienced by the couple. Each partner checks feverishly with the other to be reassured of their agreement
and accord. "Did that hurt you just now, when I smiled?"

Equalizing of Partnership

Equality is not sameness. It is represented in a male couple's relationship by an attitude. The attitude includes the expectation that each
partner will take care of himself *and* try his best to meet his partner's
needs.

Men in this culture have been trained to be competitive and to
be the powerful providers. Money and other forms of power loom as
threats on the horizon for the male couple beginning a relationship.
We found with couples in this study that they were able to find their
way around these potential hazards. When seriously threatened by
such a hazard, they found a way, sometimes uniquely their own, to
right the imbalance they experienced.

The characteristic of equalizing, so important in this stage, is
seen in the way men carefully give while sharing evenly. All money
does not go instantly into one kitty. The partner with the most money
puts in 50 percent, not because of stinginess but because he wants his
partner to have the privilege of putting in his own 50 percent. Unlike
heterosexual couples who speak of being "in this marriage together,"
the male couple is apt to *show* it as they shop, do laundry, or pay bills
together during the first stage. Tasks are assumed individually, usually
because each person enjoys his partner's ability to show what he,
uniquely, can bring to the relationship. There are no set "husband"
and "wife" roles. Each man usually can perform all necessary tasks at
some level of competence. Men together learn early that it is equally
blessed to give and to receive, even when the temptation is to prove
love by giving more.

We have observed a phenomenon that we have named *planned
incompetence*. As one man takes pleasure in a task he performs for the
relationship, whether it is cooking or carpentry, his partner is apt to
unlearn his own level of competence in this area, the better to show
his appreciation.

"For years I was able to handle a roast and potatoes, and now you
would think I can't operate a toaster. He manages to surprise me even

at breakfast. Did you ever have eggs served with a small orchid on the dish? Maybe we gays do have better taste, if not better rhythm. Or maybe my mama did raise one butch kid after all."

There is also a surprising ability to interchange tasks as need dictates. The same man says, "I don't cook much anymore, but I learned how to make crepes from him, and when he's working late and we're having company I can turn out a respectable French meal."

His partner adds, "Once I learned to read his writing and decipher his numbers, I found it easy to take over paying bills and balancing the checkbook when he's weary of it, out of town, or out of sorts."

Boys learn to be providers. Gay men learn this and bring the yearning to provide to the developing relationship. With each partner bringing this need to provide while believing that he should provide for himself, one might expect trouble on the horizon as the two men each try to take charge of all of the providing. The gay men in our study seem to have an uncanny ability to circumvent this potential trouble, and they learn to take turns providing for each other. There is usually meticulous attention to sharing finances, work, and household chores. Each resists the cultural expectation of taking care of the other. Stage One couples infrequently consider their possessions as jointly owned, but clearly think of them as "mine" and "his." They divide household expenses and may even open a joint checking account for their shared expenses but are apt to keep individual accounts for personal use. Retaining the separation of money and possessions is an important feature of Stage One.

Merging and limerence help bring two men together. Money and other power symbols seem to permit each to retain the necessary sense of individuality as the union is forged. "It's *your* house, but it's *our* home," one man says.

Another says "So what if *I* lend *us* something, as long as *we* know who *we* are?" Here again we see that healthy yin and yang, the ebb and flow that nourishes.

Rarely do two men enter a relationship as equals in the everyday sense of the word. They are not identical twins nor are the skills and possessions they bring to the relationship identical. They find a pleasing balance on the scales, not mirror images.

"Jimmy brought home every penny of his $200 paycheck, and I brought in every penny of the family inheritance. We each kept half of what we brought for our own individual use. He brought his good cheer, too. And I brought my knowledge of the world. We were exactly the same age and there was some discomfort, no doubt about it. But I needed what he offered from inside himself, and he needed what I had inside. Friends raised eyebrows if they knew about the financial differences, but good friends were right there patting us on the back for finding our own way to be equals in our own eyes and in the eyes of each other."

Of course, there are many variations among the couples in our study. One man, twenty years his partner's senior, paid for the younger man's education from the start of college to the end of his medical residency. They feel more balanced and equal today than when they began, but they report no attendant problems from those early days.

Another man tells us, "Look, it might sound grand to hear it, but when we got started he was in the film industry as an executive with big bucks, and I was on the unemployment line. He was generous, but I couldn't stand it. I worked nights as a security guard for five years until I saw that we could use his money to make a better life for both of us. But, God, those fights in the first years!"

And we should include this touching report: "He was in a wheelchair and I liked to disco, but we loved each other. No movie stuff, I didn't dance his chair in the flashing lights, but he helped me to learn more about music he listened to at home. I still go dancing sometimes, and he has the madrigal group in, but yes, I'd say we're equal."

Problems

With the absence of role models, one might expect gay men to have a natural tendency to follow the patterns of their parents, who have a traditional set of husband-and-wife expectations. Again, our experience shows that they do not. Because they lack models, it is easy to understand why male couples temporarily lose their sense of ease and balance at times.

The most common problems concerning equality arise when the two men forget that they are dealing with equality as a balance and behave like boys who count marbles to make sure each has an equal number. Again, it is the attitude of equality that helps the male couple develop.

"You know, he had everything. Before I came along his household ran like a clock, what with the gardener, the housekeeper, and his secretary. What could I bring as my share?"

His partner interjects: "I kept telling you it was empty until you came. I listened to that clock for two years. When you came you reminded me that I could still laugh and that someone cared whether I remembered to wear a warm coat. I didn't need another servant. I needed someone to bring me back to life. You did for me what I could not ever do for myself and could not hire anyone to do. I wondered how I could give as much to you."

His partner smiles: "The scales did balance finally, didn't they?"

"Yeah, when we saw that you don't have to put apples on both sides of the scale."

Couples remembering their difficulties in Stage One speak of this sort of problem often. "I didn't feel like an equal partner," Joe says. "He was making all the decisions about everything."

"But I felt I was making plenty of money for both of us," Frank interrupts. "I wanted to take care of Joe."

"And we finally learned how to take care of each other." Joe smiles at him. "We can show we care for each other by stepping back once in a while and letting the other guy do some taking care of."

Many of the longer-term couples who recall these kinds of problems emphasize the importance and sense of relief in establishing equality early in the relationship. Sometimes one partner comes to accept that the other will take care of him, causing resentment to build in the other. It is a variation on the example just cited. Both are resentful and hurt. "Why do I have to take care of everything?" is answered by, "Well, you do own everything, don't you? And you're better at everything. You're better with people. You even cook better."

"But why, just once, couldn't you have a take-out pizza waiting when I get home? That would be fine. It doesn't have to be the kind of food I cook. I need to feel taken care of sometimes."

Here's another example: "I guess I've been mad because you haven't managed the vacation like you promised. You could set it up yourself. You know the travel agent. You know the American Express number."

"I was afraid you would change your mind again."

"Don't let me. Better yet, tell *me* what to do sometimes. I know you love me. Sit on me if you have to. I don't want to be in charge all the time."

One couple reports that, while they were in this stage, the man who had been married had to be reminded again and again that being a "good husband" caused problems.

"I used to yell at him until I cried. 'God damn it,' I'd say, 'Don't pussy-foot around with me. If you're short on money we don't have to go out this weekend.' And I liked the flowers he brought home, but let the vase go dry once in a while so *I* can bring home flowers. 'I am not your wife,' I'd scream. 'I do a hundred God-damned situps every morning, and I can take care of you as well as you can take care of me. Keep on loving me, but let me show how I love you, too."

A striking factor we noticed was the good that came from apparent problems with age discrepancy. We quote Anthony, twenty-two years his partner's junior: "It seemed rosy for the first two years. I kept the house gorgeous, got the cars serviced, even made the hors d'oeuvres when we entertained his cronies. Unlike my sister, who did the same for her executive husband, the time came pretty fast when I couldn't stay locked in to the 'pretty but dumb' spot forever. More important, I wanted to become his equal and he wanted it, too. He didn't want a pretty boy. He could have rented one if he did. I went back to school and worked my way up. But there is no doubt in my mind that if we hadn't gotten together I'd be doing some dumb, low-level job somewhere."

Male couples, like all humans, have problems. Not surprisingly, they have problems in keeping the attitude of balance that serves them so well over the years. But they learn. Each partner does learn, sooner or later, to provide for and to be provided for by the man who loves him.

High Sexual Activity

Most of the men agree that sex was not the principal reason for entering into their relationships *and* that it was very important for many reasons. Merger has its most tangible expression in sexual union, and limerence finds its fulfillment in making love. There is a seemingly high frequency of genital sexual activity in these first few months.

When one listens carefully to couples describing this period, however, one hears their need to incorporate the other person's being into one's self and the driving need to transcend all male training and yield completely, vulnerably, to this one other male. It is a striving for equality, security, and peace using body and soul. "His body and mine became as one—they had to—we needed it, not to get off with an orgasm but to get whole, finally."

This high frequency of sexual activity represents a great deal more than frequent sex. A usual report is, "He wasn't my type, but all of a sudden I wanted to touch him, hold him, feel him holding me. It excited me tremendously. It sounds dumb, but I was flattered, I guess, that he wanted to explore my whole body. I had to know all about his body, too. There were endless hours of holding, nibbling, kissing, fondling. I never thought I'd nibble somebody's toes! And, oh God, the long periods of holding each other after an orgasm. I, who was raised a Mormon and kept myself covered at all times, lost all inhibitions. There was no need for shame. A glow filled the room. Anything was right as long as we could be closer. I had nothing to be ashamed of. I could ask if he liked this or that, and he could tell me he wanted to experiment some way, and I was putty in his hands. We laughed and cried and told secrets I never thought I'd tell anybody. I could lay back and let him do with me as he would, and then I could ravish him like a savage. It was serious, playful, new, adventurous—a whole new way of talking to somebody who wanted to hear all of me. And when an orgasm did come, it came from all of me."

Again and again couples remember small, surprising miracles from this period. "I was doing the same things with him that I had done with other guys, but somehow it was different. I felt the most safe and the most reassured. We could kiss for an hour, and I felt like we told each other everything."

"He could tell me one way or another what excited him and felt good to him, and I could drive him to heaven the next time. I mean, we have the same basic bodies, so I could catch on right away. I have a damned good idea how it feels to have somebody nibble you right there in that spot."

Another man remembers, "When I was married I really got into having sex with my wife, but it is different. I didn't want to *be* her, just please her. With Jim I wanted to please him, but I wanted his eyes to be my eyes and his legs to be my legs. I wanted him, and I knew he wanted me. Don't get me wrong. I knew we were still different people and which bus to catch to get to my office, not his."

Still another recollects, "There was a precision about how we touched. We learned how to fit together making love so fast! It was like he was reading my mind and my body."

One more participant recalls, "We sure did spend a lot of time in bed, I remember that. Early to bed and late to rise made us not wealthy, but it sure made us healthy and wise. It was a private adventure like two boys at camp with a secret love. It was special."

Sex is, of course, intrinsically pleasurable. For couples in Stage One it is a powerful tool used in fashioning the bond. Even more than the verbal reassurances, it stays the fear of loss of this new wonder that has come to be. It assists the couple in risking the high jumps over the fence to find each other in satisfying intimacy. Many men touchingly report to us, sometimes in shy words, how sex had helped them willingly make themselves vulnerable. The lovemaking was the protective film that permitted the pain of vulnerability.

For hundreds of years men have spoken and written millions of words to try to capture the meaning of equality. Two men in Stage One use the playground laboratory of the bedroom to demonstrate beyond words that they are equal, taking turns with power as desire dictates. All time spent in sexual activity is not necessarily driven by lust. The high frequency of sexual activity is a gem of many facets, helping the two men to grow together with or without the capricious urges of passion, driven instead by the need to learn all about each other so that they can blend and form a more perfect union.

With this characteristic, as with all other stage characteristics, not every couple is the same. One man tells us, "It almost broke my heart at first. I wanted to *live* in his bed, and he wanted to sleep there a few hours each night. I became an expert at finding ways to turn him on. He certainly liked it once we got going, but he just never had that great misty-eyed feeling for me that I had for him. I finally had to see that he is the way he is, and I had hooked up with him and not somebody else."

Sometimes one partner is more inhibited and has a more negative mind-set about sex in general. This need not be a problem unless his partner reads the behavior to mean less love. Such a couple must find vehicles other than sexual activity to carry on the process of merging. "When he'd say, 'Let's go to Roma to get some pasta,' I don't know why, but it gave me goosebumps. I knew he still loved me. Roma is a restaurant, and that's where we went."

There are couples who start out as friends, and other couples where neither partner cares much about sex. Again, they find other ways. "No, there wasn't all that much sex as I remember, but we spent long hours, evening after evening, just listening to music and looking at each other. Then I guess we had enough looking and we'd lie tangled together on the sofa and read."

Sometimes partners do not particularly excite each other in an erotic manner. "We would get very excited when we talked politics or art; then we'd go off to the baths together happy as cats climbing out of a milk pail, but we could always say anything to each other and, of course, we liked to touch—just not much interested in sex with each other."

Sexual exclusivity is a usual phenomenon found in Stage One. Not all couples decide on a monogamous relationship, and not every partner is equally enthused about sexual exclusivity. Sexual exclusivity seems to happen often in this stage because the couple is apt to be highly protective of the tender young relationship and eager to avoid threats to its development. Sexual exclusivity seems to be a natural result symbolizing commitment. Therefore, the slightest possible hint of interruption in sexual rapport, such as arriving home later than anticipated, receiving a phone call from a former sexual partner, or showing the least reluctance in responding to lovemaking, can be experienced as a threat. This potential threat can be translated into jealousy, anger, hurt, fear, and anxiety. The partner then may feel shame or guilt. Using the heterosexual model of fidelity as a guideline, other couples establish sexual exclusivity simply because of an unspoken expectation that their commitment to each other can be maintained only through the symbolic act.

As was stated so clearly by Bell and Weinberg, what may be good for heterosexual relationships may well be detrimental to homosexual ones.[2]

"I'm not the jealous type usually, but did my brown eyes ever turn green in those days! Sammy had a flat tire once, and I could not shut my mouth. I started with clever, subtle questions like, 'Whatever happened to Mark, I wonder?' (who was an old boyfriend I knew he had seen for lunch that day), and moved right along to, 'Well, I suppose Mark *was* always the best bed partner you ever found.' God, I could have cut my tongue out. The poor guy only had a flat tire, and I almost knew it was the truth, and here I was coming on like an interrogation officer."

For many, the high incandescence of the sexual attraction often begins to dim as sexual knowledge of each other increases. The high rapport of the blending, the increasing familiarity with each other, and the growing attention to finding ways to work together seem to decrease sexual excitement for many couples. The dilemma it poses for male couples is not usually recognized as a simple and usual change in the process of relationship development.

Frank giggled. "First it was sex before breakfast, lunch, and dinner. Well, breakfast went. Lunch went. Then dinner went. There was only one night and one occasional Saturday afternoon—and we both got secretly worried."

Many of the original attracting features, such as the curve of the buttocks, body hair distribution, facial structure, or lilt in the walk, may lose some allure. Many couples have some awareness of these changes and may begin to introduce new excitement into their relationships. Sometimes the playful threats that other partners are available, hints of attraction different from those found in each other, or different experimentation in lovemaking increases interest sufficiently to add fuel to the still warm embers of passion in their sex

CHAPTER 4

STAGE TWO—NESTING
(Second and Third Years)

Characteristics

1. Homemaking
2. Finding compatibility
3. Decline of limerence
4. Ambivalence

Ned, a twenty-nine-year-old accountant, and Frank, a thirty-one-year-old bank officer, have been living together for two and a half years. "We were so much in love when we started. My eyes were full of Frank. Maybe love *is* blind. We didn't pay much attention to where we were living," Ned tells us. "But things changed, and by the time we moved to this house last year we began making a real home."

"Yeah," Frank nods in agreement. "After a while I really wanted *our* home. You know, a place we were proud of, where we could have friends and family. We had a lot of fun fixing it up together. It was only a rental, but we transported half the hardware store and two tons of Macy's sale items to say nothing of the acres of topsoil and tiny plants that we nourished. The property owner was a lucky man, but we were the ones who felt lucky. He supplied the paint, and we supplied each other."

"And the recipes we invented! It didn't take long to move up from tuna casseroles to spaghetti with caviar," Ned laughs. "We thought we were real gourmets. Then I noticed Frank was *really* cooking—I mean cookbooks, fancy equipment, and all. I've learned a lot about cooking from him, but that was about the time he emerged as the master chef of the house."

"And you emerged as the master diplomat," Franks says. "I would get so damned annoyed at the clerk saying, 'If you don't see it, we don't have it,' and Ned would just smile and say something like, "But

41

we're not good at finding things, and you're busy, but could you give us a hand?' "

"Both of us thought we were total incompetents in taking care of a house," Frank says. "Remember the day the roof leaked and we both climbed the ladder just to look at it so we could call for help? And you had the idea of putting a plastic tarp over the area and weighting it with bricks, and I said, 'Hey, great! Try it. See if it works.' Now he can fix an air-conditioner at the drop of a wrench."

"Well, how about you?" Ned adds. "Remember the time the yard started to wash away and you suggested building a retaining wall with the hundred boxes of old paper we were trying to get rid of? He's now an accomplished landscaper. Please note the terraced garden on your way out."

"I do remember that house as a time of finding real happiness," Frank says. "So much seemed to come along right. I could come home from the bank and feel there just was no use trying to deal decently with anyone in the world. Ned would take over. He'd answer the phone, get the dinner going, and even help me to see I was mad and had a right to be."

"Or I'd come bustling in from the office," Ned says, "full of all the cheery big news about a new account we had landed, and Frank would sit and listen, rub my feet, or do whatever to get me landed until I knew I was home and could take off the mask. I was the accountant, but he quietly just took over the bills and checkbook because he knew before I did that I hated to have to do it at home."

Ned glances at Frank, seeming to ask permission. "There were some tough times between us, though, in pulling the house together. We had disagreements about how to do it."

Frank looks uncomfortable but nods in agreement. "I guess we both thought we could naturally agree on things like colors for the walls and the kind of furniture for the living room, but we didn't. No way could I go along with the bright colors Ned wanted in all the rooms."

"Yeah, looking back, it would have been a hodgepodge," Ned smiles. "I wanted to make it nice for us and forgot I didn't need to take care of everything. Also, I discovered I have a lousy eye for color. Frank, though, was gung-ho about getting the newest deluxe refrigerator for the kitchen; first, it was way out of line with our budget, and, second, it was too big for our needs then. Believe me, I had bought refrigerators before."

"It was like a bolt of lightning striking when I realized I didn't have to know as much as Ned about everything," Frank says. 'I always thought more was better, but I also knew I appreciated Ned's practicality. Of course, the clincher that got me embarrassed was when Ned sweetly pointed out that we couldn't get that monster refrigerator through the doorway anyway."

"In that honeymoon haven we even dared to disagree at last, and the roof may have leaked but it didn't fall in," Ned laughs.

"I hate to see the pink clouds fading now that we're growing into an old couple together for two and a half years," Frank says. "The sex is still real good, thank God, even if we don't do it as often. We're down to five times a week, right Ned?"

"Or three," Ned says. "But that's not as important as it used to be. I think I miss not sitting by the fire together as often as we used to more than running to bed all the time. But we do other things more now, like going on camping trips."

"We worry a little sometimes, I think—silly thoughts like 'Have we lost it?' " Frank is reflective. "But we know it's silly; sex can still be hot sometimes, and there's so much more we have now. I think we know each other better and feel more safe."

Both Ned and Frank admit that they are feeling sexually attracted to other men again, however, and they worry about what that might mean.

"I was so relieved that the sexual hunt was over when we fell in love, but now I'm beginning to wonder about that. We started out with monogamy, but I know I'm getting interested in other guys," Ned says and then adds, "I know it's safe when I'm interested in another guy, but if Frank started going out on me I'd be jealous as hell. It's scary."

Frank looks troubled and hesitant. "As well as things are going for us, some nagging doubts pop up in me sometimes. You know, wondering if this how I want to live my life, is this relationship right, or is this where I want to be. It's like a rerun of what do I want to be when I grow up. I can't go see the high-school counselor anymore, so I have to do it in my head. Some days it seems so good and then I wonder if the balloon is going to pop—maybe I should pack now. And what the hell do you do knowing that other guys are starting to look very tempting again?"

"We found a great poster last week at a garage sale," Ned says. "It must have been gay artwork." He points to it in the hall, a picture of a vine-covered cottage, inscribed "Home Sweet Home. Love it or leave it."

Homemaking

One of the earliest and most visible signs of a couple's progression into Stage Two is their move to new quarters or their joint efforts to fix up and make a real home for two. They make things "pretty." The purchase of two fine dishes may be the beginning. But soon, the sow's ear of an old rundown flat becomes the silk purse of a model showplace. The finery may be from hand-me-downs or garage sales, but they are selected and placed with care by the two men in constant consultation. It is a display of their union, their announcement to the world that they are joined as one in creating the future for better or worse, and they work hard to make it better and not worse. "Yes, I think we should get that tablecloth" can be translated into a moving "I do."

They enthusiastically and seriously begin to fix up the apartment or house, transforming it into a home. They buy chairs or kitchen towels, arrange furniture, and turn the weeds into a garden. Budgeting and planning begin. Couples invite friends, sometimes fellow employees, and selected family members. For these visits the male couple, rich or poor, shows a knack for creating an appealing scene. A crate and a cloth remnant in the corner becomes an attractive table.

Making the home may be restricted to rearranging the existing furniture. Not every male couple is dedicated to "making it pretty." But all male couples, as they move into Stage Two, are dedicated to "making it our home." It is not so much the purchases that please as it is the pleasure of announced pairing that satisfies.

Homemaking reflects an attitude the couple develops after the first year, and it may include opening their home to others. They invite friends for dinner or cards or TV, eager to show off their nest. In some instances there is almost a ceremonial aspect to inviting their first guests. For opposite-sex couples there is a series of ceremonial traditions surrounding engagement and marriage (showers, bachelor parties, etc.). Lacking these built-in ceremonies, male couples unwittingly create their own ceremonies.

"I remember the first time we had company over. It was like our announcement to the world that we were 'at home,' you know, we couldn't send out notices to everyone, but we began inviting a few close friends over, one or two at a time. We were proud of our new place and us, and they could see how happy we were."

Other homemaking items include budget planning, establishing priorities for future household purchases, and developing housekeeping routines. This is also a time when many integrate their clothes closets and bureau drawers and combine their books, records, and tapes into "our" library and music collection.

"The first time I saw Bob with one of my shirts on, I realized how much better it looked on him than on me. Then I decided to try one of *his* shirts. All of a sudden we were wearing each other's clothes and we both had twice as many. It just seemed to make sense to put all of our shirts in the same drawer, slacks in the same closet, and shoes in the same rack, although I'd have a hard time getting my size 11 feet into his size 9 shoes."

"We started a photo album to keep a record of our times together. I think that was in the second or third year. One of our regular routines is to get out the pictures and look at them even after all these eight years."

Some couples together for two or three years still had not "nested" in the ways described above. However, we did find evidence of homemaking in things like buying an old sailboat or antique car and pridefully refurbishing it together. Another couple had focused their homemaking energy on buying a weekend camper and finding isolated campsites in the mountains or the desert.

"In those years we were off every weekend finding a new campsite to make into a home," says Tom.

Fred adds, "Even the weekend cabin we rented got rearranged. By the time we left on Sunday, every one of those places had our homemaking seal of approval on it."

When one partner already lived in a well-established home or when there was a wide difference in age, we did find variations on the homemaking theme. For example, Bob moved into Ted's beautiful hillside house and after the first year was completely managing the household. Bob and Ted were making Ted's house their home. We found similar homemaking accommodations in couples with age differences of more than a few years.

"I had become uninterested in the house. I had begun to believe that I'd live alone forever in this big museum." Forty-year-old Pat is talking about his life before twenty-three-year-old Matt came upon the scene.

"It took almost a year before I had the courage to tell Pat how awful the place really was. He just didn't have the interest in getting it together," explains Matt.

Their home is a very attractive and attentively decorated showplace that reflects the tastes and touches of both men.

The partner who had moved in often did not notice his own dissatisfaction with the other's taste in furnishing or decoration. However, once they are over the one-year hurdle, the urge to assert individual taste and express the relationship in terms of the home they share comes to the fore.

We have seen couples who begin homemaking almost as soon as they move in together. Sometimes the couple has been dating for several months and living apart. When they do move in together, the signs of homemaking are evident from the start. The tangible evidence of homemaking provides early reassurance to themselves that they *are* a couple.

"We made our house a home right from the start. We both had some nice furniture. He had the bedroom set, and I had the living room stuff." Jeff is telling us about how he and Peter started homemaking in Stage One. "Our furniture matched just like we did. That was a sure sign to us that we were made for each other."

Other couples where both partners have a history of previous relationships with homemaking a high priority also start it earlier than Stage Two. Homemaking is one of those characteristics that appears sooner if it has been done before.

Although a few couples do start homemaking in the beginning of their relationship, why do the majority postpone this part of nesting until after the first year? The high intensity of the blending during Stage One rivets their attention to each other. As a consequence their physical surroundings are not noticed or considered that important. Gay men do not always trust their relationships to be permanent like the expectation of a marriage. As wonderful as it is, they frequently harbor the lingering concern that it might not last. As our data indi-

cate, many of these men have had a number of previous brief relationships ranging from weeks to months. Therefore, during the first year
together, despite the intensity of the emotional togetherness, they re-
serve a little mad money just in case they might need to get home
again. With these observations, it is easy to see how the process of
homemaking is truly a sign of commitment to the relationship.

Homemaking is one of the characteristics with fewer problems.
Two of the more common ones are disagreements about what and how
much to do and differences in taste and style.

"I just wasn't ready to spend so much or get committed to
monthly payments when Jeff wanted to start buying furniture. I'm
more of a tightwad, and he gets grand ideas about how our house
should look."

"One of us wants a modern theme, and the other wants antiques.
We couldn't figure out how both could fit in together in the house."

"When I moved in last year the house was already beautifully
decorated and furnished. It's *his* house, but I know it's also our home.
He doesn't want to change a thing. I feel left out of it."

Some of the sources of these problems come from individual personality and background differences. Far too often, when these problems arise they are experienced as relationship discord—"What's
wrong with us?"—instead of individual differences needing
compromise.

Finding Compatibility

Finding ways to live together in harmony is what compatibility is all
about. For some it comes as second nature, for others it is a lot of
work, and for most it is a mixture. The blending of Stage One capital-
izes on the attractions and minimizes the distractions. The nesting of
Stage Two highlights differences and minimizes similarities. Compatibility depends on how the differences are balanced. Once couples recognize their differences they search for harmony by resolving,
ignoring, or denying them.

At this time incompatibilities are not well tolerated by the
evolving couple, especially if the harmony found in blending has begun to sound discordant. It is so characteristic for men in Stage One to
ignore the faults and shortcomings of the other or to subjugate their

own ideas and feelings to the other that the sudden reemergence of differences must be neutralized. The natural trend is for the couple to seek a new balance. Some differences are disappointing, irritating, and potential sources of conflict. The deficits seen as potential liabilities intuitively are converted to assets.

Joe and Steve (from chapter 1) had major differences in their backgrounds. Joe was from a lower-middle-class, Italian Catholic, affectionate family, and Steve was from an upper-middle-class, Protestant, genteel, nonaffectionate family. In the first year the exchange of affection was generally initiated by Joe, and Steve responded appropriately, liking the touching, holding, and hugging he was receiving from Joe. As they moved into their second year together Joe was feeling that he was giving all of the affection. "I would get so disappointed when we'd spend the evening watching TV, and I'd just want Steve to hold me." Joe is talking about their second year together. "But Steve would just want to have sex. I used to go along with that in the beginning, but then I started to get bugged."

"Yeah, I couldn't understand why he was annoyed with me," Steve chimes in, "until I realized that every time Joe started touching and hugging me he wasn't expecting sex."

"You know, it took us almost a year to realize what was happening," Joe says, "and thank God we worked it out."

In this case both men had different affectional needs that were met easily in the first year because the high sexual activity satisfied both of them. However, as the sex declined, the affectional needs increased. Steve continued to expect sex to fulfill those needs, while Joe found that sex alone did not sufficiently satisfy his need for kissing, holding, and touching.

"It got pretty hairy for a while," Steve says, "and when we first began talking about something being wrong we almost came to blows."

"When I really stopped to think about it, I realized that I was missing the affection more than the sex," Joe says. "I had been getting enough sex from Steve," he continues, leaning toward Steve and squeezing his knee.

Steve learned about his affectionate side from Joe, and Joe learned that sex could sometimes be just sex without necessarily being accompanied by verbal expressions of tenderness or even a lot of affection. Their misunderstood and irritating differences were thus turned into balancing assets, restoring harmony.

This process of taking from the other what is wanted or lacking in the self, and using this newfound combination to enhance the relationship, is called complementarity. Tripp took this old idea of complementarity and simplifed the explanation by using the terms *import* and *export*.[1] One partner is importing what he needs and admires from the other while exporting what is needed and admired by his partner. In this example, Steve was importing the tenderness and affection from Joe. Steve was exporting his gentility and culture, which Joe greatly admired and wanted for himself. For heterosexual couples there are built-in complementarities arising from their different social scripting. For example, men are trained to rely on just the facts and figures in making decisions. On the other hand, women are taught to allow their intuitions and emotions to guide them. Therefore, a man and a woman who make a decision together have this built-in complementarity. Two men in a relationship lack this natural balance. How do male couples develop complementarity? That is what finding compatibility is all about. Fortunately, for most gay men while growing up there has been some variation from the usual social scripting for boys. (See chapter 9.) Childhood traits, such as high sensitivity, willingness to compromise, and lack of competitiveness, earned them the label "sissy." However, these very same traits that made the boys feel different and wrong are now the highly valued building blocks for finding compatibility and developing complementarity in their relationships.

Most gay men are positively disposed toward tasks and attitudes usually contained in female social scripting. Learning to cook, operating a sewing machine, setting a table, expressing feelings, showing vulnerability, and wanting to nurture are skills and attitudes many gay men have developed in spite of that often-heard warning, "Little boys don't do that."

Each gay man, at the start of a relationship, brings attitudes and skills that are traditionally both masculine and feminine. This allows gay partners an easy interchangeability in developing complementarity. Without thinking, one begins to take on tasks the other does not do or does not do as well. For instance, in the process of fixing up the home, one may have a talent with mechanical repairs and the other a knack for arranging furniture. Each partner can fill in for the other at any task.

"Some jobs we alternate, like sometimes we take turns making the bed, at other times we do it together," explains Steve, "but if Joe lived alone he'd probably never make the bed. Right, Joe?"

Joe nods in agreement, adding, "I guess that's true. But I always try to make it now, because I know you like it that way."

Joe and Steve explain that they both could do almost everything that needed doing in the apartment, but that in the past year Joe has done most of the cooking and Steve has done the shopping just because it has turned out that way. Yet each can do either task.

"Sometimes I like to cook, so I'll tell Joe in advance, especially if he's working hard or getting home late," Steve says.

"Actually, I'm just a better cook than Steve. You know, my Italian mom taught me a lot about good eating," Joe adds, and Steve nods his agreement.

"There were some things about the way Joe managed household cleaning like vacuuming," Steve begins.

"Yeah, I really liked doing it since it got my mind off work," Joe says, completing the thought.

"Unfortunately, as his mind wandered from work it didn't find its way to the task at hand, and the vacuum missed half the carpet and all of the corners. It used to amuse me, then it started to annoy me. So I recommended to Joe that I take over the vacuuming and suggested jogging as a way for him to get his mind off work while doing something else at the same time," Steve reports.

In other areas such as giving and receiving affection or offering and accepting emotional support, there also can be an easy exchange between male lovers. To illustrate this point, one couple devised a unique system of communicating their needs for affection and emotional support. They talk about a "needy person (NP) scale" they invented using numbers one through ten. The higher the number, the greater the neediness. When one of them had a particularly draining day, he gave an NP number to the other and would get taken care of accordingly. Taking care and being taken care of go back and forth with interesting ease, often without dialogue.

Although this fluid interchangeability exists, some tasks get fixed with one partner or the other. In fact, we saw partners willingly unlearn previous skills. For example, both may have been skilled cooks, but one unlearned his cooking and the partner became the cook. Again we have labeled this phenomenon *planned incompetence*. It helps to divide the responsibilities. There are limited ways in which partners can be truly complementary, so they invent them. It helps to develop and strengthen compatibility.

"I was always able to get my bills paid before I met Steve, but I don't do bills any more. Steve does it so much better." Joe laughs a little as we all recognize that he is capable of paying his own bills but that he now counts on Steve to do it for him, just as Steve depends on Joe to do the cooking.

When couples block the search for compatibility, problems surface. Some of the blocks include stubborn refusals to compromise, reluctance to accept their differences, and attempts to change each other. Because of the intensity of blending, the glaring mismatches of some couples were muted during the first year. Extreme personality differences and discrepancies in values and backgrounds contribute to the difficulties they are experiencing in finding ways to be compatible.

George and Matthew have been lovers for almost two years. Both describe the first year as marvelous, but the past six months have been miserable. Each is a strong person, but the limerence of the first year made mutual compromising easy. Now Matt says, "George doesn't even know how to wash the dishes right. I don't do it the way he wants them done, so neither of us does them."

"We can't seem to compromise anymore." George sees the problem: "We're both too stubborn to let the other person do it his way."

"For the first year I did everything his way; then I started doing it my way and he got really angry with me," another man tells us.

His mate takes up the narrative. "I was really upset when he stopped doing things the 'right' way. I was after him all the time. Finally I realized there was no 'right' way; I just wanted him to do everything my way."

Couples with severe mismatching can go in several directions. Some establish role fixity by definition and lack the fluid exchange of tasks and attitudes. These we see as negotiated "labor settlements." These couples do not have to find compatibility; they are kept together by respect for each other's differences, and each functions in his own domain. Some couples, once out of limerence, find the differences so glaring that they separate. Others, recognizing their mismatch, work harder and more painfully at finding ways to be compatible. The intensity of their blending, despite the mismatching, gives them stamina in the struggle to remain partners.

Decline of Limerence

Few characteristics have potential as far-reaching as the decline in feelings of passionate, romantic love. The whole magic of being in love, which seems to be the foundation of the relationship, begins to give way under the ordinary pressures of daily living. Analogously, if the relationship is seen as a chemical solution, the limerence has partially maintained the blending, but as the limerence begins to evaporate those elements dissolved in the solution begin to precipitate out. So, with our couples in Stage Two, as the intensity of their emotional attraction to each other diminishes, the rose-colored glasses tinting the other with perfection become less rosy. They begin to see each other as they are—the imperfections along with the perfections.

"It was real gradual, like I would feel aggravated which I had never felt before when he changed the TV channel, or I'd want to be alone in the bedroom and he'd follow me in, or suddenly I couldn't stand the noise he made chewing his food. I just wasn't floating on air as often as before. I got real scared thinking I was falling out of love."

Another recalls, "For the first year I was always jealous when old friends would call Bob. I hated myself for it, but I was waiting for him to leave me, taking my emotional high feelings with him. Then, gradually I found myself being uninterested about his phone calls, like I wasn't so jealous anymore. When he saw that, he began to accuse me of not loving him."

Still another remembers, "We used to call each other four and five times a day. Then the calls tapered off. I found I was concentrating better on my work. I wasn't so preoccupied with him. It actually was a relief. People at work noticed my renewed interest. I couldn't help but wonder what was happening to him at the same time."

When limerence or being in love is considered to be the foundation of a relationship, and then limerence begins to crumble, partners justifiably expect the relationship to topple. The consequences of this misunderstanding often lead them to believe that their love has been lost, and the relationship breaks up.

On the other side of the coin there are positive outcomes, especially if the decline in limerence is recognized by the couple for what it is—a shift in the way they love each other. There is a quality of selfishness in the loving that accompanies limerence. For example, there is a moment-to-moment preoccupation with being loved by the other and a demand that the beloved's every word and action be moment-to-moment reciprocation and reassurance of that love. Limerence has certain illusory qualities, blurring the imperfections and magnifying the desired and admired qualities. These illusions fade with the decline in limerence. Partners see each other as they really are. If lovers are not devastated by the loss of limerence, the shift in the quality of their love changes from the highly charged romantic feelings to care and concern for each other characterized by more selflessness and giving. Lacking the urgency and illusions of limerence, the men develop a deeper, more knowledgeable understanding, establishing more firmly the foundation for a constant and enduring relationship.

"What a mutual admiration society we had going! We were constantly whispering sweet nothings, writing notes, and devising countless ways to show how much we were in love. We didn't have time for much else but ourselves. It was a wonderful time, and we don't need that as much now. Fixing up the house and making it into our home gives us different ways to say how much we love each other. We have lots of fun. Our love is less frantic. What a relief!"

"I was just about worn out, constantly worried and jealous about Tom's every move. He was a few minutes late getting home, and I'd know he was out with someone else. I was a terror. He couldn't give me enough reassurance. Yet he was always around. He kept loving me the same. Actually, I was glad to let go of the infatuation. It made our lives much easier."

Limerence paves the way for the growth of a different kind of love, and it does fade as it is outshone by components of the maturing. Intimacy, affection, vulnerability, deep sharing, concern for the well-being of the other, loyalty, and dependable companionship are developing. The seeming decline in limerence is not necessarily a negative characteristic here, but rather a bridge or stepping stone to future stages.

More often than not, limerence persists well into the second stage. There usually is a decline in its intensity for one or both partners during Stage Two. Its decline does not happen to both partners at the same time. All too frequently one partner maintains high emotional intensity while the other's feelings change. Couples who are not aware of the elusive nature of the romantic aspect of their love begin distancing themselves from each other. The change in feelings may be feared as an omen of the possible end of their relationship. As has been observed by other researchers (Saghir and Robins,[2] Bell and Weinberg[3]) many male relationships end at about this time. A misunderstanding of these changes in feelings is frequently the cause.

What makes limerence waiver, diminish, or disappear altogether? For one thing, the mundane invades the romance. Prince Charming, the object of our every desire, ends up leaving the dishes in the sink, his dirty socks on the bathroom floor, and hair in the shower drain. Limerence is maintained by a certain adversity, implying mystery and creating even a momentary distance from the other. Familiarity does not really breed contempt, but it can and does reduce limerence. It removes the mystery and imposes reality on the romantic illusions. The magical becomes the known. As with most highly charged emotional experiences, there is fatigue. The intense glow of limerence loses its incandescence by burning out or lowering the glow.

There is a concomitant decrease in the frequency of sex and lovemaking. For some couples this creates serious problems, especially when one partner has continuing limerence. Far too often he interprets the other's decline in sexual interest as a loss of love when it is only a shift. If sex becomes the principal measure of the expression of their love for each other, a decreasing frequency can cause chaos.

"He didn't seem to be calling me by my special nickname anymore, which caused me to feel insecure. I responded by wanting to make love. He hesitated like he never did before. That made me more insecure. I was convinced that something was wrong and that he didn't love me."

Jealousy, with all its attendant feelings of rejection, loss, anger, and self-doubt, can tear such a relationship to shreds in short order.

"He wasn't talking to me as much. He seemed real mysterious, so of course I got jealous. I'd say I worked up such a lather that I could have killed him. I was sure he had a new boyfriend. The more he denied it, the surer I got. I would go to bed at night thinking of ways to get away, but I loved him so much still. When we did finally start talking honestly, I learned that he was afraid he didn't love me anymore because his feelings had changed."

The loss of limerence also can be accompanied by depression, as happens with the loss of anything important. The loss of the feelings of togetherness and well-being—the sense of oneness in the relationship—can result in separation anxiety and despondency. Misinterpretation of loss of limerence raises the specter of the end of the relationship.

For most people, limerence is a highly valued human experience. It does wonders for relationships. Most people would like to be able to control it so that it could be turned on and off at will. We do not know how to do that. On the other hand, we do know some ways in which the positive effects and feelings of limerence can be reawakened or rekindled by a couple. Doing the things that have contributed to making the limerence more intense in the past will often bring it back for a moment, an hour, a day, or even for weeks.

Ambivalence

The simultaneous attraction and aversion to the relationship is expressed in a variety of ways during Stage Two. Ambivalence is the mixture of positive and negative feelings, thoughts, words, and deeds that are sometimes expressed and sometimes not expressed. Ambivalence emerges in the process of the development of the other characteristics in Stage Two. Finding compatibility becomes disappointing because it takes work but is also very satisfying when it begins to happen. Homemaking can be a mixture of highs and lows in agreeing and disagreeing. The decline of limerence can be both a relief and a sad loss when it occurs. The well-being induced by the merging and limerence of Stage One prevents ambivalence from appearing earlier. In fact, for most couples it usually does not begin to make itself felt until late in Stage Two.

Ambivalence about the relationship parades in many different disguises. For example, the decline in intensity of newness and the discomfort generated by knowing so much but not yet enough about each other increase the temptation to find a new limerence. Other examples include changes in behavior, like a decrease in verbal tenderness or omissions of previous thoughtfulness, and changes in feelings, like diminished erotic attraction or affectionate impulses.

"I used to love getting him flowers every Friday after work, but then it sort of got to be a chore. The fun went out of it. I kept doing it, thinking that his response would be my reward. He just started taking it for granted, like I was bringing home a quart of milk."

"I'd get angry at him and then begin thinking of how great it would be to be single again. That never happened last year."

"One day I'd be gung-ho about us, and then the next I'd be wishing I was alone again. My thoughts about us were on a seesaw. I was confused. Nothing special was happening to make me feel the way I did."

The impact of changes like these causes confusion and upset because the changes are occurring along with all of the positive features of homemaking and finding compatibility. Some individuals experience considerable self-doubt at this time, wondering if something is wrong with themselves. "What's the matter with me? Can't I keep a lover?" Such questions often get turned into introspection and withdrawal. The other partner will then attempt to discover the source, believing that he has provoked his lover's withdrawal by doing something wrong. Not being able to figure out what that is, he may try to be extra attentive and do extra special things. Unfortunately, the response evoked from his lover may be absent or may further distancing.

"When he got home from work I got a peck on the cheek, not the usual bear hug. I sensed he might be disappointed with something I did or didn't do. Who knows what? But I sure made every effort to make the dinner special that night. He sat through dinner in strained silence and afterward he kept telling me nothing was wrong. I started thinking the worst. I figured he must have made it with someone else. I started feeling jealous. What a mess it turned into!"

After the complete sharing of Stage One, couples usually do not talk about their ambivalence. It is hard enough for them to understand and deal with it individually, let alone talk with the other about it. A conspiracy of silence begins. They withhold the ambivalence in hopes that it will disappear. Intuitively, the partner knows something is wrong, and it is easy for him to think the worst. This is called dishonesty by omission.

For the most part, the ambivalence is overshadowed and contained by the positive features in other characteristics of this stage. It might be fueled by the decline in limerence and the struggle to find compatibility, but it is dampened by the security and excitement of homemaking and the harmony and balance of complementarity.

Another impact of ambivalence is its ability to arouse jealousy. Although jealous feelings may come along in any stage, Stage Two couples report them most often. The jealous partners reveal their fear of losing each other. Anger, insecurity, and wishes to get revenge are painful. Jealousy appears most often, of course, around other potential sexual partners. "I hate feeling jealous. I didn't want to feel it, but there it was."

"Ted was so jealous that he'd keep track of my every move. He was smothering me."

"It was OK for me to be with other guys, but I couldn't stand the thought of his doing it. I knew I would come home; I wasn't so sure he would. The togetherness is wonderful, but it can smother you, too."

Jealousy can and does generate competitiveness in some couples. One may attempt to attract more sexual partners or win attention from the partner's new friends. Competition also takes other forms, such as income production or even a degree of dedication to the nesting process itself. We found the most evidence of competition among couples who were closer to the same age and generally in their twenties or early thirties. Excessive competition can be resolved by finding and creating greater complementarity.

All of the effects of ambivalence are not negative. Actually, some of the positive spinoffs are among the most important for relationship maintenance.

Out of the struggle with opposite feelings, thoughts, and deeds come the need for dealing with conflict and the reemergence of the individual. These are both characteristics of the next stage. Couples who work at finding harmony despite a decline in their highly romantic attachment reap the satisfaction of discovering new depths in each other. Often, from these discoveries the pair finds that there is much more to their mateship than the feelings they have shared. They take stock of what they have together and find that the sum is greater than each of them individually, despite the problems. It is at this time that both men make some cognitive commitment to each other and to their relationship.

"I had been in two relationships before I met Tom. Both broke up after a year or two. This time, despite the ups and downs, we've learned how to be together. I want this relationship more than anything, and I'm ready to work to keep it. I guess I used to think a good relationship would just go on its own steam. Now I know better."

"The romance went out a couple of seasons ago, but we're still together. But I guess we know how to get it back now and again. We've got enough sense to realize that no relationship is perfect. I can't get everything from Bob, but there are plenty of reasons to stay together."

Another example of how ambivalence positively influences relationships is contained in the stories we've often heard about the increased passion and excitement found in sex after an argument or a particularly difficult disagreement. This reaction is generally recognized, but most persons do not realize the direct connection between the distancing in the dispute and the increased erotic attraction. Ambivalence sets into motion a series of opposing interactions that are, in turn, often responsible for increased sexual activity that ultimately brings the couple closer. (See chapter 9.)

Beyond the sources explored above, there are many others that generate ambivalence, such as anxieties related to intimacy, concerns about getting hurt by being too vulnerable, homophobia with its self-invalidation, or totally adopting the heterosexual model of marriage.

"I was expecting to take care of Mark. I didn't want him to work. I made plenty of money for both of us. I guess I really wanted him to act just like a wife. Wow, did that cause us problems! He tried to do what I wanted, but it just didn't work. He told me he wasn't my wife."

"I know that I'm gay, but it sure would be easier to be married to a woman. I think marriage is more natural."

Although ambivalence is most frequently mentioned in this stage, it continues to reappear as couples deal with the stresses and strains of other stages. One of the great risks that ambivalence has for male couples is the pressure it can exert on their pairing. Lacking legal ties, a male couple can dissolve a relationship simply by packing their suitcases.

CHAPTER 5

STAGE THREE—MAINTAINING
(Fourth and Fifth Years)

Characteristics

1. Reappearance of the individual
2. Taking risks
3. Dealing with conflict
4. Establishing traditions

What strikes us about their home was that you could see Tim's touch and Phil's touch working in harmony. It looks like a carefully put together home. And their pride shows as Phil gestures to the living room and says, "This is us."

When we sit down to talk the two elements of harmony are present again. They watch each other so as not to interrupt. Tim and Phil are thirty-five and thirty-four and have been a couple for nearly five years.

Tim is a lawyer, and Phil is an architect. Each has two children from previous marriages, and both take pride in their mutually owned home. All four children visit on the same alternate weekends and spend time together as a family. Tim's boys are nine and eleven; Phil's daughter and son are eight and ten.

"The kids try hard to get along together," Phil says.

"My two are happier than they've ever been," Tim smiles.

"I've been teaching my older son and Phil's daughter tennis," Tim says. "I had forgotten how good it feels to get out on the courts every week. I think it's good for them."

"Yeah, somehow I never made it as a tennis star," Phil chuckles. "When Tim and I tried playing together, it was pretty clear I was better at chess. So I've been playing chess with the other two while the jocks head off to the park. It's the Eggheads versus the Terrible Tigers, and we're going to have a home series one of these days with the losers cooking the spaghetti."

In individual interviews, Phil confesses that he feels uneasy. "You know, when Tim is off doing tennis with the kids, it's different from when all six of us used to do something together like going to the planetarium. I guess it's sort of that way when the kids aren't here, too. Sometimes I'm reading and Tim is downstairs talking to old friends on the phone. But I've enjoyed rediscovering a couple of my old friends, too, so I guess it's fair, but nonetheless I'm alone reading while he's on the phone. We used to be together more."

And Tim says, "It's crazy but sometimes I feel like I'm losing Phil. It makes no sense. Just because he's reading again doesn't mean he'll leave me. I have wondered if that's related somehow to the way I find myself telling Phil that I don't always like the way we are together in bed. It scares me to hear myself say it, but I keep saying it. He's terrific about being willing to experiment with sex. Maybe I'm afraid he'll start experimenting with more people. This is all crazy," he laughs. "We're really happy."

Tim also tells us, "In the kitchen yesterday I found myself saying, 'For God's sake, Phil, can't you ever remember to keep the hair out of the drain in the tub?' I guess it's bugged me for a while but it didn't seem important. But it does bother me. Why I chose that moment when we were cooking dinner as opposed to a thousand times in the past few years, I'll be damned if I know. Maybe it had something to do with the way he had looked at the guy in the supermarket. It's confusing. It led to a bizarre fight, nothing physical, that lasted three days, and then I sulked for one day."

Tim's brother and his wife are close to both men, and all regularly visit one another's homes. Tim had a long talk with his sister-in-law, asking her advice about the trouble they were having. She made some helpful suggestions that got them talking again.

"Sometimes I think we're learning from the kids," Phil tells us. "When they have a fight none of them rushes for a suitcase. They have to find some way to work it out. My daughter said something to Tim yesterday at breakfast. She said, 'I can tell you guys love each other because Daddy always fixes your oatmeal, and you always bring flowers for Daddy on Friday after work.'"

"I think she hit it," Tim says. "When I'm most scared I think about how many little ways we've found with each other, and I know in my heart we've got a home."

This is a stage during which maintaining the relationship relies on establishing a balance between confusion and understanding, individuality and togetherness, conflict and its resolution, and autonomy and independence.

Each partner usually has found such deep satisfaction in the early years of the relationship that the startling discovery of faults in the other precipitates withdrawal or arguing and bickering over minor issues.

The shocking realization is that the same person who was once the object of high passion and the paragon of all perfection has now become the partner who leaves his dirty underwear on the bedroom floor and dishes in the kitchen sink.

Reappearance of the Individual

The totality of the blending in Stage One and the nesting in Stage Two places the relationship at center stage. The early merger of two individuals into one entity maintains the momentum for the first three years. As satisfying as the blending of Stage One was, and as fulfilling as the nesting of Stage Two was, both contribute to the oneness of the pair. Now, the reappearance of each partner as an individual becomes central to maintaining the relationship through Stage Three. During Stage One and well into Stage Two, couples function as if they were one. Just as individual self-sufficiency gives way to a dependency to create the relationship, so the reappearance of each partner's self-identity is the next milestone in the process of relationship growth. After three years together, the couple's mutual confidence in the relationship supports the emergence of former individual traits, habits, and characteristics. As a consequence of the relationship's history and maturation, it not only can tolerate these new additions but it also needs each partner's individuality to avoid stagnation and to assure growth. Couples begin to sense that too much togetherness is stagnating. Each partner moves to rediscover old interests as well as to develop new ones that are his alone. This process establishes new individual autonomy. Figuratively speaking, for most couples until now there has been only one entity, the relationship. With the new individual autonomy, there are now three entities—each partner and the relationship.

In the above vignette, Phil and Tim demonstrated the reappearance of the individual. As benign as the example of playing different games may seem, it is really the tip of the iceberg. They used to do everything together, even when they might have preferred to do some things separately. Sometimes. without knowing it, they would submerge their individual desires to do "what's best for us." Phil used to play tennis, and Tim used to play chess. They both stopped and went to the planetarium instead. At the time neither missed the surrendered activity because the sacrifice was made generously in the service of the relationship.

Needs that are not being fulfilled within the relationship find other safe avenues of satisfaction. They find others to participate in activities in which the partners do not share, such as sports, theatergoing, or politics. They also develop new interests during this time. Interestingly enough, their different new interests are often complementary. One partner becomes interested in real estate, and the other develops skills in remodeling houses. One partner takes courses in cooking, and the other becomes interested in auto mechanics.

"For a while Wayne had me working like crazy in the garden. We'd spend hours out there, and most of the time I liked doing it because it was a project we were doing together. But gradually it dawned on me that before Wayne came along I hated gardening. I like the results, you know, like the flowers and all those fresh vegetables we no longer have to buy. I've learned dozens of ways to cook vegetables. Now I stay out of the garden but tell him what vegetables to plant. He really didn't need me out there with him."

For some couples the reappearance of individuality occurs smoothly and with a minimum of difficulty. The transition is so easy for some couples that they do not even recognize that it has happened. It is only in retrospect or with questioning that they see it for themselves. For others, there is a sense of confusion and a fear of too much separation and possible loss of the relationship.

Chris and Steve are talking with us about how they slipped into individualizing without even knowing what was happening. "I'm not really sure when I got the idea that Steven couldn't satisfy all of my needs. I guess at the start I really expected he would, but both of us knew that wasn't so but still felt like it should be. When he started going out with some old friends without me I sure got some evenings alone that I really had wanted."

Chris chimes in, "I had some second thoughts about going out without him, but I wanted to do it so badly that it was easy. Steve was continuing to satisfy so many of my needs that I figured I was really lucky. He couldn't be everything for me."

Another couple illustrates the same point. "I went through hell when David told me he was joining a gym without me. He hadn't ever done anything like that before. I was irrational about it. It didn't make any difference that I wasn't interested in the gym; it was just the idea that he would do it without me." Peter smiles as he reflects on the past. "He was doing a lot of other independent things, too. He started buying his shirts without asking my opinion. He even started going to the movies with friends. I was terrified that I was going to lose him."

Still another example: "Peter had such a tight hold on me before that when I did get a little freedom I just went wild," David tells us. "I tried to tell Peter that doing some things with old friends and going to the gym wouldn't change how I felt about him, but he wouldn't believe me."

For couples like David and Peter, one of the major consequences of this process of individualizing is conflict. They begin to fight over little things that gradually escalate into major battles, threatening the foundation of the relationship. Couples feel the togetherness of their mateships threatened as each partner begins to branch out.

Actually, finding outside sexual partners is part of the next characteristic, taking risks. However, the return of sexual interests outside the relationship generates fears of loss and abandonment.

Although Steve did not have an early expectation of sexual exclusivity, after the first few months, he and Chris slipped into a monogamous relationship, which excluded outside sexual contact. Steve tells us, "Yeah, the tables really turned on me when Chris started talking about going to the baths again. I couldn't believe him at first. I figured he was tired of me and that I was going to get dumped." He is talking retrospectively about Stage Three.

"When I starting thinking about sex with other guys again, I couldn't help but figure Jim was having sex with his old friends. For me, I knew I could do it and I'd come home for sure, but when I thought about him doing it I went crazy. Sort of like a double standard, I guess."

As with the results of other characteristics, there are some positive effects of individualizing. It does set the scene for the development of the other characteristics, especially taking risks and conflict resolution, both of which become important elements in the continuing growth of the partnership. Some couples report that the return of individual interests and activities enriched, stabilized, and invigorated the relationship, adding strength and security.

Tim tells us that when he began to have sexual contacts outside the relationship early in Stage Three, he knew he would not leave Phil, but when Phil had the first outside sexual relationship, Tim was terrified.

"We went through the whole trip of trying to reassure each other. You know, 'You're my number one man,' and all that. But the words didn't help all that much."

"It was repeatedly finding him coming home to me no matter how terrific the other guy seemed that finally calmed the fear," Phil says. "I'm not going away. I may go play. But I'm not going away. And I don't think Tim is either."

"When we first started living together I couldn't stand Steve's friends." Chris is telling us how things changed in their third or fourth year together. "I think I was really jealous so I made all of them bad guys. He stopped seeing them, as I recall. Then he started seeing them again despite my previous objections. I relented and told him to bring them home. Well, I really started to like them. They've become part of the family now, and we get a lot out of being together."

"I was almost always a loner before we got together. Then for three years I never had any time to myself. I'd get irritable and wouldn't know what was wrong. I finally started taking some time alone again—long drives, walks in the park, even a few days backpacking in the mountains. At first George had a fit, but when he saw how happy I'd be when I got home, he was eager for me to get the time alone. In fact, he likes his time now, too."

In this stage men learn that they can move away from the relationship and gain confidence that each will be present and available to the other upon return.

Variations

The individual's reappearance is most sensitive to and affected by differences between men, such as their ages, backgrounds, or previous relationship experiences. Some relationships never experience loss of the individual in Stage One. Instead, the partners accommodate each other and find complementarity earlier. Their experience of individualizing is merely a change in direction for their relationships.

It is formidable enough when both partners begin to reemerge as individuals around the same time. However, more frequently one partner begins before the other. This confounds an already complex source of tension in the relationship. Most couples are not aware of what is happening and, therefore, cannot understand that it is a normal part of the growth of their relationship. During these difficult times, frequently mentioned thoughts and feelings emerge. One may think, "What's wrong with me? Don't I love him anymore?" Another may find himself wondering, "What's wrong with him? He seems not to want me anymore. He's changing; he's not the same guy." Yet another person may confront a painful thought, such as "What's wrong with us? Is this a mismatch?"

This kind of discrepancy in individualizing is one of the most common problems we see in our clinical practice. The discrepancy also can manifest itself earlier when one partner begins with individual reappearance in a previous stage.

Though some couples desperately try to avoid the reappearance of the individual and, by vigilant avoidance, postpone it for a time, most are carried on the tide of its natural development. Couples continually remind us that this issue never goes away completely. The longer they are together, the deeper and richer is the bond of the relationship and the more necessary it is to develop as individuals at the same time.

Dick and Michael have been together for five years. "We still do everything together. We get teased a lot, called the Bobbsey Twins. One guy told us that the prom was over, but we're still dancing the same waltz. Guys who start doing things apart are headed for a breakup for sure. Our relationship is number one for us, and we're not going to let anything get in the way."

Couples can use many different reasons for postponing

individualizing, such as fear of the loss, belief that is it wrong to have needs that the other cannot fulfill, or the reluctance of one partner to individualize.

Problems

Of course, the major problem is the fear of losing the other. It can become a major obstacle. Couples often report that during this period the accompanying fear of abandonment is so painful that dissolution of the relationship seems the only way to solve the problem. Other researchers (Saghir and Robbins,[1]; Bell and Weinberg[2]) have discovered that male relationships commonly end at around the last part of the third year together. We believe that these terminations often are attributable to the reappearance of the individual.

Couples can get so involved in their individual interests that they drift apart and distance themselves from the relationship. As mentioned above, the time discrepancy in the reappearance of the individual can wreak havoc with a couple. More often, couples do not understand the process and interpret the need for individualizing as something far more sinister than it is. One individual may be more inclined to dependency than the other, causing him to cling to the partner when the partner wants to do things on his own.

Taking Risks

Although couples start taking risks from the moment of meeting, the reappearance of the individuals now forces and permits each partner to take risks of increased magnitude. In Stage Three risks are taken with the lover. The partner dares to bring up something about the other that he finds to be less than wonderful. With the lover, risks may include not only new sexual friendships but also more time apart, disclosures of dissatisfactions ranging from their own lovemaking to expressing negative feelings for mutual friends or the other's family. Risk also is taken with the relationship. The silent question is there: "If I do this, am I going to damage our relationship?" The third risk seen at this time is with the self. The fear emerges that "I am not all that he thinks I am." The person confesses flaws, first to himself and then to his lover. Taking risks with the self may include intense looking inward and dissatisfaction.

These three areas of risk permit the individual to move along his own path of growth. This movement counteracts stagnation and helps in the maintaining that is the hallmark of this stage. Each partner becomes more aware that he wants the relationship even if he does not know why. A result of risking is new knowledge of the self, of the other, and of the relationship, and risking the disclosure increases personal vulnerability.

Taking risks occurs not only with the lover and the relationship, but also with others, including friends, fellow employees, and family. These risks include coming out to people at work, taking assertive career actions, or trying new activities like learning to fly or water ski.

Earlier in the relationship there are various reasons why male couples were not visible to some friends, family members, neighbors, or colleagues. Some of these reasons include the couple's own insecurities about the relationship and their fears of coming out to others. The usual fears range from estrangement from the family to loss of a job. By the time of Stage Three, families have gotten accustomed to seeing the men together, and many couples, if they have not already done so, take the risk of coming out to their families.

Paul cringes when he remembers finally coming out to his family. "The worst was the family. First no one ever mentioned him. That made more distance from the family I loved. Then they called him my roommate. Then the first holiday came, and I went back home alone and missed him so much. That damned denial and pretending! We slid right into it, in collusion with them—the unspoken agreement. All that chatter with Mom and not looking at each other. He was the most important person in my life, and all of us, including me, denied his existence by what was carefully not said. I guess I was afraid of being rejected by them. We'd never talked openly even about my being gay. Lo and behold, after three years, I couldn't stand the charade any longer. We talked to my folks together. Of course, they already knew but were just as afraid to ask about it as we were to tell about it."

Some men move closer emotionally to their families. Parents may offer advice, and letters are now addressed to both. There is a reconciliation of some sort except for those families who choose prejudice over blood ties, or the male couple that insists on isolation because of feelings of shame. Older couples in our study were awed and sometimes made uncomfortable by young male couples of today who are able to establish these ties with their families. For male couples who reconnect with biological families at about this time, they report relief and appreciation. "It came at a good time," Paul says. "We needed that boost just about then."

Risking becomes a tough fact of life, with the threat of loss never out of sight. "If I'd tell him what I really thought about how his family is treating us, I'm afraid he'd walk out on me. At the least provocation his mom won't invite us to a family gathering. The whole family is short-tempered and hypersensitive. If I bring it up to him, his temper flares just like the rest of them."

"When I started looking at other guys and going to the baths for outside sex, I was keeping everyone I met at a distance, afraid that I'd fall in love again and lose what I had with George. The last thing I wanted was to harm our relationship, yet I couldn't resist my urges for new sexual adventures."

Parents take more risks with three-, four-, and five-year-olds than with younger children. So, too, male couples take more risks as their relationships move beyond three years. They now trust it sufficiently to dare to tell the partner more. It was easier to tell what one liked earlier. Now the time has come to tell more of what is disliked about self, partner, and relationship. It is distasteful medicine that helps to maintain the health of this increasingly sturdy relationship.

"Somewhere along the line we started having talks that were like encounter groups—you know, we started telling each other what we didn't like. Our gripes and annoyances started coming out. It wasn't easy to risk hurting each other. We were so used to saying only the good things. That seemed risky enough, let alone adding the bad stuff now."

"The first time he told me I had bad breath I thought I'd die, but then if your own lover doesn't tell you, who else would?"

There are immediate benefits from taking risks as well as the long-term benefits. A partner may respond to being told about an annoying habit in a variety of ways. Once told he may see it and respond positively. The relief at the moment is a small celebration. The couple has done something difficult together and has taken a step forward.

After three years, Joe summoned his courage one morning and said, "Paul, those double-knit slacks are snagged and out of style. They look awful."

"Oh. I never noticed. What would be better?"

Joe tells us he had thought Paul's lack of concern about clothes was cute in the beginning but increasingly felt he did not want his lover to be seen by other people that way. "After I told him and he was OK with it, I realized that helping him dress better was something I could do for him. He was doing a lot for me already."

From these small risks, larger ones become more possible. "It was one little thing like that after another," Joe tells us. "Before I knew how I had gotten there I found myself telling Paul I wanted to try having sex with a friend who had been at our house for dinner. That was harder than criticizing his slacks. But the time had come."

Taking risks begins differently for different couples. Some leap right into it like diving into an icy lake; others try the waters one toe at a time.

"You can't imagine how I felt when I came into the apartment and found Bob making out with this cute guy right in the living room! I knew we shouldn't have hired a male maid. They both tried to get me into a three-way, but I was so taken aback I just stomped into the bedroom and slammed the door. Bob's explanation was innocent enough, and God knows how often I had wanted to trick with him myself. Still, I put up a righteous front. After all, we both were committed to monogamy then. I had such mixed feelings, like how could he do this to me? What would the guy think about us? Did this mean Bob and I were finished? Yet, I wanted to do the same thing, only Bob beat me to the punch," Les explains.

Bob jumps in, "Hey, I'm the guy who took the risk. You were just jealous. We were both interested in outside sex but hadn't leveled with each other. We had talked about how cute the maid was and what it would have been like to fool around with him. I really didn't plan it; it just happened. I did feel guilty and defensive, especially when Les caught me and got so mad. But it did get us to start talking about risking outside sex. We both wanted it but felt that something just wasn't right about it. It was a good thing, as it turned out, but it was hell at the time."

For all couples in our study some outside sexual activity had begun by the end of this stage. Often it had begun in Stage Two. There is a difference in the level of sexual risk-taking in Stage Three, however. Sexual activity with others was limited previously to sex for the sake of sex. There were the baths for casual, one-time contacts. Now, one or the other partner may form a friendship including sex that can threaten the unincluded partner.

"It used to be that going to the baths or meeting a new trick at the gym was OK. Andy started working out with Tim twice a week, then brought him home one afternoon to meet me. I suspected he was interested in having an 'affairette' when I got the vibes that Tim was more than just a new friend. At first I kept quiet, then finally asked him about his relationship with Tim. I was afraid Tim was my replacement, but I decided that if Andy was replacing me he was crazy. Anyway, the situation got us to talking about more than casual outside sex, but about having sex with guys who became ongoing friends."

The realization has come in Stage Three that the world has told another untruth. There is no Santa Claus, and one limited human, no matter how wonderful or willing, cannot meet all the needs of his lover. Nor is this bittersweet dawning of shared awareness limited to sex. Life is broad. The relationship is now sufficiently strong to help each person avoid this culturally insinuated pitfall of expecting all needs to be met by the other. In this stage, risk permits one to look to others to meet some of those needs. Sometimes couples talk a lot, and sometimes it is simply done. The behavior tells the story. It is scary, but one does go to others and return home.

"I hadn't played basketball in almost three years when my friend John invited me to join their new team," Peter recalls. "I used to play a lot, but I stopped when I moved in with Frank. He hates the game, thinks it's silliness for ten men to run back and forth chasing and bouncing a fat ball. Anyway, I was really missing the game and the fun I'd had with the other guys. So, I joined John's team, even though Frank wasn't so happy about it. He figured I'd drift away from him, but I knew it was going to be OK for me."

Another said: "It was wrong. I knew it was dead wrong, but there it was. I couldn't give Don the kind of companionship he got from men his own age. I was older but always thought we would be everything the other needed or wanted. Now, here we were four years later. He's out 'with the boys' because I don't want to go. I'm fine that he's out there, and I miss him when he's away. Still, having fun with his peers makes him happier at home."

The male double standard plagues the couple at first. Joe says, "I knew what I was doing was safe, and I finally saw he was doing the same thing. It's a thing about being men; we both had to see what was good for the gander is good for the other gander, too. There it is! We learned there was no goose, just we two ganders."

"I feel it's really OK for me to have outside recreational sex," Carl tells us. "I know that I can handle it and not get so involved that our relationship is in jeopardy. I guess I don't trust him to do the same thing."

In the above vignette about playing basketball, Frank had some mixed feelings about Peter's activities away from him. Peter had his own mixed feelings. "I knew that playing basketball was just for exercise and some time with the guys, but when Frank started playing bridge every week and spent so much time with his new duplicate partner, I felt real uneasy about it. I think I was jealous and didn't want him to do it."

The double standard is a well-established cultural attitude that finds its most glaring example between husbands and wives. Gay men sharing the same male attitude come to grips with the accompanying problems with greater ease.

Insecure and fearful of damaging the relationship, some couples have difficulties in taking risks. They express their dislikes in covert and indirect ways. Sometimes their negative feelings toward their partners are expressed through joking or campy sarcasm.

"I guess I was afraid of rocking the boat. We got along so well in the first few years without many disagreements or real differences. Taking a chance on losing what we have by criticizing him seemed too much to me. My parents divorced early because of all the disagreements they had. I didn't want to follow in their footsteps. My annoyances began to get expressed by making jokes and pretending like it didn't matter when it did."

Joe, ordinarily a deep baritone, stands up with his hand on his hip and says, "Listen, honey," in a high whiny voice. "If you don't do something about those scattered dresses of yours, I'll divorce you." He is referring to not liking his lover's clothes dropped on the bedroom floor. They both laugh, but the point gets across.

Taking risks appears to be an inevitable occurrence in the process of relationship growth. Most couples start with careful risks and proceed into this period of increased risk. Individualizing is partially responsible, and often the process includes considerable conflict.

Dealing With Conflict

Although for most of their lives gay men have avoided conflict at almost any price, now is the time in their relationships when they must come to terms with it. Conflict is not necessarily new and in earlier

stages the couples have been handling their disagreements and differences in many of the ways we have outlined. However, in Stage
Three, couples generally devise definitive means of neutralizing,
resolving, or completely avoiding conflict for the present and into the
future. Dealing with conflict is a developmental task that can be
avoided no longer if their relationship is to continue to grow. Finding
effective ways to manage conflict usually results in the couple establishing a system. The system may not resolve discords, but the discords
are better managed. When such a system is not developed, maintaining the relationship becomes a much more unstable process.

Again, after their first years together, couples find the mundane
invading their romance. Formerly tolerated annoyances become more
irritating. Leaving the cap off the toothpaste or hair in the shower
now comes up for discussion. During Stage One the threat of conflict
is experienced as potentially lethal to the relationship. Couples move
quickly to restore harmony. During Stage Three the expression of anger, disagreement, and disappointment is not as frightening. With the
reappearance of the individual there are differences. Conflict is natural and expected as the couple remembers that they are two separate
individuals as well as a couple.

Now they begin to tolerate the discord and also to develop styles
of managing conflict in an attempt to restore peace. Anger does erupt
more easily, whereas in the past it had been too threatening. Now the
expression of negative feelings becomes an important ingredient of individual growth and relationship maintenance. Ways of dealing with
conflict are different for each couple and usually evolve slowly over
time. Couples use trial-and-error methods to discover the most effective ways for themselves.

Sources of conflict are multiple. Conflict may arise from within
the relationship. It is just as likely, however, that the root of the conflict comes from within the individual or from outside the couple. The
conflict is not experienced in terms of where it has its beginnings. The
couple simply wants to be rid of it. They learn with time, however,
that they must locate the source if they are to effectively come to
terms with the conflict. Otherwise, a partner is apt to think, "It's my
fault," or "It's his fault," or "Our relationship is just no good." In fact,
the conflict may have little or nothing to do with the quality of the
relationship.

Having learned to tolerate or contain the conflict or discord in the relationship, some couples move to resolve it as quickly as possible. Some will deny, ignore, or avoid. The mutual impulse in either direction is to seek quiet after the disquiet caused by a conflict. Whether a couple finds resolution or peace in some momentary means of restoration or balance, they are learning that conflict does and will exist in their relationship and that they will find some way to allay its disturbing influence.

Most couples in this stage intuitively recognize the need to develop skills in managing conflict. Some do it far better than others. Some learn sooner, some later, and some try to avoid it altogether. Every couple does learn to live with it.

Ways to Handle Conflict

Some couples head off most conflict at the pass, by nipping it in the bud early or at least before it becomes a major confrontation. Others try to deny discord and put off dealing with it. Nevertheless, whether early or late, the following are some of the ways couples in this study have dealt with their conflicts.

At the top of the list is compromise. It is a means they have been using almost from the beginning. The compromises of Stage One were easy and unspoken surrenders to the blending. Those of Stage Two contributed to the satisfaction of nesting. The compromises of Stage Three serve to maintain the relationship. The difference in Stage Three is that the conflict is on the table and the compromise is more deliberate. For those couples experiencing power struggles with each other, compromising becomes very difficult. If power is not a major issue, compromise is an easy and effective style for dealing with conflict.

Joe says he will never forget the day he found himself admitting, "Look, we've been going to visit your family one Sunday a month for three and a half years. I'm bored with it. They're *your* family. You go today. I want to stay home."

Stan is surprised to hear this. "You never gave any inkling that you didn't like going. Sure, I'll be glad to go alone, but would you be willing to go again next month?"

"I've been trying to get David to go to Europe with me for the last four years. I was willing to pay for the whole trip, but he's always said no." Peter is a physician, and David is an intensive care nurse. David has consistently refused to allow Peter to pay for expensive vacations. Wanting to pay his equal share of vacation costs, as they do most other things, David feels he couldn't afford the trip to Europe. The disagreement has continued all this time. Peter continues with the story. "I kept thinking how much I wanted to take David to Europe with me, and I also knew how stubbornly he was sticking to his guns about paying, so I figured out a compromise that he accepted. I'll pay for the airfare, and we'll share the other expenses."

Another means of dealing with conflict is illustrated by another couple. Andy and Jake are telling us about the early days of running their hardware store. "We were really excited about finally getting our business going. We'd had so much fun planning it. Then we started competing with each other to wait on customers or make a better window display. We'd almost come to blows about things. Actually, we could both do everything pretty well." Andy is chuckling as he recalls those past days.

Jake says, "Yeah, if we hadn't been smart enough to begin to divide things up between us, our store wouldn't have been the success it is today. I took over the upstairs jobs, like bookkeeping, ordering, financial management, billing, and that sort of stuff, while Andy took over the downstairs jobs, like hiring and firing sales staff, displays and the rest. I make the upstairs decisions, and he makes the downstairs ones. Actually, we never make any important decisions without talking together about them, but the division of responsibilities saved our relationship and our store."

Each had the training and skills to run the business by himself. Their conflicts began to arise over differences in ways of doing things. They finally divided the tasks along functional lines, and each assumed full responsibility for his particular area without interfering with the other. This resolution is much like the planned incompetency we discussed in Stage Two. We referred to it as developing complementarity.

"I could begin to feel a real fight coming on. We were always overdrawn or behind in our payments, even though we seemed to make enough money." Ted is telling us how he and Wayne dealt with the difficult conflict over money. "I'd get really angry with him when we'd get the overdue notices from the gas and light company and get our credit card rejected because it wasn't paid. One month I just sat down at the desk with him and started writing the checks and making suggestions about which bills to pay and how to manage the others. Before many months passed, I began taking full charge."

Wayne completes the story. "I was so relieved when Ted took over that I didn't even know how to thank him. I don't know why I couldn't ask him to do it before. I mow the lawn now while Ted is balancing the checkbook."

Couples establish fixed roles. Wayne took charge of financial management early. As the financial situation deteriorated, they switched tasks. There was no resentment. Once again, male couples do not have the role expectations that heterosexual couples experience.

A few couples orchestrate sham fights in front of others to express their dissatisfactions with the hope of changing the annoying attitude or behavior. This method often is employed to handle discord over relatively minor issues. By making humorous comments in a sham adversarial tone, they deliberately exaggerate the importance of the point. Tensions get discharged, and the point of the disagreement becomes clear and frequently gets resolved. These performances allow for options other than direct confrontation. This method permits discharge of tension. The partner, meanwhile, does not feel attacked.

Conferring with friends and family, as Tim and Phil illustrated in the opening vignette of this chapter, is a very useful way for some couples to deal with serious conflicts. Having the advice and support of loving friends or family can give perspective, help reduce emotionality, and provide useful suggestions.

A very helpful way to handle conflict that was reported by many couples was developing a specific system. For instance, when a conflict would emerge, one would say to the other, "Let's have a family conference." This code phrase meant that a disagreement was recognized and would be dealt with at an agreed-upon time in the near future. Other couples have set aside time on a weekly basis for "gripe sessions." Some always talk about it in front of close friends; others agree never to discuss differences with others. Some agree that conflict should always be discussed as soon as it happens, while others carefully wait until they calm down before trying to deal with the conflict.

Establishing Traditions

Tradition usually refers to customs handed down from generation to generation. For gay couples, traditions are formed from the customs each man brings to the relationship and the customs created by the couple. By this stage, the customs that get incorporated into the routine life of the relationship become traditions. Along with traditions we also include customs and habits that serve similar functions. Establishing traditions expresses the life of a relationship like no other characteristic discussed thus far. Those customs and habits of the first few years that become traditions are visible indicators of relationship history. Traditions are an outward sign of a couple's special partnership. Traditions announce the existence of a past history and the expectation of a future one, while maintaining the relationship through this stage and naturally propelling it toward the building of the next.

"Both of us came from families where Christmas was a big deal, but there were lots of differences, like who gets to participate, when things get done, what special foods are prepared. His family always went to midnight Mass and opened presents afterward. My family went to church on Christmas morning and didn't open presents until after Christmas dinner. Over these past five years we've worked out our own special way of having Christmas together."

"I'm Jewish. For me it's more ethnic than religious. Those roots are really deep, even though I don't really believe in the old rules. I like some of the traditions like Passover. There is some parallel in being gay, I think. My lover grew up a Christian, but he also likes some of the Jewish traditions. For instance, we always celebrate Passover by having a Seder on one of the nights."

"We didn't go to the altar for approval, so we never really had a date for our anniversary together. We've celebrated it at different times over the first three years; then last year we picked the date—the day we moved in together. There's a regular ritual that goes with celebrating. We take off for a weekend camping trip in the desert and do all sorts of things we never get to do in our usual day-to-day lives. Cooking over a campfire, long walks, sleeping on the ground together, getting away completely from the hustle and bustle of the city, help freshen us up *and* freshen up the relationship."

For male couples beginning a relationship there is a sharp contrast with heterosexual couples, who usually bring many shared traditions to their new pairing. There is going steady, getting engaged, and
the engagement ring. Families plan weddings, with a reception, the
cake, the rings, and the vows. Wedding anniversaries are yearly re-
minders that family and community honor this union. Gay culture is
not old enough to have established a similar set of traditions and
therefore male couples have none of the time-honored celebrations,
recognitions, and privileges.

A wedding ring, that ancient tradition, is an honored symbol
that the wearer is half of a couple, with a relationship that is recognized. If your spouse is ill you are legitimately excused from work;
airlines give "spouse take-along" discounts; death and its attendant
mourning are respected as natural privileges of this bonding. For the
first three years male partners themselves have confirmed their
mateship. Recognition of their togetherness by others came slowly.
After three years there is the beginning of community recognition
from family and friends.

In the absence of cultural traditions, gay couples have the definite advantage of creating their own. As indicated in our introduction, this lack of traditional rules allows the men greater freedom and
more choice in establishing the matrix for their couplings. They do
not have to fulfill preconceived expectations. By trial and error they
develop their own blueprint for a relationship that is customized to
their needs and individual expectations.

"I knew it wouldn't be like my sister's relationship with her husband, but part of me really wanted to have a husband, too. Tim and I
started going out together. Then I moved in with him. We talked a lot
about commitment to each other, but both of us wanted to go
slowly—well, actually, I didn't. I was so in love with him that I
wanted to be with him forever right from the start, and I wanted him
to marry me so that he'd have to be mine forever. I think those feelings were sort of silly and immature, but I sure felt them. In the long
haul we've both changed and tried lots of different ways to be
committed to each other. First it was monogamy, then it was anonymous sex only, and now we're trying new friends. Also, in the beginning I tried to play the 'wife' because I thought that's what I was supposed to do. I found out real fast that it wasn't for me. Tim caught on

quicker than me and suggested that we switch our roles around and change household jobs. That made a difference. We learned fast that we couldn't have a relationship like my sister's."

This couple at first used monogamy as their sign of commitment to each other. Gradually, as they started making outside sexual contact, the sign of their commitment was to be found in the customs and habits they had established as a couple. For instance, both partners report the importance of their Friday nights alone together, their weekends working in the garden, and the dependable affection of always sleeping together. These and similar customs and habits became the most tangible evidence of their commitment to each other.

Tim tells us more about their relationship. "In the beginning, monogamy was our way of showing our commitment to each other. It was easy then. When we started having outside sex, we were constantly reassuring each other. Chatter, chatter, chatter—words of reassurance were cheap when we were so insecure with each other. What else could we do then? With all the other reassurance we now have from each other, we don't have to depend only on the words."

When traditions, customs, and habits get established they do provide reassurance. Traditions establish a structure that now adds to the foundation of earlier years, to help maintain the commitment, increase the security, and add to the feelings of well-being and stability. Traditions become important in Stage Three as a stabilizing balance to the insecurities associated with the reappearance of the individual and risk-taking. Recognizing the structure and security created by their traditions, customs, and history, the couple begins to feel more like a family.

With this new awareness of their status as a family unit, they automatically begin to choose where and how they will celebrate holidays and special events. As Don Clark has noted, the couple creates new ceremonies as they draw from their respective family traditions.[3] With these created ceremonies, couples report a new feeling of their own family formation. They see the Friday flowers in a new light. They can and do honor their own traditions, whether established by chance or by conscious intention.

In one form or another over the years, older or younger individuals and couples have found their way to others like them. This is the beginning of what the younger couples refer to as "our gay family." Holidays may be shared together, and they see one another through joys and crises, poorly understood by the rest of the world. It is an alternative family, chosen, but no less strong than the family of birth.

"Glen and Ernie are like my family," Mike says. "No, they *are* my family. We always have Thanksgiving together. I take my new boyfriends over for them to meet and decide about. It seems funny, but that's how it is."

"The thing I like most about being in my 'gay family' is that it's not just gays, but some straights belong, too. All of those people I want to be with. I've been part of that crowd for over four years now, and we stick together through thick and thin—like a real family."

The notion of an extended family is certainly not new. Gay people have been forming them for years as have many others. Some have different ground rules, but for the most part members of extended families are treated like blood relatives with mutual responsibilities to one another.

One of the most rewarding outcomes of establishing traditions, customs, and habits is the enrichment it brings to the couple's relationship. The traditions the couple creates come out of an intermingling of their backgrounds and an investment in their life together. Innovative styles can arise from the freedom of choice these men have to make life together better and not worse.

CHAPTER 6

STAGE FOUR—BUILDING
(Year Six Through Year Ten)

Characteristics

1. Collaborating
2. Increasing productivity
3. Establishing independence
4. Dependability of partners

"Sometimes we look at each other and just shake our heads. I think I know what he's thinking and he knows what I'm thinking too often. That's more than just being lovers. Nine years together means a lot of water under the bridge and a lot more, too." Walt, forty, has been living with Manny thirty-eight, for those nine years. Walt has been a barber for almost twenty years, first working for someone else and then owning his own shop for the past ten years. He grew up on a small farm in the Midwest and left home at seventeen to get away, joined the Navy, and spent time in San Diego. He learned to cut hair while on active duty. After his discharge he stayed in "America's finest city" where he has lived ever since. He had finished high school before leaving home. He says he liked school but has only taken a few courses in junior college since. He came out during the last year in the Navy and had several relationships before settling down with Manny nine years ago.

Manny also had a Navy career. He grew up in northern California near Oakland. He stayed in the Navy for eight years before taking a discharge. He also had graduated from high school but didn't have any college time. His recent courses in plumbing were the most he had wanted. He took a job with the Postal Service and has been delivering the mail in the same neighborhood for the past ten years. He claims he was out of the closet before joining the Navy but never got caught in the service. He also tells us he is a recovering alcoholic, mainly because of Walt's support.

"We haven't always been such good friends." Manny looks to Walt as he speaks. "But the roughest days are behind us now. They'd better be. I know he's reliable because he's been hanging in there even when I used to get so drunk nobody else could handle me."

Walt shifts uncomfortably in his chair, clearly not wanting to comment on that last remark. "We each have our separate ways. Manny plays golf on Saturdays, and you couldn't drag me out there with a team of wild horses. I go off to the beach to muscle watch."

We are impressed by the number of rituals these men have: dinner on Friday nights at the Copper Kettle, Sunday nights for TV, last week in June means the lake, French toast on Christmas morning, and "a bath before bed every night," Manny adds proudly.

"Old Iris over there has been with us ever since he got run over seven years ago. Manny fixes that dog a hot meal every morning. I say he babies him too much. But, what the heck, he's only going to be around another year or so anyway. The vet says he's going blind."

Walt, walking past Manny, slaps him lightly on the back of the neck. "Manny's good for a few more years, I hope. He'd better be. He's the one who nursed Iris back to life and he does everything for him. And we have a lot of things to see together."

We learn that while sex with others no longer disturbs either partner, they do continue to enjoy sleeping together every night as they have from the beginning, and they make love a few times each month.

They own their own home together. It's in a comfortable middle-class neighborhood where working-class couples live and rear their families. The lawn is neatly trimmed, with flower beds across the front of the house, all carefully weeded. The living room is furnished with a practical, sturdy living room set, a vinyl-covered recliner, and a Mexican blanket in front of the small fireplace for the dog. There are a few plants in the front window and the lace tablecloth on the dining room table is visible from where we are seated. Manny and Walt have a small circle of mutual friends, mostly other male couples with whom they socialize several times in an average week. They admit that they do not talk together as much as they did a few years back. Both agree that they could say anything they wanted to each other although they rarely need to talk so seriously anymore.

Manny laughs, "Lord, there was a time when you couldn't shut us up, particularly Walt. We would talk the flowers right off the wallpaper. It was one night after another of thinking we were making sense out of a bunch of junk. We just had to agree everything right into the ground."

Walt sits up straight. "That pair of lamps there on either end of the sofa came from a big furniture sale, and we spent one whole week talking about whether or not to get them or save up for a recliner chair."

Walt and Manny are just in the process of combining their savings to invest in some acreage. "We just finished fixing up a tiny little ranch and selling it. We did all the work ourselves. Manny learned plumbing and I learned the electric work without killing myself," Walt says.

"But we had to fight about who would sew the curtains," Manny adds wryly.

"Anyway, from here on in there are certain things we each know how to do, and this next ranch should be a good project for us."

"Don't get the idea that we're in each other's back pockets all the time," Manny says. "I still do my own things, and Walt does something, I suppose." Walt pretends to try to kick Manny. "He's just jealous because he cannot get into my bowling club," he says.

"To tell you the truth, his bowling night is great for him and for me," Walt says, "even on a night when I just watch TV. I think some people smother each other."

"I suppose even if we're together another nine years, there will be some things to get used to with each other," Manny says. "But the truth is, when Walt had his appendix out last summer I thought it was me that wasn't going to make it."

"Get right down to it," Walt says, "we get on each other's nerves sometimes, but I always know Manny is here."

"Yeah, and so's Iris," Manny says with a wink.

Collaborating

Collaborating means working together. It also has the connotation of cooperating in a negative manner, as when one strikes a bargain with a seeming enemy. In either case it means working together to make the best of what there is. Our findings about couples in this stage support the dichotomy.

There is a quality of working together in the couple's life whether they are joking, doing dishes, or making a difficult decision. They know each other. They finish sentences for each other. They are finely tuned to each other.

There is so much ease with the relationship and comfort in this family of three—the two partners and their relationship—that they cooperate in moving closer together and making sure that there is room for each individual at the same time. There is an ebb and flow or a push and pull in their loving. The collaboration arises from both the earned familiarity and the developed complementarity of the couple. Often the two seem to function as a single person in the tasks they perform.

Each reports the feeling of knowing what the other thinks and feels at such a highly intuitive level that it reminds them of the first year, but without the illusions. There is reality and depth now. The fear of loss has lessened so much that the couple finds they have not only each other, but more, something intangible and unanticipated. The couples have passed through the initial threats caused by the reappearance of the individual in Stage Three. A new unspoken rapport is with them. They no longer require the elaborate verbal exchanges and clarifications. The men know and trust each other deeply. Collaborating is easy and rewarding.

The negative side of collaboration is far more subtle and is rooted in the positive feelings. The constant communication of Stage Three led to the present rapport. Communication about each other and about the relationship itself happens intuitively in Stage Four. The danger is the resulting complacency.

The energy of the couple now is directed outward easily, and the relationship gets neglected. The very comfort and reliability of the relationship that lulled the couple into complacency blinds them to the continuing process of change. They do not see that they themselves are changing. Their relationship is changing, too. And the relationship needs attention and nurturing. It needs new excitement, renewed romance, for the couple together to reestablish facets of the past that have gradually slipped away. Ironically, the easy relationship has become a threat, almost an enemy.

This comforting, quiet, ironic "enemy" may lead to boredom and empty routines that partners independently fear as traps. The collaborators, of course, do not recognize the relationship as an occupying enemy, but they do move instinctively to protect each other and the mateship by devising mechanisms for both moving away from each other and, at the same time, consolidating their partnership. In actuality both the distancing and consolidating, seemingly oppositional forces on the surface, are critical ingredients that aid in the continuing stability and vitality of the relationship.

The collaboration that sustains and increases the strength of the relationship leads the couple to find or create more and more areas of complementarity. Walt learned electrical work, and Manny learned plumbing.

There are some direct results of the increased smooth collaboration. Couples invariably have increased financial security and usually an increased comfort of lifestyle.

"Once we really began working together on making more money, it was almost like nothing could stop us. We pushed day and night, both of us, making contacts, working weekends, not taking any time off. We sure wouldn't be here in this house if we hadn't done that." Doug is a real estate agent and his lover Bill is an interior designer. Bill works weekends with Doug, helping to hold open houses, returning phone calls, and doing whatever is needed. Doug helps Bill get more jobs. Doug and Bill live in a spacious, beautifully appointed, expensive home. "We know we have slipped into living a bit beyond our means. We're sure continuing to work hard to keep it all together," Doug admits, and Bill nods in agreement.

For this next couple, the high collaboration has brought them financial success and upgraded their life situation, but in the highs of collaborating they overextended themselves. They lost some of their individual objectivity and were both carried along on the deceptive tidal wave of mutual cooperation.

"We tried working together to make more money, and it was a disaster," Ben tells us about their efforts at collaborating. "At home we always worked well together, no problems at all. We thought investing in this bar would be a bonanza. Wrong! It's opened up too many areas of disagreement and different ways of dealing with things that never happened to us before. Our jobs fit us to a tee, but this business was just too much. Some couples can't be involved with each other on everything."

Couples who enjoy and do well with high collaborating at home might not be able to carry that into every aspect of their lives together. The above example demonstrates this well. Often enough these couples have established fixed roles at home, which increases the smoothness of their working together there, but when they try to move away from that structure problems result. Usually these fixed roles also have created a high level of complementarity. When the game shifts to new ground, the old complementarities are no longer effective.

Collaborating sometimes also means one partner supporting the other in striving to achieve certain goals. However noble the intention, one partner can be misguided in his estimate of the other's ability and can encourage him to pursue something beyond his reach. In such a situation, they are collaborators in the failure of one or the other, and both feel badly about it.

Ron was a hot-shot, aggressive, outgoing real estate salesman. Ted, his lover of eight years, was a shy, thoughtful, sensitive man who saw how pleased Ron would be if he, too, could make as much money. So, Ted announced to Ron that he could sell real estate, too. Ron actively supported Ted's efforts, but despite everything Ted was not successful.

Highly tuned, intuitive communication results from the give-and-take of Stage Three. As a result there is a decline in verbal "checking in." Partners believe they know what each other thinks and feels, but often changes have taken place in one or the other, thus, unwittingly, the partners misinterpret each other.

"I thought I really knew what he wanted. He'd always told me in the past that he would love to do some foreign travel. I worked for several weeks to plan a surprise trip, and when I sprang the surprise on him he seemed much less than enthusiastic. I was flabbergasted."

His lover replies, "A few years ago I was interested in going abroad. In fact, then I would have given anything to go. Now, I'm more interested in buying a sailboat and staying in town. I guess I haven't made that clear to you."

Sometimes couples collaborate so intensely that old competitive feelings get ignited. In these cases there can be monumental power struggles, resulting in relationship collapse.

Sam and Frank started their business together two years ago and have been very successful. Each had made large sums of money when they started to compete to see who could make the most. This led to a serious struggle over who should run the business, and it almost ruined their relationship. What had started out as an effective and enjoyable collaboration stimulated their individual competitiveness and turned them against each other.

Sam is talking in retrospect: "We had such a good thing going, and we almost lost everything because we lost sight of each other. Our successful working together got us away from attending to our relationship. I'd rather lose the business than us. At any rate, we got smart to that just in the nick of time."

Increasing Productivity

As is so often true in nature, from the union of two beings something new is produced. Male couples are no exception. The collaboration so characteristic of Stage Four leads to a smooth interchange, an ability to think, feel, and work together. With couples in this stage, we saw some like Manny and Walt, working together to restore property, sending one of the partners back to school, joining a local business association, or creating a vegetable garden that yielded much more than items not found at the produce market. One rented a rototiller and set to in the garden while the other read books on horticulture or plant diseases and their cures. We saw the pride they took in their accomplishment and production. There was pride also in the manner in which they were doing this together as a team. Learning with the effort seemed as important as the product.

Individual productivity is increased during this stage. Men talk about greater success and satisfaction with their jobs. Individual achievement is encouraged and supported by partners. We found many career changes and much job advancement in this stage. It is easier to walk strongly into the world when there is a strong, well-functioning home where one is nourished.

"Academic life has advantages and awful drawbacks." Brian is telling us about his job at the university. "Like the politics of getting promotions. For a long time I just couldn't get committed to jumping the hurdles, especially at the start of our relationship. Greg was far more important to me than my job. Then, a couple of years ago I found new energy to put into teaching and research. Greg really got behind and pushed me."

The increasing productivity of this stage is not limited to possessions, specific projects, or tangibles, but extends to expansion of attitudes and horizons for the individuals and the couple. For example, Brian's increasing attention to his academic life probably was made possible by the dependability of Greg and the collaboration of Stage Four. There is less concern about attending to the relationship, making energy formerly directed inward to the couple available to be directed outward to the job or other project.

Sometimes male couples put so much energy into projects that they become like proud parents focused on rearing children, getting the job done well, while paying little conscious attention to their marriage. Without children, male couples often turn their attention to their projects as if they were offspring and in so doing pay little conscious attention to their relationship. Usually there is strength and resilience enough to manage the problems brought on by the neglect. For Manny and Walt, their ranch and all the work it required became much like a child. As if they were parents, they took pride in the project, how it was developing, and the recognition they got from others for a job well done. They were telling us about how they were plagued at the ranch by a leak that seemed to change its source with each rainstorm. As is so characteristic of couples in this stage, they paid less attention to the strain it placed on each in relation to the other than to getting the leak fixed once and for all.

Couples express greater ability to get projects completed together with each person assuming his own responsibility, resulting in a smooth working together. For instance, some couples describe the ease with which they now entertain. One partner plans and executes while the other takes the assisting role. Their mutual productivity is supported by a trend toward one partner always doing one task while the other always does his. Such rigid roles block changes that need to be made in the relationship. It is precisely this kind of situation we had in mind earlier when we described the relationship as the occupying enemy. Couples speak less often but with no less feeling of the troubles that go hand in hand with the smoothness of their working together. There is the sudden unexpected outburst. "Why don't *you* do the party this one time and let *me* just do the dishes?" Although their entertaining comes off like clockwork, what was once a fun activity together has become a fixed routine. The various chores become expected and hardly noticed, as if they are running a restaurant but without earning salaries. Couples miss the fun of doing it together, and in the process of routinizing everything they forget to recognize the part each plays in making things function.

From Stage One onward there usually has been at least an attitude of financial equality. Although in previous stages couples may have purchased a home or condo together, it is at the beginning of Stage Four that they begin combining their money and possessions, which contribute to the increasing productivity. It is unusual for all of their money to be merged, but it is not unusual for them to combine resources more creatively at this time in order to make more. We have observed that the gradual merger of money and possessions is clearly a symbolic and actual commitment to the relationship, often unspoken and unrecognized.

Establishing Independence

Each partner in a male couple does become more of a partner and more of his own person during this building stage of the relationship. The pursuit of a separate hobby, friend, entertainment, sport, or activity may take partners in divergent directions. "My" new friend may or may not become "our" new friend. Partners confer less on decisions that do not affect both of them. This is very different from the beginning of the relationship, where partners talk and confer about minute matters. One partner now may invite someone to dinner the following week without first consulting the other. It becomes, "Oh, by the way, I invited Joe and Tom," rather than "What would you think about inviting Joe and Tom?" One partner may make an individual commitment, "Oh, by the way, I agreed to be on the bowling team next Tuesday," rather than "How about our going bowling some time soon?" Independence is rooted in years together, and by this time each partner has learned to remain as sensitive as possible to the other.

The insecurity and fear of loss that accompanied the reappearance of the individual in Stage Three has given way to a sense of reliability and dependability that not only allows but indeed boosts partners into more individualizing. Individuality is not synonymous with rejection. It is a step out, not a push away. It is a natural development, but it is not always smooth and easy. Sometimes old ghosts of competition, hurt, and misunderstanding reappear, but the couple has learned to identify these potential troubles and has developed skill in calming troubled waters.

"We had been working so closely together that when Tom had a chance to direct a play at the local volunteer theater I was really pleased," Jim starts to explain, "but when he was out so much and started having such a good time away from me I got jealous about it."

Tom tells us his side of the story. "Yeah, Jim was eager for me to do it; then all of a sudden he got angry and complaining about it. We struggled with it until after the first play was over. Then we talked."

"What I needed was something equally satisfying for myself, so I started taking piano lessons again and I couldn't be happier," Jim says.

When partners express dissatisfaction or anger, it is less threatening. "No, I don't really want to do that" no longer sounds like the end of the world or the end of the relationship. Partners can say no to each other more easily and with greater frequency than in previous years.

The independence touches all aspects of the couple's life. While separate sexual contacts with others are not new events at this stage, they may well change form. There may be friendships that include sex and are more separate. Again, the security the male couple has been building now permits this sort of risk. However, if the partner is truly threatened, the private sexual liaison is apt to fail.

Fred tells us that at this stage, "I used to go to the baths occasionally and just trick out, but then I met Jack and we saw each other a few times. Finally, I told Al about him, and Jack came home with me. Al told me he just couldn't handle the situation. Even though the sex with Jack was great, I stopped seeing him. Al was far more important to me."

The growing independence helps to keep the relationship vital. Ralph says, "There were times when it felt like cold water in the face, but it left us awake. I mean, here he was changing right in front of me. He went back to school. I was looking at my lover, the A student. I was used to my good old lover, the bank teller, but this student in the house upset the balance. We had less money, he was studying all the time, and he might get to be the bank president some day and not want to be with me. I guess I had to see it in his eyes that he still wanted me. And I had to see it enough days that I could start to breathe easy again, even if I was breathing new air. And you know, I think that's what got me interested in computers and got me into this business I own."

Men report the importance of each partner being able to import new things into the relationship from his outside experiences. As an example, outside sexual experiences can broaden and vary their sexual repertoire. With both partners gaining new independence, a new equilibrium is formed within the relationship. Independence serves to distance each from the other, a distancing that is necessary to keep their mutual attraction viable and minimize boredom and stagnation. A major signpost of Stage Four relationships is the balance between individual independence and dependence on the partner. These oppositional push–pull forces strive for homeostasis and in the process provide the high and low emotional punctuations mentioned above.

In this stage the individual partner finds he has new work to do. He finds he can do interesting things on his own. The solid relationship permits the fresh steps of the individual. The other partner has the opportunity to reestablish balance by means of his own growth. It becomes difficult when old fears of loss reappear. It is a time for the couples to learn that they can count on each other, even in the midst of change.

Dependability of Partners

"When Fred decided to go back to school because he was tired of being a teller, it did make the money a lot tighter," Al tells us.

"That made me feel guilty," Fred says, "but it really was good. Al told me that he did mind that we didn't have enough money to do everything we wanted, but he was really behind my going back to school even if it was a pain and scared him a little."

While each characteristic has its negative and positive aspects, the dependability of partners we saw in this stage was a remarkably consistent factor that helped the partners in their building. The productivity we saw in this stage was made possible by the reassurance of knowing that the partner was ready and willing to help without necessarily talking about it. One partner may begin to pick up the shirts at the laundry after nine years of expecting the other one to do it. Or the presumed noncook may have dinner ready so that his partner can make it from work to night class on time.

Some men in this stage mention knowing that they could count on their partners in some particular way because they had seen it in their first months together. "I knew Mike was generous because he always had been, and I knew he was good at tightening the belt in a pinch because I saw him do it when we first met."

Here is where we saw that it was not only the strong relationship that had been built that was helping, but each partner was counting on something special about the individual person with whom he had chosen to pair. They knew each other well after these many years together. Walt puts it his own way when he says, "I ain't no fortune teller. There's lots I don't know about. Old Iris could start talking tomorrow for all I know. But I sure as hell know Manny don't have no screws loose. And I sure as hell know he does have some shortcomings. If I didn't do the arithmetic on the checkbook we'd be two years behind. And if I didn't call his sick Aunt Ida in the rest home once a month, she'd have thought he died long ago."

Again and again we hear the phrase "I knew he'd be there." There is a tone of relieved comfort that is not surprising in the face of the growing independence seen in this stage. In Stage Three the dependability rested more on the relationship. Although the relationship structure is continually building, now the dependability shifts more to the individual.

Every positive feature seems to have its negative counterpart. The dependability of one's partner is wonderfully reassuring. But it is predictable, and it is too easy to take it all for granted. The teamwork oils the machinery of growth and change during this stage, but misunderstandings happen most often when all is taken for granted. Like the hero of *Fiddler on the Roof*, one member of the male couple may stop suddenly to look into his partner's eyes, knowing all the household chores are done, and ask, "But do you *love* me?" There is independence in the air. Change demands active reassurance. We observed how consistently couples in this stage, whether or not they talked about it, seem to know that they must handle this period of change *together*.

Another problem seen in this stage is that an actively changing partner can take the dependable backup for granted and fail to notice that the other person also is starting on some new path of change.

"We worked together for almost five years." Steve is telling us about how he and Michael developed some new independence after six years together. "Then I had a big job offer for a lot of money that I just couldn't refuse. It meant a real upheaval in our lives, more hours for me, lots of trips and times away. At first Michael was real supportive, then he got jealous, I think."

Michael tells us his side of it. "At first I was really proud of Steve's new job. Then I started feeling like I was carrying all the burdens at home plus all the work we had done together. Steve was out having fun, traveling, meeting new people and new sex partners, while I kept the lawn mowed. It took me a few months to realize how bad I was feeling. I told Steve we had to talk about it. We hadn't had one of those heart-to-hearts in over a year, and I really needed it."

"I hadn't realized how much things had changed for the worse for Mike," Steve says. "I was so wrapped up in my own excitement that I just took us for granted. He has always been so dependable."

There may be temporary hurt when one partner points out the imbalance in dependability. Stage Four couples have learned earlier how to manage these hurts, and they do rebalance when necessary.

One partner may be going too fast in his individual change and may need to hear the alarm sounded. It may slow or temporarily stop his moving out into the world. This can be uncomfortable, but, again, male couples in this stage find a way or use accustomed ways to keep their relationship alive, well, and balanced. This is a period of balancing. The couple balances dependence and independence, going separate ways and coming back together, going outward into the larger world and coming home. By the end of this stage the two people have established a reliable recipe for balancing the sweetness of individual freedom and the safe blandness of mutual security.

Commentary

The building stage is a time when couples reap profits from having managed the characteristics of the second and third stages. The way they have found compatibility through developing complementarity was an early foundation for the smooth working together of collaboration. The resolution of the ambivalence felt in Stage Two helps lay the groundwork for the dependability of this stage. How the individuals reappear in Stage Three can make the independence of Stage Four satisfying and stimulating for the couple. Taking risks and dealing with conflicts allow the collaboration to lead to higher productivity. Establishing traditions creates a reliable skeletal structure so that the relationship becomes an even more tangible reality, allowing the individual partners to move away from home base, knowing that the relationship will be there upon their return.

Once again returning to our analogy between the relationship and the developing child, there is a slowing down of physical growth in this five-to-ten-year period. A child grows physically five times as much between birth and age five as he or she does between five and ten years. On the other hand, during the second five years the child acquires a different kind of growth, measured in skills acquired and integrated, such as reading, arithmetic, and motor coordination. During this five-year stage, there is a general slowdown in the process of change. The differences are more subtle, which accounts for problems when couples are not really aware of the changes in each other. This is a stage where earlier characteristics often appear again. For instance, some of the ways of dealing with conflict learned in Stage Three may fail to be effective when differences arise over productivity, as we saw in the story of Steve and Ted above. Taking risks may appear in greater force during this time, especially with couples in their desire for greater productivity or for some individuals in their striving for more independence. The old fears of loss experienced in Stage Three may be felt strongly as partners move away from each other in their seventh or eighth year together. These are but a few examples of how the stages can and do lose their rigidity and must be viewed as being on a spiral progression rather than a strictly linear one.

Some other occurrences are so commonly found in Stage Four that they must be included here. They do not qualify as characteristics but can be seen as problems by the couples when they are simply stage-related happenings. For example, the familiarity and comfortableness that have developed between the pair frequently reduce their sexual interest in each other. As Tripp says, the price they pay for the old shoe comfort of the relationship is found in the ashes of the bedroom.[1] Our findings do not fully support his thesis, but there is clearly a reduction in sexual activity together some time during Stage Four. We believe that the high intuitiveness and accord between the partners reduces the resistance between them to such a low level that it extinguishes much of the erotic attraction. Again, almost intuitively, by developing greater independence and by introducing outside sexual partners, some couples reestablish a level of resistance that stimulates sexual interest and activity again. This problem of decline in sexual interest as high compatibility is established occurs with opposite-sex couples and female couples as well.

"I guess I didn't realize that our sex was less and less frequent, until one day he asked me why it was so. We had always slept together and cuddled and kissed and held each other. I don't think either of us could sleep without doing that, but, indeed, the high sex of earlier days was gone."

We also found some difference in the attitude of couples toward dealing with their antihomosexual attitudes. (See chapter 9.) Couples who had been together for more than five years in 1975 appeared different from Stage Four couples we interviewed in 1979. The rapid influence of the gay rights movement did seem to have some effect on lowering some people's homophobia and prejudice about themselves and other gays. Many books had been written, new models had begun to surface, and openness of talking about relationships between gay men had increased dramatically. We still find, however, that homophobia and other antigay attitudes take their toll on the lives of couples, especially when they are not identified and neutralized.

Another common occurrence here is the development of a new limerence by one or both partners. Falling in love is such a powerful human adventure that it certainly is not surprising to find that gay men do it over and over again. It does become somewhat disconcerting to partners, however, when they do not realize the usual transient nature of the feelings and experience the terrifying threat of relationship dissolution. New limerence is a fact of life, and old couples only laugh when they hear the younger ones worrying about it. Couples in this stage must allow each other the freedom to have such new romances but must also safeguard their mateship with mutual agreements and understandings about the new lovers.

Some Problems

As mentioned in other stages, where one person moves more quickly into the next stage or the other remains longer in the previous stage the discrepancies created cause unduly severe distress. In Stage Four, the most common discrepancy is found in the couple where one partner is holding tenaciously to the usual dependencies that arise from five years together, while the other partner is moving rapidly to be more independent. The dependent partner grasps at every straw to keep the other from moving too far away. He may develop illnesses or other ways of being even more dependent on the partner, holding him back. This is usually not a consciously contrived process but rather a normal human defensive response. Change does not come easily for all, especially for couples who have different experiences when growing up that influence their current responses to their partners.

Jealousy is an enemy of the relationship at every stage. It never seems to disappear completely, but with the frequent development of new romantic attachments it can and does get intensified in Stage Four, especially if the couple has not prepared for it. In couples with stage discrepancies, a new limerence can spell doom for the relationship.

As the dependability of the relationship increases from Stage Three and the independence of Stage Four grows, partners can find themselves spending less and less time together. This insidious isolation from each other and from the relationship can create distance of such magnitude that the couple begins to feel like housemates and not lovers. This distancing often leads to arguments, which in turn create more distance. It becomes a catch-22 that must be stopped, or they will become only roommates.

Conclusion

Stage Three provides the foundation for the building that happens in Stage Four. Each partner in the male couple goes about his individual tasks that result in the team productivity. The couple's eye is on the future. Their comfort is established in the present. The hallmark of this stage is the acquired ability to balance. The usual danger is a temporary lack of perspective during which all attention is on the accomplishment and, for the moment, the couple become too separate, forgetting that the primary earned reward of their years together is the relationship they have created. The couple then must rebalance. They learn in Stage Four how to be individuals, growing and changing, separately and together, reaping more than twice the reward that might be found individually.

CHAPTER 7

STAGE FIVE—RELEASING
(Years Eleven Through Year Twenty)

Characteristics

1. Trusting
2. Merging of money and possessions
3. Constricting
4. Taking each other for granted

Their house fits the neighborhood, though it has been given more attention than those on either side of it. The paint is fresh and flowers are in bloom. The yard is neatly kept. There is a locked wrought iron gate in front of the short hall leading to the front door. The sun is setting as we arrive adding color to the potted plants on the porch. When we ring the bell, John buzzes the gate open immediately. He and Francis greet us together at the front door.

"Hi, kids, you're just in time for cocktails. But none for you, Coco, you go downstairs and see Mommy," Francis says to the blue-eyed Siamese cat looking at him expectantly.

Once inside the door we see a well-kept and carefully arranged home. While they are informal in manner and dress, we wait to be told where to sit. John is wearing a San Diego Padres hat, open shirt, jeans, and Adidas. Francis wears slacks and a cashmere sweater. "Don't mind Miss Butch," he says. "She hasn't gotten over the game on TV yesterday yet." Francis is referring to the San Diego Padres baseball team victory.

There is a small collection of crystal paperweights on the coffee table. "We have got to move those damned baubles, Jean Louis," Francis says, as he quickly reaches for a bar tray on the tea cart next to the fireplace. "There's no room for a martini, let alone their pads and

97

pencils. Oh, I forgot, you boys said on the phone no drinks until our chat is done, didn't you?"

On our first visit, Francis is fifty-four and has been with John just over fifteen years. After finishing his two-year stint in the Army, Francis had returned to San Diego and started teaching music in high school. He tells us he has had many opportunities to move into educational administration, but he likes teaching too much to leave it. He also mentions something about his gayness making it difficult to be too visible. Francis was born, reared, and educated in San Diego. His father had a plumbing business and his mother was a piano teacher. Growing up was generally a pleasant experience and Francis gives us the same story of being "different" from the other boys because of his homosexual feelings. He was always a very talented and accomplished pianist and loved music. He had lived with several different partners, one for almost nine years before he moved in with John. His father had died twelve years earlier, and John had built an apartment in their house for his mother eight years ago. She lives with them.

John was born forty-five years ago in Atlanta, Georgia, where his father had a contracting business. John was the youngest of three children. "I'm not sure my mother knew the Civil War was over," John jokes as he talks about the airs he always saw his mother putting on. He left home after high school to attend a small college in Ohio, where he met and married Joline. He worked in various businesses in Ohio and had a modest home in a Cleveland suburb, two children, and much unhappiness because he knew he was gay and had not really faced it. He was traveling alone on a business trip sixteen years ago when he met Francis in a San Diego bar.

"Can we show you the mansion?" John asks. There is an elaborate kitchen, surprising in such a modest house. "Jean Louis does all his pancakes in there," Francis says, waving his hand. Each has his own bedroom though they usually sleep together in the larger one. The garden extends quite far behind the house, with flowering hedges that protect its privacy. There is a small workshop in a separate, small prefab building in the garden. "This is where I hide out. Francis thinks I should put shingles over the aluminum, but it suits me." Each tool is neatly arranged on the wall inside.

"He pretends he can only build knickknack shelves, but he's the one who built the entire apartment under the house, which is where my mother and Coco live," Francis says proudly.

"Next I have to build a shed for Francis's tools. This garden looked like the city dump when we bought the house. Francis put each and every plant you see growing here in with his own two hands," John says.

"Well, let's go back inside and face the music," he adds with a nervous laugh. "I don't think they drove all the way out here to see our arts and crafts fair."

At the start of the interview, Francis and John rarely look directly at each other, seeming to know the other is there without looking. We notice how often they speak positively about each other. "I guess I have been teaching piano for about thirty years now," Francis says. "Or is it a hundred and thirty? I just can't remember."

"He really is a gifted pianist," John says. "His mother taught him and he gave his first real recital when he was only seven years old. We even have the newspaper clippings."

"Oh, I'm just a tired, old, used-up high-school teacher. You know, a sort of dropout."

John wrinkles his brow and looks serious. "Francis was teaching during the McCarthy days. It's hard even to remember how hard it was. Several of his friends were fired. Everybody who was suspected of being homosexual was called a Communist. There were no gays then, you know. He weathered the storm OK by minding his ps and qs. That's when he started teaching at home, too, to lay in a little extra money just in case. That was before we met, of course, but I'll tell you, this boy had guts to get through that time without getting married."

Even Francis looks sobered by John's remarks. "It was a tough time. I was just out of college and had no girlfriend in sight. A lot of those kids got into bad fixes. The parties were different then, lots of booze and pretend. God, it's hard to realize I'm fifty-four now. There was so much fluff."

"Well, thanks a lot," John says. "I may be only forty-five, but I'm no air-head and no twinkie."

"No, seriously, meeting John was the best thing that ever happened to me, but I never guessed I'd end up with a married man."

"I was one of those guys who kept hoping it would go away," John says. "I got married when I was nineteen and have two kids in Ohio. The boy is twenty-four now, and the girl is twenty-two. I met Francis sixteen years ago in a bar. A year later the marriage was done, and we were living in a little apartment where Francis paid the rent."

"He felt so bad he just gave Joline everything," Francis says. "The real hurt was having to let go of the kids. The judge said he could only see them once a month, and he had to be alone then. It might have been nice to have them with us sometimes. You know, it's his own flesh and blood."

In our individual interview with Francis, he tells us, "I like the guy just the way he is. I know he's here with me and here to stay. It's easier to let him be who he is now. I mean, for years I tried to change his name to the French pronunciation of Jean-Louis. It sounded more elegant. But the truth is he was named after John L. Lewis, the coal-mining union guy, and he's just plain John from Ohio. I guess we're old enough to relax now. He's happy in his workshop, and I'm happy learning a new piece on the piano or puttering in the garden. He doesn't need me to play Carnegie Hall, and I don't need to pretend he's anything more than an office manager at the electric company. It's a relief, I guess."

John tells us, "I handle the family money. At the start we had his money, my money, and our money. Somewhere along the line, it all got to be our money. I mean, I guess the woodworking tools are mine and the piano is his, but everything is ours. It would be one hell of a mess to try to separate things now. When I got married everything was ours the day of the wedding. I know it took Francis and me a while to get there, but we're just as there now as I ever was with Joline—more, really. I mean, we're really married now, though that word still doesn't sound right to me for two men. We have our wills and everything goes to the other, that's for sure. Francis knows I'd take care of his mother."

About two months after our first interview we received an invitation from these two men to attend their annual World Series party. They have a tight group of friends—mostly other gay couples—who socialize together regularly. Many of the other couples have some sort of traditional annual party. We can't resist the temptation to attend: we're eager to get more couples for our study. The party is a goldmine for new participants. We could meet couples who never went to bars or any gay events beyond the parties held by their network of friends. Many of them are blue-collar workers, fitting none of the usual stereotypes of gay men.

Although we have visited with Francis and John several times in the intervening year, we return to interview them four years later, as we have done with a number of couples. We want to see which of our findings remained the same and what changes have occurred.

The outside of the house has the same fresh, well-tended look. The wrought iron gate once again opens immediately. It is a chilly winter afternoon. There is a welcoming fire. Both men wear corduroy trousers and wool sweaters. "It's good to see both you again," Francis says. "We were just remembering our last interview with you."

"As you can see, nothing much has changed," John says. "I think Francis has a couple of new rosebushes, and I have a food processor, but life goes on. Mom had her gall bladder out last month, but she's on the mend. Coco is a little slower. I guess we're a little slower, too." He smiles. "Maybe it's the new five pounds each of us is wearing."

"Well, there are some changes. We don't have the gang over as much anymore," Francis says. "I guess we've been busy."

"I don't think it's busy so much as getting tired of hearing the same old stories. The TV isn't much better, but you get a laugh once in a while."

"Maybe I should get a face lift," Francis says, striking a theatrical pose. "Or maybe a whole body lift."

John laughs. "No. Things are as fine as ever. We're going to be having our nineteenth anniversary next month. We're taking Mom with us to the desert for a big weekend. We thought about all sharing one room but got two just in case one of us gets a perverted urge to make love this month."

"Will you send me roses, my dear?" Francis asks. "Remember how you always sent roses on our anniversary?"

"Yeah, and you always found some wonderful kitchen gadget for me," John says.

Francis laughs, "Well, we have our own rosebushes now, and there is no gourmet kitchen shop in the desert." He gives John a perfunctory pat on the knee as he blows a speck of dust from the crystal.

"I guess after nineteen years together you have everything you need," John says.

Trusting

The two partners in a male couple begin their trust in the first embrace. It grows with them through the years. It is not new here, but couples in our study in this stage use the word *trusting* most often. It seems to us that the quality of the trust has changed and become more tangible. Illusions are gone, and the man they see is the real person with his endearing qualities and his imperfections. This permits a new freedom and a new security, but even with these there is some lingering sense of loss as the old illusions vanish.

By the time the two have been together for ten years, each has slowly been releasing or letting go of hopes and fantasies about how his partner might change. He also has let go of false pictures of his partner that he tried to superimpose earlier in the relationship. He knows who and what his partner is. The secrets have been told. There may be a sense of loss when one stops thinking, "If only he were. . . ." Couples we interviewed in this stage often used remarks such as, "Oh, he's always been that way, and he probably always will be. It used to bother me, but he is what he is." There is a new quality of appreciation. What was once an irritant can become endearing. "We used to fight like cats and dogs every time he discovered he had a hundred dollars less in the checking account because he had added it wrong again. But for some reason it makes me smile now," one man tells us. "I mean, it's how he is. He'll always think we have a hundred dollars more than we have."

The person feeling appreciated now feels more secure and content. He knows he is accepted. He no longer fears the discovery of the arithmetic error. He can say, "I made a deposit today, and you know what that means." There are no more hidden land mines that may go off unexpectedly. Sometimes, at this point, the person, no longer fearing criticism from his partner, may use the comfort of acceptance to try out new behavior. Facing his habitual mistakes in the checkbook, he may try buying a pocket calculator. Or the partner who has lived with his beloved's defective arithmetic for ten years may realize it would be a relief for both of them if he took over the checkbook. This is apt to happen in a spirit of acceptance rather than annoyance after the first decade shared.

A major payoff in Stage Five is the friendship the partners have established. Although it started early in the relationship, the emphasis then was on being lovers. A subtle change begins in Stage Four. When the development of a new limerence is integrated and the establishment of fidelity becomes dependent upon emotional commitment and not sexual exclusivity, a different level of friendship starts. It is carried into Stage Five where love and respect ripen into a fidelity of unquestioned positive regard, where friendship and comfortable companionship are the most important components in forming the matrix of the partnership.

In the early years of a relationship there are often problems with the feeling of possessiveness. With the acceptance and support seen in Stage Five there is a lessening of the intensity of possessive feelings. Both now are aware that they are two individuals who have chosen to join together. There is at times an almost puzzling sense of loss when the partner does not show the old jealousy. One man says, "I began to wonder if we were just best friends—not that there's anything wrong with having a best friend—but I wondered if he really still loved me. It took me a while to see he loved me differently from before. He doesn't have to be jealous all the time. He knows I don't belong to him but my love does. Number one is number one no matter who smiles at whom or who sleeps with whom."

Two men who have worked together through their first ten years have lost much of the fear that something drastic may go wrong. They have learned how to talk with each other and find balance. Each can be his own person. He may go out to dinner with someone his partner does not like. He does not risk great displeasure. There may be a dispute, but each knows the other will be near when the dust has settled. There is less willingness to create unnecessary trouble.

The edge of uncertainty present in other stages created tension. The tension now has eased. Often people spend so much of their time thinking about and planning for their future lives that they miss the here and now, as if the moment is somehow only practicing for the future. The partners know that life together is not a dress rehearsal but the real thing.

The price may be a new sense of emptiness or ennui. As John says, "There comes a time when the scare is gone but so is the thrill. It's like our old TV. The picture's real clear, but the color just isn't what it used to be. But we can count on it working unless somebody pulls the plug."

Some couples do not deal well with new conflicts that arise in Stage Five. The tendency to accept the other as he is leads to a resignation: "Oh, well, that's how he is and nothing will change him." This attitude usually blocks formerly effective strategies for effecting reconciliation and causes withdrawal, adding to the constriction seen later in this stage.

"We used to fight over things like that, or at least have some heated discussions. Now I figure he's just that way and won't change. Then I keep boiling inside. A teakettle with no steam vent."

Some couples take extreme measures to block trust, like being preoccupied about a partner's past shortcomings or transgressions.

"Look, we lost so much on that deal a few years back that I just don't trust anything you want me to do with my money now."

A level of deep trust is necessary for full commitment to each other and to the relationship.

Merging of Money and Possessions

Men are trained to pay careful attention to money. It represents power and a sense of self. The personal significance men attach to their earning capacity correlates with their independence and their ability to take care of themselves. It is a proud accomplishment of male couples to find it possible in Stage Five to develop a true sense of "our" money and "our" possessions. A man may learn to say, "What is mine is yours." These men have learned to say, "What is ours is ours." This is a process, not an event. It starts when one man pays for the movie simply because the other man is engrossed in telling an event of the day. After ten years they are no longer the Stage Two couple, proud of their shared contribution in buying a new chair. They are no longer the Stage Three couple who pay for their vacations out of the joint household account. Over the years they have learned how to invest in the relationship and in each other. "Our" money buys the new chair, "our" money pays for the vacation, and "our" money pays for one partner's unexpected tax audit.

"When I look back and think how jealously we guarded our own possessions for all those years, I can't help but wonder what was going on. It was almost as if we didn't trust each other or that if one got too indebted to the other there'd be hell to pay. As it now stands, we couldn't tell whose was what if our lives depended on it."

The recognition of shared funds and possessions, which may have started much earlier, is now more an attitude of mutual surrender to each other and releasing to the relationship. Couples speak of this development as an important new symbol of what they want, hope, and expect to be a permanent relationship. This is the single most consistent finding among all couples who have been together longer than ten years. It is the single identifiable phenomenon signifying ongoing commitment. In heterosexual marriage, this fact of sharing comes legally on the wedding day and attitudinally shortly thereafter. Although male couples share from the beginning, their mutual expectation of each paying his own share does get in the way of earlier consolidation of resources. They may have bought a house together before now, but each knows what his share of the costs and profits are. There is some essential symbol of trust expressed in the final merger of their money. It takes male couples ten years to create a state of full voluntary sharing. Amusingly enough, Detroit's advertising of the automobile as a man's symbol of pride and ownership has influenced male couples. In this Southern California sample, even cars jointly owned were referred to stubbornly as "his" car and "my " car. Perhaps as men change with the changing times even this last vestige of male "me" will fade for male couples.

Sal, a plumber, and David, a draftsman, became lovers after they were thirty. They met in a bar fourteen years ago and started living together a year later. They now own a small home, which they show off with great pride. They are both in their mid forties. Though they seem to have limited psychological insight about themselves or their relationship, they talk warmly and intensely about each other during our interviews. They had kept their bank accounts and possessions separate until about three years ago, when they each recognized that life without the other would be unthinkable. Although they do not talk about commitment, they express a sense of "feeling right" about pooling their resources when it happened. From the preceding years, they both offer numerous examples of a gradual awareness of mutuality in their decision making, which they express as consensus and not compromise.

It does not surprise us, on reflection, that in a society so concerned about the symbolic use of money and possessions there comes a point in the development of a male couple's relationship where the expected permanence of the relationship is recognized through the marriage of money. Men dared to say "I love you" earlier in the relationship. In Stage Five they put their money where their love is. It represents the surrender of each partner's last major symbol of independence.

In this stage, where the individuals release themselves to the relationship, we find that couples who had not already done so now made wills in which the partner was protected financially should one of the individuals die. Though other biological family members might be protected in the will, there was an emphasis on making sure that one's chosen lifemate had due legal protection.

"We hadn't really thought about wills until one day when a lesbian couple who had been friends of ours for years were in an accident. One of them was killed, and her lover had to fight the family in the courts for almost two years just to keep the house they owned together."

One major problem can arise for couples after they have merged all of their resources when dissolution of the relationship becomes inevitable.

Constricting

Some cloth shrinks when it gets wet. Its fibers draw closer together, making it smaller but stronger. The cloth of the male relationship, woven over a ten-year period, gathers the moisture of various nutrients year by year as the partners find their way in life together. The very factors that make it strong seem to make the relationship less expansive in the latter half of Stage Five. The gentle squeezing begins to isolate the partners from each other. As the constriction occurs, the individual notices his worry, the relationship is invaded by boredom and monotony, and the outside world fades with a decrease in social contacts.

"Well, life has gotten really boring these past few years," Clyde sighs. "Things between Jeff and me are calm, cool, and collected, but we're in a rut." Clyde is forty-six, and Jeff, his lover of seventeen years, is forty-three. Both have excellent jobs and own their handsomely decorated home filled with carefully selected artwork and other fine furnishings.

Jeff says, "Clyde worries about being forty-six and no longer attractive. He worries about burglars, inflation, politics, the Russians, whatever. Me, I think about getting older, too. Clyde couldn't get along without me. He still can't boil water without burning it."

It is no longer news that men go through a midlife crisis. This period of crisis is a time for self-examination, reexamination of basic assumptions, and a search for more durable meaning. It is a time when a man is no longer content to climb the ladder or stay in harness. The reflective man, seeing the end of life ahead, tries to establish markers along his road that will reassure him of satisfaction and the ultimate worth of his daily efforts. For many men this period is initiated by noticing facial wrinkles, graying hair, or loss of muscle tone. The men in our sample are affected by these same changes. Some notice the changes, others feign panic, and some begin to feel truly unattractive in a world that sees beauty only in youth. While this period of personal constriction is subjectively unpleasant, it is the road that permits some men to move ahead in life.

"It gradually dawned on me that I had to find something else to focus on besides my body. When I turned forty I was almost preoccupied with it. I got real competitive with Tom over how many new tricks we could get, how many pushups I could do, how much work I could do in a day. Suddenly one day I got this terrible pain in my chest. I was sure it was a coronary. It wasn't, but I got scared as heck.Then I began to think about taking it easier, slowing down, and finding other things besides the physical to keep me occupied, not preoccupied."

If one man begins to experience this period of change, the other may wonder if there is a problem in the relationship or if he is doing something to trouble his partner. For men at this time of life and this stage of a relationship, the ghost of doubt may reappear. "You must remember that for my whole generation being homosexual or gay meant everything was doomed to failure, or so we were told. When the 'midlife meanies' attacked I just thought, well, there it goes. I should have known better than to think I could have a happy home and scmeone who would want *me* for life."

The person in midlife crisis may not know anything is particularly troublesome. He may feel minor discomfort, try a new hobby, or pull away from his partner emotionally. The well-developed relationship makes it seem that all is going well, but this can be a dangerous time. The two men may adeptly bypass overt examination of the distance developing between them. It could be the beginning of the end of the relationship they have crafted with such care. They may find that ignoring the small, inexplicable outward signs of midlife crisis has left them beached after an unnoticed storm, amiable roommates who once loved each other deeply. It was the strong relationship, gathering its fibers closer together, constricting, that squeezed the life force from this union.

By the end of the first decade the male couple seems remarkably able to take turns marking out individual problems. One seems to gather strength and hold off his own problem until he has helped his partner negotiate a difficult turn in the road. In this sample we were struck by the near absence of any couples who both were involved deeply in midlife crisis at the same time. Even when both partners were caught up in the struggle, however, being conscious of what was happening, talking it out together, and extending a hand—one man to another—helping themselves to come through the experience stronger as individuals and as a couple.

We were impressed by the male couple's ability not only to survive but also to thrive as a result of this period of constriction. Francis says it sagely: "You're talking to people who are outlaws. We may not look it, but we certainly grew up knowing we were not Jack Armstrong or any other all-American boy. We had to find a way to survive and get life to work for us, or most of us would never have lived long enough to vote. I've seen friends go through this middle-age slump thing, and they know just like I know, it's get through it or don't. And you'd better find something new you didn't think of before and not just try doing what everyone does because we are not everyone. We are different. It's like in that movie *Outrageous*—if the world says you're different, you'd better make it work for you somehow or you'll be sitting around like Coco, with pretty blue eyes, hoping somebody will reward you with a dish of milk sometime. John and I have worked hard for what we have. We'll break a rule here or there if it doesn't hurt anybody to make sure we can get our jalopy back on the highway. We didn't come this far waiting for somebody else to change our flat tires."

Many Stage Five couples need to draw away from others, including friends and families. There may be less desire to participate in social life. Others may view them as fed up with the struggle or having hostile attitudes. They may appear to be critical of other gay people and are often the recipients of like criticism. In truth it would seem that many Stage Five couples are occupied with other matters. We found more couples in this stage sleeping in separate bedrooms or maintaining them for appearance's sake. We believe this phenomenon is a product of negative self-image that may be related to the period in history in which these relationships have developed. When couples find this happening they frequently misinterpret what it all means.

They may feel something has gone wrong. Some report a quiet desper-
ation, feeling trapped, and thinking that they could not split up even
if that was what they wanted. When couples have some understanding
of the various forces acting upon their lives as this withdrawal occurs,
they can take active steps to right the balance.

Taking Each Other for Granted

"Life goes on," John says. It is a phrase he uses often. Like so many
male couples in Stage Five, John and Francis have a life that seems to
work smoothly and easily. Their relationship has been built with great
care. But somewhere along the way, in this second decade, the individuals no longer feel special.

"It sounds silly," one man says in his private interview, "but I
keep remembering how Eugene used to tell me he loved my arms or he
loved my legs or he loved my chest. I am embarrassed to say it, but I
miss him telling me he loves to kiss my stomach. I mean, that stomach
is a lot bigger now than when we were twenty-five, but just once it
would feel nice, even if it is silly, to hear him say again that he loves
my stomach or loves to kiss it. I guess I'm in my second childhood
already, and I can't help it. I want to feel special again."

Couples reported frequent expressions of love and praise for each
other in earlier stages. There were plentiful examples of romance and
mutual attentiveness. We find these references lacking in Stage Five
interviews. While these men, because of repressive circumstances,
may have been less overtly expressive of affection throughout their relationships, the expressions that were there earlier are now missing
and missed.

"I used to ask him how I looked in the morning, and he'd make a
little fuss over me or suggest a different tie or shirt. Now if I ask, he
just says I look fine."

"He always used to kiss me on the back of the neck when we were
alone. Now he just gives me a good-night hug."

The security a couple feels in a strong, durable relationship has-
tens some degree of neglect. "I expect my heart to beat, I expect my
lungs to breathe, and I expect him to be there." It's the dark side of
security, and it takes its toll in Stage Five.

"I miss it." This faint complaint can be the straw that breaks the
camel's back. It is too apt to bring back ancient suspicions about not

being good enough or attractive enough. The individual may silently search the horizon for greener pastures—someone who will tell him he is noticed and appreciated. Worse, the individual may silently agree with the ancient accusation and give up hope of being genuinely valued. A sturdy relationship can end with the arrival of a new suitor. Or the relationship may go on and on, giving neither partner much more than company. It is the paradox again that plagues developing relationships. Out of the strength appears the weakness. The fortunate couples are the watchful ones.

The faint complaint can lead to other consequences as well. It can lead to psychosomatic expression of the sadness. Developing hypertension or irritable colon can be related directly to the stress of neglect and sadness. As a result of the illness a person may learn just how valued he is after all. It is a costly way to learn but may provide the beginning of necessary healing in the relationship.

"I almost lost him after his heart attack," John tells us, "and somehow we learned. We learned to take better care of ourselves, and we remembered to take better care of each other. I say 'I love you' every night before we go to sleep now. And I mean it. We had stopped that ten years ago. It seemed like kid stuff, I suppose. But, I'll tell you, it's good medicine."

Francis tells us how he discovered he missed the old days. He was puzzled because all seemed better than ever, yet he felt down. "John and my mom always liked each other. She taught him all about opera over the years. One day it dawned on me that it was more like *they* were married. He would compliment her on a new dress, and she'd bake something special for him and tell him how sweet he was, and nobody was paying any attention to me. That was just before the heart attack. I mean, she's been living with us for eight years. When my dad died, my brother and sister had ten kids and a hundred reasons why she couldn't stay with them in Ohio. And we do both like her. But I don't want to be left out."

Couples who move on from Stage Five do something about their previous neglect of each other. And what is done is more than sitting down for a chat. One way or another they rediscover that what they have in life is each other. They take stock and take a fresh look at their partner. That which seemed stale and empty is warm with life once again.

Commentary

This stage has been named *releasing* for two reasons. First, it is during this decade that the couple learn to give the self wholly to the relationship. It is the final giving up of an aloneness that was never wanted. The "me" is now safe in the arms of the "we." Second, toward the end of this stage the individual and the couple take a new lease on life. The troubles of Stage Five act as a springboard.

As in other stages, there are some general occurrences in Stage Five that are worth mentioning because they are too often interpreted as failures or incorrigible flaws, when they are only some of the unpleasant manifestations of time together.

Some couples feel something is wrong when they have lost all of the romance at this stage. There is fatigue from being together that squelches the thoughtfulnesses of past years. There is generally a lack of tension from disagreements, and there is little evidence of jealousy. With most sources of resistance decreased, there is little or no sexual activity together for many couples. Some manage to maintain sex together by introducing other partners and experimenting with new outlets together.

For most men there is some ambivalence about the relationship, just as in Stage Two. Most feel trapped but think that this may be their last chance to find another partner, so they think about "getting while the getting is possible." Sometimes, as one or the other passes through a life crisis, they may start arguing again. Most often the one in crisis brings up past hurts and disappointments the other thought were settled years before. When the men do not understand that there are adult stages of development to be lived through, powerful misunderstandings can develop.

Couples report a lessening of affectionate interchanges just at a time in their lives when their needs are greater. Not sleeping together feeds this loss. They usually report a general decline in their overall sexual interests on the part of one or the other or both. This does not need to be problematic, but it can become so when there are wide discrepancies.

This stage appears to have more unpleasant features than some of the others. We have not played up the positives as much as we have highlighted the problems. The second decade of any relationship brings the high rewards of being friends, having dependable companionship and strong emotional support. Aging is a human problem we cannot avoid, try as we might. It brings wisdom and peace if it is accepted gracefully. Stage Five couples come the closest to showing us some of the ways to do that.

CHAPTER 8

STAGE SIX—RENEWING
(Beyond Twenty Years)

Characteristics

1. Achieving security
2. Shifting perspectives
3. Restoring the partnership
4. Remembering

"One of the important things that's happened in the past few years seems to be some kind of rejuvenation, like we've had a new look at each other and decided that we weren't such a bad choice after all." Ted squints as the setting sun's last rays bounce off the glass coffee table between us.

Ted and Phil were introduced in the first chapter. Two school teachers, together for thirty-three years, Ted is fifty-seven and Phil is fifty-six. They had met in 1944 in Europe when they were both in the Army.

Ted was born and reared in northern California where his father had a management job with a stove manufacturing company. He had an older sister and a younger brother. He started working in the company plant right out of high school. "It was 1938 when I graduated from high school. Let me tell you, things were mighty tough in those depression days. I wanted to go to college, but Dad insisted that I work for a while. After two years and putting away some money, I went to San Jose State College for two years and then got drafted in 1942. I think I was twenty-two then. I took their tests, and before I knew what happened I was in Officers Candidate School. I hated the infantry but had some damned patriotic ideas. I remember Pearl Harbor so clearly —that terrible Sunday morning in December of 1941." Ted digresses often in the interview to fill me in on side details, bits of history that he wants to include, just as if he is teaching a class.

113

Phil was born in central Texas, and even though he hasn't lived there since 1942 there is still a slightly detectable drawl and an occasional "sure enough" to remind the interviewer of his origins. Phil's father was a sheriff. "Something like Matt Dillon in that old TV show *Gunsmoke*," Phil says, "except not that far back and not so glamorous." Taking up the thread of his history once again, Phil continues, "I finished high school when I was seventeen. I really loved school. I got excited about music, especially opera. I remember the first opera I ever saw was in Dallas—Lilly Pons singing *Lucia di Lammermoor*. It was a long time before I saw the next one—that was in London in 1943 at Covent Garden, *La Boheme*." Phil worked on his uncle's farm managing the cotton pickers and other hired hands because there just wasn't enough money for college. "I played the piano," he says "I guess I was a little too queer for my father's tastes. He was always riding me about playing ball and dating girls, neither of which I was doing. I knew I was interested in other men but felt really terrible about it. It was Ted who got me out of that. When I saw him, I was in love forever, as far as I was concerned. Fortunately, it seems to have been the same for him. Don't get me wrong—we have had our ups and downs."

Both men were discharged from the service at around the same time in late 1945. They each visited the other's homes after arriving back stateside at different times. "We didn't want to be separated, and I knew I didn't want to go back to Texas." Phil fills in some of the missing details. "California was offering some of the best veterans' benefits and had the best college programs for getting teaching credentials. We both saw the growth potential out here. When we were visiting Ted's folks in Newark, we bought a 1942 Plymouth coupe and drove down along the California coast all the way to Tijuana. Yep, you guessed it, when we drove into San Diego in February of 1946 we looked at each other and, just like Brigham Young, we both said, 'This is the place.'"

To shorten a much longer story, we came back here in the summer and started the fall semester at San Diego State. We had our first home together, a little apartment out near the campus. In those days it was mostly fields and sagebrush on the mesas. I got a job with the city schools just after I finished, and Phil got one a year later, even before he finished his degree. We both got Master's degrees later on. We loved every day. Looking back it all seems so wonderful, but actually there were some terrible times. Like the first time I got VD and brought it home to him." Ted chuckles now as the twinkle in his eye lets the interviewer know that was an old problem.

Ted and Phil had built their own home on a beautiful acre of land in a San Diego suburb in the mid-1960s. Before that they had owned a home together closer to the downtown area. They have other real estate holdings and marvelous collections of paintings and statues in their modern house. They had built a guest house on their property for Phil's mom after his dad died. She lived there until her death a year before our interview.

"We never talked to Mom about our relationship. The families never questioned us or mentioned it, yet after the first few years we were always included in everything on both sides. They just never think of two men like us having a sexual relationship. It isn't part of their world." Phil is telling us more about the gay side of their lives. "We have lots of friends, mostly man-woman couples that we visit and entertain. We've never been very big on gay life, although Ted would love to get out there and be more actively involved. I don't like the idea. I'm content just to hold back. I remember how scared we got with that Proposition 6 deal. If that thing had passed it would really have upset our applecart. We sent some money in but were afraid to do more."

Proposition 6 was an initiative on the California state ballot in 1978, making it illegal for homosexual people or even those supportive of homosexual people to teach in the public schools. The measure was soundly defeated, but there was a very heated debate over it for many months.

"We both could retire from teaching, but then what would we do? We've invested wisely and have plenty of money and property to keep us going for years. As important as the money is to us, some things are more valuable. I'm having some trouble with high blood pressure, and Phil's arthritis kicks up. We just aren't getting any younger," Ted says.

Achieving Security

When couples talk about security, they refer to financial, personal, and relationship well-being. Almost all of the couples in this stage have reached a moderate or high level of financial comfort with retirement funds, investments, real estate, and other incomes. Dual-career couples combining their incomes and other resources for more than twenty years, usually without dependents, do achieve financial security, or at least see its achievement in the near future. The collaboration and productivity of Stage Four and the complete merger of money in Stage Five generally result in accumulations that account for those with combined incomes of more than $50,000 yearly.

Alan and Ken are a good case in point. They will be discussed as individuals in chapter 11 and as a couple in chapter 12. They are both very wealthy men by any standard and have accumulated the bulk of their wealth by working together for the last twenty-seven years. "We planned it after our first year together. Alan was the smart guy, and I provided more of the brawn," Ken tells us.

But Alan interrupts. "That's not exactly right. If it hadn't been for your steady hand and heart at times I would have blown the whole show. You always come through in a pinch."

Most couples who have been together more than twenty years have a feeling of permanence in their relationships that provides the security of companionship and the lack of loneliness. Most of us fear loneliness as we grow older, haunted by the movie and TV images of old men and women abandoned in sleazy rest homes or other less than desirable retirement settings. These couples who have retired are usually very busy with things they had planned before retiring.

"I know it sounds a little corny, but it really is true that I've been far busier since I retired than when I was still employed. I've finally been able to take on a lot more responsibility with the symphony. And now there is time for the garden. I enjoy it so much that I hardly know when to quit. I'm on the phone more often than I would like with someone somewhere about my old work." This man is a retired university physics professor with several textbooks to his credit.

The feelings about the importance of security seem strongest in couples in the latter part of Stage Six. These men are usually older, with a stronger need for security.

"I wouldn't know what to do without Paul," says Fred, referring to his sense of security with his lover of forty-six years. "I thank my lucky stars every night for his persistence in sticking with me." Seventy-two-year-old Fred is referring to how he had tried to chase Paul off when he was pursuing him so insistently almost fifty years earlier.

"I feel like what we now have together is like a return on the investment we've made in each other and in our relationship over all these years. We're reaping the profits from what we did and collected. The good Lord has been watching over us and still is." Paul feels the same way as Fred does about their mutual security.

Men talk about the challenge of their goals, then the absence of the challenge once the goals are achieved. "We have nothing to drive for like we used to. Having the carrot out in front kept both of us in harness."

Some couples establish new goals, such as collecting art or antiques. One couple is dedicated to developing a retirement community for other gay people. In the few instances in which couples have not attained at least some of their goals, there is some degree of estrangement and evidence of unresolved conflict.

Achieving security produces strong feelings of well-being in the couple, feelings they recall from Stage One's blending and limerence. The difference, however, is that the early feelings were built on *expectations*, and the renewing experience is built on the *reality* of themselves and their shared history together.

Shifting Perspectives

One of the very best examples we have found of how couples' perspectives change was provided for us by the last couple quoted above. Fred and Paul are one of those Stage Six couples we did not meet until after we stopped collecting our data. However, as indicated in the introduction, we have used as examples some of the couples not included in the data because their stories are so illustrative of some characteristics.

"Just last month we had to rush down to the bank on the fifteenth to prevent one of our six-year investment notes from rolling over." Fred is talking. "Because if you don't get to the bank on the very day of maturation, the money is automatically reinvested for six more years. When you're our age, six years is a really long time. We may not be here in six months, let alone six years. Even when we first bought those notes, six years didn't seem like long. Now, I really can't expect to live that long."

As we get older, life gets shorter. It is just that simple, but not all of us can face it in quite the same simple way. Besides concerns about life expectancy, men in Stage Six express shifts in many other concerns. They talk about health problems, growing old, fear of their lover's death, fear of loneliness, and concern about their attractiveness to others. Some deal with these concerns by withdrawal into the self, being depressed and isolated, while others rush out to confront them actively. Many exercise regularly and frequently, playing tennis, swimming, jogging, or going to a spa or gym. Others are diet watchers, worrying about cholesterol and blood pressure, too much red meat and alcohol. Others have dealt with health concerns by denial.

These men deal with the fear of aging in the same sensible and foolish ways that all people do. Some give in to the aches and pains of aging. While some appear to age with grace and tranquility, being even more attractive than in younger days, others have their face lifts, and eye tucks and dye their hair.

Pride makes it difficult to discuss all concerns as one grows old, yet there seems to be a need to tell. Harold tells us, "You know, I used to run down those steps and now I take hold of the handrail. I don't use the bike anymore because of the arthritis in my knee. I do still walk downtown, but I take the bus back because it's a little uphill."

We see the look of concern on Harold's face when Sam repeats the same humorous anecdote just a few minutes after its first telling. We have to rely on our guess that Harold worries about Sam's memory lapses as signs of gradual deterioration.

There are poignant references to future loss. "You know, we have to use those six-month investment things because we don't know if we have five years."

"Our old friend Robert passed last week, and now Russell is sick."

"Well, that's for the future and that's God's worry, not ours—we just try to stay well."

"Sex used to be such a big deal. I guess it still is in a way as long as it stays."

"Learning that this disease is degenerative was the most depressing."

Russ is fifty-nine and blind, and Peter is fifty-eight. They have been together for thirty-one years. Russ had gradually lost his vision from progressive glaucoma three years earlier. Russ says, "I need Peter now more than ever, not so much because I can't see, but because I love him more."

Peter's rejoinder is, "An important thing for me all my life has been a need to be needed. Russ has needed me more since his illness. The satisfaction I have gotten from that fact alone has been as great as anything in my life. We're closer now than ever. Russ doesn't really need me because he's blind. He could function very adequately without my eyes, but the real truth is that I need him as much as he needs me."

The emergence of these personal concerns can bring the partners closer together and contribute to repartnering, or it can increase distancing. If the communication between partners is open and they have been able to share their feelings, each realizes he is not alone. On the other hand, if they are not communicating, feelings of isolation are almost assured. The most difficult anticipated loss, of course, is death of the partner. Harold says, "When one of us goes it will be all over. Oh, the other one will hang on until he's taken, too, but it will be just a matter of waiting."

Some couples tell us they welcomed the seclusion that retirement provided, because it was voluntarily chosen by them. On the other hand, there are couples where one partner sees retirement as a voluntary seclusion while the other sees it as an enforced solitude when he longs for social contact with others. In these couples, one partner has become more isolated and the other expresses his concern for the withdrawal. We usually can identify some depression in the individuals.

The new butcher might take the order without looking at them. They feel literally unrecognized. Perhaps even the partner responds in such a habitual manner that he hardly seems to notice the other's presence.

While these changes are not limited to male couples there are some changes that are specific to our population. These are men who have appreciatively noticed and been noticed by other men. Attractions between men have played an important role in life satisfaction. In Stage Six some men speak with feeling about being ignored by younger gays. "Those youngsters get it all on a silver platter and have no appreciation for how we survived at their age. We could teach them a thing or two, but they look right through us." At times it is the younger men excluding the Stage Six couples, at times it is these older couples dismissing "the youngsters," but there is sometimes a tension between the generations.

One of the positive features of shifting perspectives is found among couples who talk about their relationship representing a place of retreat, like an oasis in the desert where they could stop for refreshment and linger in the quiet shade together for days on end. "We take refuge in each other because it's so well known and so secure."

Restoring the Partnership

Like a marvelous old Victorian house that has passed through years of neglect, some relationships need mending and restoring; others have been tended to with greater caution all along.

"We've been with each other more than half our lives. I can hardly remember it being otherwise." George is recalling his thirty-five years with Jerry. Both men are still working, although Jerry tried retiring and found he couldn't stand it. They have a beautiful home, small, neatly kept, and stylishly furnished.

"We've fought often and hard over the years, but mostly when we get mad at each other we both pout and shut up," Jerry says.

George continues, "Jerry developed high blood pressure a few years back. I got real concerned about him and then about myself. We had to stop and realize we're not spring chickens anymore. I made him promise to go easier. We started working less, taking some trips together again, just being better to ourselves and to each other."

Not all of these couples are aged. Some are in their late forties and fifties. "Twenty-two years seemed like a long time to be with the same man," Ron says. "Some years back Doug and I got into such a fight that he moved into his own room, and we just existed together, not too comfortably, for a few years. There was a time when we didn't even talk to each other for six months. Doug had his life and friends, and I had mine. Gradually we slipped into living together as roommates. Although we did do some things together, we stopped any attempt at sex or even being affectionate. Then, about two years ago, Doug told me he was planning on retiring from his job as a salesman. He was just forty-five and I was forty-three. I began to think about all the plans we had made years ago about retiring around this time. Actually, we had put our money in good investments. When I look the whole situation over, I could see my way to retiring, too, but what would it be like if he and I weren't together? Doug is the quiet one in our relationship, so I decided to take things into my own hands. I told him I was taking him away for the weekend. I reserved a little hideaway in Palm Springs, and we talked the entire weekend, the first time in almost five years. It was the beginning of a whole new life for us."

If couples have not learned to communicate with each other earlier in their lives together, it rarely starts happening in this stage. If, however, somewhere in their history they remember a time of close communication, it can be restored by effort. More often than not, with the advent of a crisis, personal or otherwise, the couple can pull themselves together and breathe new life into their partnership.

"When Russ came back from the doctor's office that morning, I knew something was wrong." Peter is telling us how he learned about Russ's impending blindness. "He had been complaining about needing new glasses for months, so I stopped paying any attention to him. I hadn't even considered the possibility of something as bad as it was."

Russ's vision deteriorated rapidly, and the couple faced the problem together. "I was depressed and scared at first, feeling like life was over and I just wanted to die." Russ tells his side. "Peter jumped into my life with new energy and wouldn't give me a chance to get down. He told me I had to learn to read braille, and we had to set the house up so that I knew where things were. Almost from the start of my visual failure, he insisted that I use a blindfold and learn my way around the house, the garden, and everything."

"Yeah, we got so busy preparing for it that neither of us had much time to think. I started using the blindfold around the house, too, so that I knew what it was like. We would keep the lights out at night. We marked all our stereo albums so we could read them with our fingers," Peter tells us. "We tried to see it as a new challenge. We weren't going to let it get us down."

"Peter felt I really needed him, like in the old days, I guess. And you know, I did need him. We've slept together every night since, haven't we, Peter?" Russ asks.

Couples together for more than twenty years tell many stories of changes in their relationships. As we age, maintaining flexibility is one of the secrets of continuing vitality, yet changing becomes progressively more difficult as we get older. Rejuvenation of relationships depends on many factors, but change can be a key to it. Functional complementation becomes less flexible and reversible with these couples, but emotional complementarity continues to be interchangeable. "I can take care of him just like a child, but he can do it for me, too. That's a nice thing about our relationship."

What might be responsible for the restoration of partnerships at this time in life? The habit of being together helps keep them together but does not always assist with improving the quality. Self-appraisal and a new look at the partner sometimes start the ball rolling. With couples who have a positive past history, especially those who have faced some serious adversity earlier, restoration is easier.

When we ask Albert and Jacob about the most difficult thing they had faced together, they both answer immediately and without hesitation that the three-year enforced separation during World War II was the most difficult experience they had endured. Jacob says, "He wanted everything to be exactly the same when he came home, so I worked my tail off getting the apartment set up as close to the original as possible. I was so nervous when I went down to the train station. You'll never be able to imagine my shock when I saw him. He was fifty pounds heavier and almost four years older, and he didn't want anything to be changed! I sent a boy off to war and here he came back a great big man."

Albert adds his observations. "In those first few weeks we went from the highest peaks to the lowest depths. We really rode the roller coaster for a while. If we got through that, we can get through anything."

Jacob gives us more insight into his feelings about Albert. "I still get down on my knees every night and thank God for giving me Albert. I also think about whether I have told him everything I want him to know, because I don't sleep well if something has gone unsaid. I might not live till morning."

"I think there was a new awakening for us when we sold the ranch and moved back into town." Albert recalls what had happened a decade earlier. "It was definitely a different phase in our lives. We started homemaking all over again. We decorated and planned together like newlyweds."

Sometimes there is a quality of romance in the repartnering that is a little redolent of limerence. Some couples know how to regain a flash of high romance now and again. One couple tells of a trip they took down the Nile two years ago. Amidst the exotic and ancient surroundings they experienced a return of feelings for each other they had not had in years. They speak of their mutual awkwardness in dealing with them. Another couple describes a serious financial crisis that forced them into clinging together and rejoining forces against this

outside threat to their security, in a way that intensified their emotional bonding. As noted with Russ and Peter, illness in one partner
also can precipitate reexamination and repartnering. Couples in other
stages can be affected similarly, but it just seems to happen more with
couples in Stage Six.

Remembering

These people reminisce a lot. They tell anecdote after anecdote about
the past, checking with each other about this recalled fact or that remembered date and name. Sharing their long relationship history,
rich in memories, is clearly pleasurable.

These couples are storytellers. In telling the stories they are able
to relive the events. Sometimes one partner corrects a detail, adds a
bit of remembered dialogue, or smiles and nods agreement. It is oral
history being passed along the generation chain. They seek out willing
audiences, usually younger people, as grandparents might do. They
have lessons to teach. They want others to profit from their experience. Again and again, the message in the story seems to be, "Don't
expect it to be easy, but remember to take care of each other and find
out if this relationship is the real thing."

They muse about how it would be to be starting again together
now. "We really needed each other so much back then," we learn
more than once. Like tolerant elders they might listen to the stories of
younger people and say, "Well, maybe you need to be single for a
while and then find the right person."

So often the gift they seem eager to give is the knowledge that
two men can love and support each other through good and bad times
for many years. They want it known that male couples have existed
always, that it takes willingness and effort, and that the reward is
great. There is the natural human desire to have younger people learn
from one's own errors.

Stage Six couples remark again and again on how different times
are today. Harold says, "It's easy to go from one relationship to another nowadays. Maybe it's too easy, but maybe it's good. Who knows
if Sam and I would be together now if we had started out in times like
this? Who knows what's best? It's different, that's for sure. And now,
just like thirty years ago, we fellows are getting together anyway and
doing it our own way because it's our nature and we need to. We'll

always find a new way, I guess." He continues, patting Sam on the leg, "Maybe the rest of the world will learn from watching us now. They could do what they need to do, too. You know, last week the man and woman next door were asking us advice about their daughter and the young man she's living with. It's new for them but old for us."

Many of the couples in Stage Six make observations about time passing quickly or slowly. Some feel their mutual perceptions about the passage of remaining time bring them closer together. Some seem sad about time passing; some are challenged. It is always easy to get these couples to talk for a long time about their past. They talk with each other in our presence as if we were not there, recalling events, persons, and other memories. It is this shared past, ultimately, that seems their most prized possession and the intangible that offers security and peace.

There seems to be a desire to pass on the folklore and wisdom. There are money, possessions, security, and time. There is the desire to use all of this in some useful way. Some Stage Six couples find it too difficult to adapt quickly to the new world available to male couples. Others plunge in, joining organizations and finding willing offspring who value them and want to listen. "It seems like we have sons, and I guess before we know it we'll have to call new ones grandsons. And it's not a one-way street. You don't think we did all this gardening, do you?" Sam is referring to the younger gay couple who come every week to tend the garden and have dinner with them.

One Stage Six couple, who had built their own home, built a new home on the lot next to theirs. "We talked it over and decided we should make it more than an investment of money. So, when we rented the old place, we looked for younger guys who were settled with each other and would want to visit back and forth. We usually see them two or three times a week for dinner or lunch. I know my sister doesn't have anything that good with her kids."

There seems to be a strong reaction to any hint of being patronized. "All of the waiters in that restaurant are so cute and talk kind of seductively," Sam says. "But some of them are too stuck on themselves. I reached out to touch one just like I would with anybody, and he jumped like I had fire in my fingers. I said, 'Young man, I am more interested in getting my steak than your buns.' Hell, who does he think he is, and what makes him think I'd be interested in him? Years count for something, too, you know. Nobody should be pushed aside because they're older *or* younger. It's what's inside that counts."

Commentary

This has been the most difficult stage for us to examine. It is the one about which we seem to know the least, yet it has fascinated us mainly because of the couples we have met who have long relationship histories. The world believes that homosexual men have a lonely and isolated old age. These data discount that old belief. Although some men are isolated and even lonely, it is not the rule for most. Among the common problems of this stage we do see some depression from a variety of causes: illness, death of family or friends, feelings of being excluded, and similar occurrences. During this stage the problems tend to shift from the relationship back to the individual. Sometimes poor management of past stage characteristics causes problems. Some couples still have not learned to deal with conflict effectively and establish a truce or moratorium that breaks down over minor points, causing each to compartmentalize. The rigidity of aging can block compromise and cause couples to undo some previous characteristics, like trying to separate their finances again. Like Stage Two couples trying to avoid conflict, some Stage Six couples have come full circle and are trying again to avoid conflict at all costs.

We found an increased dependency, as if the reappearance of the individual in Stage Three and the hard-won independence of Stage Four have been dissolved in the renewed dependency of Stage Six. This seems natural and expected.

Couples start out together by losing themselves in the blending of their individual personalities in Stage One. The continuation of their partnership over time depended upon their ability to separate and find themselves individually without abandoning the relationship. The balancing act of togetherness needed complementarity and independence, conflict and resolution, constriction and restoration. In these later years, there is a return to the need for togetherness that gets expressed in their renewing. As we said above, it is not exactly limerence, but men do describe a rejuvenation of their relationship with an emphasis on the pleasures they get from doing things together again, such as traveling, gardening, or cooking. As in Stage One, they spend more time together again in Stage Six. We find tenderness and playfulness, as well as feelings of contentment and satisfaction with their years together. Stage Six holds the rewards sought in earlier years.

There is a stage beyond the sixth that might rightfully be called "surviving." It is a stage in which one is alone again after many years, following the death of a life partner. We have encountered several of these men since our research was concluded. They face unique problems, yet in some ways seem no different from widows or widowers; relationships were wrenched from their embrace by death, and they are struggling with the solitude while comforted by the happy memories of the past.

CHAPTER 9

A RELATIONSHIP— DEVELOPMENT AND MAINTENANCE

The social nature of people, with their natural need for one another, makes finding and initiating a relationship a relatively easy task for most. We begin to learn about the processes of seeking out and identi-fying others who attract us from early childhood onward. Establishing relationships with friends, companions, and eventually lovers is part and parcel of our developmental maturation. Making contacts and validating the mutual chemistry of loving seem to be natural to hu-mans, but the skill needed to maintain these relationships to the continuing mutual satisfaction and fulfillment of the partners is an en-tirely different proposition.

Although we did have an interest in what attracted men to each other, our principle interest was in what keeps them together. How do they maintain their patnerships? We originally assumed that we could find a single factor, like love, or a group of factors. It quickly became obvious that our speculations were naive and incorrect. It should have been obvious that what brings and keeps a couple together in the be-ginning and during the first year is very different from what keeps them together in their fourth, tenth, or thirtieth year. In fact, we learned that the continued presence of some characteristics of the first year, like mutual possessiveness, if maintained, are serious detriments to the continuation of the relationship.

There are different components in the formation and develop-ment of the male couple. Some are similar to, but most are different from, those affecting heterosexual and lesbian relationships. For in-stance, the presence or absence of male bonding is different for gay and nongay men. Although many of the same factors affect female couples, the unique influences of antihomosexual attitudes and the process of coming out have their own parts to play in affecting the male couple. What part does social scripting play in their relationships? Gay men frequently vary from the usual social scripting for males. What effect does that have on their relationships? Complementarity is an important feature of all relationships. As you have already seen, gay men begin a relationship with some natural complementation, but more often than not they must develop it together.

Relationship Expectation

Society places a high value on relationship formation, specifically marriage for heterosexual persons with the expectation of childbearing and family development. For heterosexual persons there are only a few acceptable alternatives to marriage, such as religious life. Although there is less pressure and expectation for partnering among gay men, there is still a high value placed on finding a partner and settling down. Gay and nongay persons alike look upon themselves and are frequently looked upon by others as having problems if they are not involved in a primary relationship. To complicate this picture further, the expectation that relationships follow a set pattern of romantic attraction, falling in love, courtship, marriage, and family also has its effect on male couples. Gay men are apt to share these same hidden expectations. Society makes no provision for and has no expectations of a percentage of the population being gay. Gay people, therefore, are expected to follow the norm for nongay people. Sometimes they try, with varying degrees of success. Sometimes they create new patterns, also with varying degrees of success.

What does society do to help prepare people to fulfill its expectations of marriage or coupling? It provides role models in the form of parents and others, relying on assumed, built-in biological complementarity of opposite genders. It also molds further complementarity between males and females by encouraging the development of skills, emotions, and behaviors in one to the exclusion of the other, thus insuring mutual need.

Social Scripting

One of the ways in which complementarity is established is through a process labeled *social scripting* by Gagnon and Simon.[1] Gay men usually depart from the expected male script, but the pressures and influences of social scripting are significant.

From the moment of birth, children are taught different attitudes and behaviors that society considers appropriate to their gender. For example, infant boys are treated more roughly than infant girls. There is even an observable difference in the ways mothers talk to their male and female offspring. Broadly painted, males are taught to be goal-oriented, to play or fight to win, to seek conflict and adventure. Contact and competitive sports are encouraged. The male script includes aggressiveness and tight emotional control, exemplified by the popular saying, "Big boys don't cry." Men are encouraged to develop confidence, decisiveness, and assurance—to be the protector and avenger. The social script for the female is intended to complement that of the male. She is to be submissive, attentive, and nurturing. She is taught to be process-oriented instead of goal-oriented. She learns to be a peacemaker and to settle arguments, not to win them. She is taught social skills and homemaking and is encouraged to make her body attractive to the male. Females, unlike males, are encouraged to express their feelings.

In addition to these scripts, society idealizes many masculine traits and endows them with inordinately high value when compared to feminine ones. In fact, traditional feminine characteristics are held in contempt by some. If a female deviates from her programmed social script and manifests some masculine traits, she is praised and more highly valued unless she deviates too far and becomes "unpleasantly aggressive." In sharp contrast is the male who manifests certain feminine characteristics. He is stigmatized and devalued by his peers and society according to how many of these feminine traits he has and how obviously they are manifested. There are limited acceptance alternative social scripts for males. Young boys who fail to follow the traditional script are in instant social jeopardy, especially with their peers. They are teased and harassed for not conforming. Females, on the other hand, often have been able to get by with more in-between scripting, such as the tomboy who usually enjoys increased social acceptance in childhood and early adolescence.

Persons who stray from the cultural scripts encounter special problems. For example, if a macho male and a feminine female marry, the chances of their relationship surviving are greater if both partners maintain their learned scripting. If, on the other hand, the female begins to alter her scripted responses and the male maintains his macho orientation, the marriage can be in trouble. This picture characterizes many contemporary heterosexual couples in which wives have been influenced by the women's liberation movement. In contrast, consider two women forming a relationship, with each coming from the same feminine model. Although there may be difficulties without one or both making changes, there is a much greater probability of satisfaction for both. Two women who both listen, nurture, openly express their feelings, and are concerned and sensitive would seem to have a firmer basis for relationship satisfaction and survival. Another example, and one more to the point of this study, is a relationship between two macho-scripted males. The obvious potential for clash, competition, and dissonance is very high. Such a relationship probably could not endure without one or both changing a great deal. However, the majority of men in this study have strayed from the full macho scripting. Although they often suffered ridicule and rejection for these differences while growing up, it is these same developmental differences that become critical ingredients in male couples.

There are signs of mild change. Educational trends encourage cooking classes for boys, carpentry for girls, and athletic participation for both. Mainline psychological thinking has begun to isolate masculine and feminine characteristics in both sexes, extolling the values of androgyny (Singer,[2] Bems,[3] Farrell,[4] Nichols[5]). However, the participants in this study all grew up in the past and a large number report differences from the traditional social scripting for boys. Their average age is 37.5 years. As we said above, variations on developmental scripting have been beneficial to their current relationships.

Variant Social Scripting

Sissy is a pejorative label leveled at boys with attributes and behaviors usually ascribed to girls. Sissy usually evokes images of boys jumping rope, playing with dolls, and dressing up in their mothers' or sisters' clothes. Sissy also connotes characteristics such as passivity, feminine sensitivity, emotionality, and bookishness—none of which is part of the usual scripting for boys. These boys did not hew to the traditionally prescribed sets of attitudes and behaviors. More than 75 percent of the men in this study report being called sissies or seeing themselves as "different" from other boys at a very early age. (Table 2.)

TABLE 2
PLAYMATES BEFORE ADOLESCENCE

	Number of Participants	Percentage of Participants
Boys	203	65.0
Girls	87	28.0
Both sexes equally	22	7.0

Were You Called Sissy?		
No	73	23.4
Yes	239	76.6

Was Nudity Acceptable in Your Family?		
Yes	44	14.0
No	268	86.0

A boy who during childhood and adolescence believes himself to be different and is treated differently, especially by his peers, often feels very badly about himself; these are the years when being different is perceived as being wrong.

"But I really liked to jump rope, and I was good at it, I might add. It just seemed to me that girls' games were far more fun. I hated myself for liking them because the other guys would make so much fun of me."

Another participant says, "I got called 'sissy' because I was always reading. My dad called me a bookworm, but the other kids would tease me for being clumsy and inept at their games."

And still another reports, " 'Crybaby' was what my sisters called me because I hated to see an animal hurt or a bee killed. My sisters would catch butterflies and tear off their wings just to get me upset."

Some boys are also labeled as sissies for certain effeminate traits that become an affront to sex-role scripting. Some men in this study do recall effeminate mannerisms such as wrist, hand, and hip movements, or head and body inclinations that they developed in childhood but lost when they became teenagers as a result of parental pressures or peer ridicule. Some continue to carry effeminate characteristics into their adult lives.

One participant reports, "I haven't thought about it in years, but when I was real young I was limp-wristed and tended to swish. Then I stopped somewhere before high school because I took such teasing from the family. When I finally came out a few years ago, I turned into a regular queen, taking on every campy mannerism I could. I surprised even myself, but it seemed to be the best and easiest way for me to be 'in' with the boys."

Some men in our study do have effeminate characteristics, some have a few, but the large majority have none. On the other hand, many are quick to mimic, imitate, or exaggerate female mannerisms in what has come to be known as camp behavior or "camping it up." Men who enter relationships with other men without being threatened by their own or others' lack of clearcut gender-related roles and mannerisms do so with a valuable asset that may contribute to the quality and durability of their relationships.

While attending an International Symposium on Gender Dysphoria (Coronado, California, February 1979) we heard Rev. Cannon Clinton Jones make an observation that often the campy, effeminate, cross-dressing behaviors of gay men are nothing more than the need to "sometimes open up the old trunks in the attic, take out the hats and dresses, and put them on to play." The audience roared with laughter and then burst into applause. Some forms of cross-dressing behavior in gay men simply express their liberation from established gender-related roles. Such behavior does not seem to threaten their masculinity, and consequently their ability to play with cross-gender expressions increases their repertoire of available fun and games. This is not true for all expressions of camp.

Another way society encourages heterosexual relationship formation is by providing patterns or formats for experimentation and rehearsal with romance and falling in love during adolescence. One is expected to experience first limerence. As was explained in chapter 3, *limerence* is a new word coined by Dorothy Tennov to describe the experience of falling in love with the accompanying obsessive ruminations, desires for reciprocity, and single-minded intensity.[6] We use the word because it expresses the concept of romantic love as neutrally as possible without the pejorative tone of words such as *infatuation* and *puppy-love*. When limerence strikes, emotional and behavioral discharge is available in dating, petting, and similar overt expressions among nongay adolescents. For the gay male adolescent experiencing these same feelings for a boy of his own age, there are usually only covert expressions of the feelings or complete suppression. More often than not, the gay adolescent feels guilt, anxiety, and confusion.

While he does not experience romantic or sexual feelings for girls, frequently he does go through the motions of dating. Some gay men, therefore, lack the opportunity during their teenage years to experiment with and rehearse their feelings of romance and love for other men. It is not unusual to find gay men in their twenties or thirties experimenting with seemingly adolescent relationships. This is not to say that "falling in love" feelings are limited to adolescence—far from it—but their first appearance usually occurs in this developmental stage.

Resistance Theory

Society fosters heterosexual coupling by supporting male and female differences. C. A. Tripp advances a theory to explain the importance of these differences.[7] Tripp says that a certain degree of disparity or resistance between partners is necessary for sexual arousal. The gender differences between a man and a woman establish a dominance–submission hierarchy and thus provide one form of resistance needed to generate and maintain sexual attraction. Although this resistance can be manifested in far more subtle ways than the obvious disparity between sexes, generally speaking, Tripp believes that some kind of resistance or distancing is necessary for continued sexual activity. In other words, the mystery of the other provides a continual spark of excitement. This theory of resistance implies that, as couples develop greater intimacy, closeness, and parity, there is a reciprocal decline in their sexual activity caused by the decline in resistance. The theory further implies that similarities of gay partners diminish the availability of the built-in resistance of opposite genders. Gay couples must generate other sources of resistance.

Even in men with many similarities in background and socialization who can and do experience high rapport in their early mateships, we find clear evidence that they import and export from each other; that is, each gets from the other what he wants, desires, or needs for himself. This complementarity initially helps foster tension required for ongoing eroticism, but quickly fatigues as a source of resistance. For many gay men their deviation from the "normal" social scripting partially explains the development of complementary skills, feelings, and behaviors that contribute to their relationship formation and continuation. The male couples in our study have proven themselves adept at finding unique ways to keep helpful tension alive. Still, the equality and similarities found in male couples are formidable obstacles to continuing high sexual vitality in their lasting relationships.

Male Bonding

In every society and culture scrutinized by scientific observation the curious and uniquely male experience of close-knit group formation is found. These groupings may have clearly purposive explanations, such as hunting and gathering, protection of the tribe or territory, or merely team formation in competitive sports. But close-binding male partnerships and groups form even in the absence of overtly purposeful reasons in order for men to be together (e.g., Lion's Club, Masons, fraternities, and other male-only clubs). Within these groups individual associations between men develop into male friendships. Although the forms and rules vary from culture to culture, the male bond is universally characterized by friendship, loyalty, and affection (Brain,[8] Tripp[9]). In some instances these friendships are ritualized and life-long. In some societies, like our own, the bond is acknowledged but is not characterized by intimacy, vulnerability, and sharing of feelings. Among the earliest manifestations of this bonding are the exclusionary playmate selections of boys in childhood and early adolescence. Girls are not only excluded, but boys openly express aversion to them and their presence. A function of the bonding, or at least one of its effects, is the learning of male attitudes and behaviors and the internalization and solidification of a masculine self-image. Within these childhood and adolescent peer groups, the developing male ego is molded and sculpted by social scripting, more often than not leaning toward the most macho attributes as representative of the societal ideal. There are exceptions to this pattern. For instance, the loners, leaders, and, often, the geniuses who isolate themselves from the world also avoid this male bonding.

If male bonding is such a ubiquitous phenomenon—as most assuredly it is—what part, if any, does it play in the formation and maintenance of male homosexual relationships? In the preceding section on socialization we indicated that many of the men in our study do not fit the stereotypically expected model. Other research data (Green,[10]

Money and Ehrhardt[11]) indicate that boys who select opposite-sex playmates in childhood are more likely to be homosexual. Although these data do not make playmate selection a causative factor in the development of a homosexual object choice, there is some implication of it.

We believe that in boys with effeminate childhood traits and opposite-sex playmate selection, the eroticizing of male attributes already has occurred and is probably more responsible for the behavior than the opposite being the case. We strongly suspect that the presence or absence of male bonding is connected with the development of a homosexual orientation among men. We do not intend to imply a causal connection, but we do speculate that the early eroticizing of male attributes blocks male bonding because boys do not bond with persons they eroticize. Similarly, nongay boys do not bond with girls.

The development of sexual attraction to the same or to the opposite sex requires eroticizing the attributes of one or the other. This issue touches on the roots of sexuality; that is, what makes a person heterosexual or homosexual? The origins of homosexuality, as well as those of heterosexuality, are multiple. Whether homosexual attraction is prenatal and inborn, parent-induced, environmentally acquired, or socially learned, its appearance occurs at different times for different persons. Among the homosexual men in this study there is a wide variation in the times of life when they recognized their homoerotic attraction and engaged in homosexual behavior.

Some men report awareness of their erotic attraction to males at very early ages, such as five or six, while others do not experience that awareness until adolescence or even later. The earlier the eroticizing occurs, the less likely it is that the male will have experienced male bonding. Those men who have the earliest recollections of attraction to males apparently failed to make close-knit associations with other boys, and, thus, their developing ego formation was not influenced by the powerful molding forces of peer conformity.

In those men whose awareness of eroticizing occurred later, early male bonding was part and parcel of their internalized development. At the point or time period in which eroticizing occurred, however, the probability of male bonding diminished or became impossible as a consequence of the predominant force and influential power of the sexual attraction.

Setting aside this discussion for a moment, what can be said about the inherent possibility of sexual attraction occurring within the context of the male bond? Assuming the biological and psychological theories of the intrinsic bisexual nature of humans (Freud,[12] Sherfy[13]), the possibility for each individual to eroticize his or her own or the opposite gender would seem to provide male bonding with a natural incubator for the development of homosexuality. Actually the opposite appears to be true.

Male bonding provides the matrix for the expression and fulfillment of men's homosexual needs, which are far less genitally erotic than their heterosexual needs. Bonding propels them in a satisfied state toward erotic fulfillment heterosexually.

The existence of strong peer and societal taboos against homosexual behaviors is a further bulwark against the development of homosexuality and supports the establishment of a heterosexual orientation. The presence and availability of life-long male bonding serves to satisfy homosexual needs minimally—sometimes inadequately—without the expression of frank and open sexuality. In the face of the failure of fulfillment in the male bond, apparently large numbers of heterosexual men seek homosexual genital outlets on occasion while living seemingly fulfilled lives as heterosexuals. Humphreys found that more than 50 percent of the males seeking homosexual sex in public places were heterosexual.[14] Kinsey's research showed that close to 50 percent of men had homosexual outlets between adolescence and age fifty.[15]

With the possibility of erotic expression within the male bond established, the original question about the part it plays in male homosexual relationships takes on increased significance. We find that male bonding is far less important in gay couples than is the fulfillment of the need for erotic expression.

Among some couples we do find evidence supporting the presence of male bonding while in others we could find none. The initial formation of male homosexual relationships is highly dependent upon eroticizing the partner's attributes, whether physical, psychological, or spiritual. In such early relationship formation the absence of male bonding seems to be more critical than its presence. However, as relationships pass through stages, the reemergence of male bonding certainly contributes to the stability and longevity of some.

Antihomosexual Attitudes

Responses to homosexual behavior vary greatly from culture to culture. Its expression between males within the male bond is tolerated and even encouraged by some cultures. Some even institutionalize it in puberty rites and ceremonies of manhood. Others have implicit or explicit rules against it. Our western cultures incorporate and institutionalize vehicles for the expression of the male bond that attempt to exclude the potential sexual and erotic components. In *The Male Machine*, Fasteau discusses the American male's difficulty in dealing with tender and affectionate feelings:

> A major source of these inhibitions is the fear of being, or being thought, homosexual. Nothing is more frightening to a heterosexual man in our society. It threatens at one stroke to take away every vestige of his claim to a masculine identity— something like knocking out the foundations of a building—and to expose him to the ostracism, ranging from polite tolerance to violent revulsion, of his friends and colleagues. A man can be labeled as homosexual not just because of overt sexual acts but because of almost any sign of behavior which does not fit the masculine stereotype.[16]

The participants in our study have been reared and live in a culture with strong antihomosexual attitudes. These special and unique circumstances are really not comparable to any other minority group because the attitudes are shared not only by the larger society and all of its institutions but also by parents, families, and, in many instances, the men themselves.

In addition to homophobia,[17] which is described in the quotation from Fasteau above, we have identified three other categories of antihomosexual attitudes, each of which affects the process of male–male relationship formation: prejudice, ignorance, and oppression. The additional complication of sexual repression—not in the personal psychoanalytic use of the term, but closer to the societal sense in which Foucault uses the term in *The History of Sexuality*[18]—is shared by participants with the wider society of mankind. The antihomosexual attitudes of our culture, however, are supported and intensified by the more generalized evidence of sexual negativity that is partially derived from the repression.

Homophobia

Any living language allows for the formation of new words to express or define experience, things, or people. This neologistic tendency is nowhere more prevalent than in psychology and modern technology. However, one of the difficulties with the introduction of new words into the language is the stabilization of their meanings so that the function of language—the communication of ideas—can be served faithfully. The invention of the word *homophobia*[19] came at a point in time shortly after the emergence of the gay liberation movement. Although intended as a psychological term to mean fear of being or being thought gay, and fear of gays, it was quickly incorporated into gay liberationist language as a political epithet to be hurled as an insult at any and all opposition to the progress of the gay rights movement. This extended popularization of the word has diluted its significance and in some cases obscured other antihomosexual attitudes.

While recognizing the value and importance of fear as a protective and motivational emotion, as Kessler has noted, its presence in phobic proportion becomes debilitating in many instances.[20] Isolated phobic reactions, such as claustrophobia, fear of heights, fear of the dark, or fear of snakes, can be managed by avoidance or by mastery. The much more subtle fear of being homosexual can manifest itself in personality defense mechanisms. Some mechanisms may function quite well for individuals through isolation of affect, projection, rationalization, or even reaction formation. For many persons, however, the defense mechanisms themselves, which are protecting the person from feeling guilt, shame, or anxiety caused by his intrapsychic conflict over homosexual wishes, impulses, or behaviors, become detrimental and debilitating in his life, his work, and especially his relationships.

Prejudice

Prejudice is defined here as the prejudging, irrational attitude of hostility toward gay men and women. Although there may be some ignorance involved, even when the missing knowledge is supplied the hostility continues. Prejudice implies a strong emotional component that cannot be removed by learning more about the subject. Studies have shown that prejudice is overcome best when knowledge is accompanied by an experiential and emotional involvement with the person or group against whom the prejudice is held. This has been demonstrated in the case of blacks when prejudicial attitudes of nonblacks have disappeared with the formation of friendship links.

Ignorance

Lack of knowledge is included in our list of antihomosexual attitudes because we have discovered that the perpetuation of long-held negative myths about gays, even among gays themselves, is often sustained by ignorance. Information gaps are caused by the lack of research on the subject, ineffective dissemination, and resistance to reading the accurate data that are available. Two of the old myths—that homosexual men do not have lasting relationships and that they are child molesters—still carry surprising weight among gays and nongays alike.

Oppression

The unjust exercise of power and authority over others is a facet of life of which we have become more conscious today. Blacks, women, Jews, Arabs, Poles—the list is seemingly endless—all have experienced oppression. In the past decade, gay men and women have joined those demanding release from what they have experienced as oppression by the majority of society. The truth is that many homosexual individuals who have not been visible or open about their sexual orientation have never even reflected on the possibility of being oppressed. The increasing visibility of homosexual people has called attention to particular aspects of oppression, such as in federal employment, military service, and teaching. The fact of the matter is that some gay persons *have* held all of the positions and jobs from which they would be excluded had their sexual orientation been known or not been deliberately overlooked. Self-oppression is an issue when gay people themselves assume that they will receive prejudicial treatment from others and act accordingly.

Coming Out

Coming out is the phrase used to describe the process and events surrounding a person's awareness and disclosure of his or her homosexuality. People who are not open have been described as being "in the closet," and the term *coming out* carries the connotation of "coming out of the closet."

Other researchers and writers have postulated steps in the process of coming out among gays (Warren,[21] Cass,[22] Coleman,[23] Dank[24]). Although we generally find agreement with the observations of others, our research resulted in identifying the following five steps of coming out:

1. Self-recognition as gay
2. Disclosure to others
3. Socialization with other gay people
4. Positive self-identification
5. Integration and acceptance

These steps are not necessarily linear in their progression. Coming out is not a one-time event.

Self-Recognition as Gay

This first phase is more than having an awareness of attraction to same-sex persons. In fact many persons may engage in homosexual behaviors in childhood, adolescence, and even adulthood without ever recognizing themselves as gay. The obverse is also true, where persons may never engage in such behaviors either before or after their self-recognition as homosexual. More often than not, this self-recognition is accompanied by certain subphases, usually initial denial with attempts at suppressing the feelings and fantasies, then a process of bargaining about it within the self by trying to develop romantic and sexual feelings with the opposite sex, by seeking counseling, or by using religion to block the feelings. For some gay people, self-recognition or self-labeling comes early and easily, but for most it is a struggle.

Disclosure to Others

This step has many variations, but its common theme is the time at which the person either overtly or covertly lets his self-recognition be known to others, usually significant others such as family members, a close friend, a therapist, a minister, or a teacher. The first disclosure may be a halting one. It may be taken back a number of times before the person becomes comfortable sharing his sexual orientation. First disclosures may be to other gays and may occur after sexual exploits or visits to gay bars, baths, or discos. The response of the person to whom the disclosure is made becomes important in the process of coming out; rejection may retard further disclosures, and acceptance may facilitate more risk-taking. Initial rejection also may push the person back toward the first phase, accompanied by self-doubt and questioning. Covert disclosures may take the form of introducing male lovers to family, leaving evidence of an interest in homosexuality in places where it will be found—books, articles, magazines, and so on. However disclosure is made, it is an important step that must be taken—disclosure must be made to some significant other, even though family and former close friends may not be the first to learn about it. In fact, they may never learn about it.

Socialization With Other Gay People

This phase may precede or follow disclosure, but the steps involved in socialization with others is a vital one that influences both thoughts and feelings about being gay. Initially most gay persons feel they are totally alone with their gayness and the discovery of others like them affects their thoughts and feelings about themselves. The development of self-identity and acceptance is greatly advanced by support and validation from other members of the same stigmatized group. Replacing former negative ideas and feelings with positive experiences with others like themselves who are happy and well adjusted makes a necessary bridge in the process of coming out.

Positive Self-Identification

In using this term we do not intend to open a discussion on the issue of identity and the attendant points of view about it. What we mean is the positive identification of the self as gay accompanied by the ability to express the self in fulfilling and satisfying ways. This kind of self-identification requires knowledge about gays and homosexuality that replaces prior ignorance and bias. It requires positive feelings and experiences that mitigate against the prejudice and the homophobia. It means moving in the direction of total self-acceptance, regardless of the means one chooses to express the self. The self-identified gay person may still be partially in the closet or may be completely out of the closet. The final determinant of a positive self-identity is found within the quiet confines of each person's personality—how he feels about himself and how he acts with those feelings.

Integration and Acceptance

This phase of coming out is more dependent upon the presence of the other phases than any of the previous four. The variations in the ways this phase is manifest are multiple. A major characteristic of acceptance and integration is the "taken for granted without any fuss" attitude held by those who have achieved this status. For some this may mean being publicly open and nondefensive about sexual orientation. Some are moved to taking active roles in advocacy causes for other gays, while others live their lives quietly without announcing or even reflecting upon their gayness, but always willing to be open and not needing to deny it.

The myth commonly held by gay men and others is that coming out is a single process or a step that is taken in a one-time occurrence. Nothing could be further from the facts as revealed by our study. Men slip back and forth in the phases of coming out.

"I was pretty open about being gay in high school. Then when I got to college I was right back in the closet. In fact, I was dating girls again and almost got married."

"I was so mixed up about it for so long that my closet had a revolving door on it. I was out to a few friends, then not to others, then denying it, then being an activist. It took my relationship with my lover to finally get it all together."

In addition to this vacillation, there are many subphases of coming out. For instance, making a contact with another man for sex may precede discussing it or disclosing the fact to someone else, or vice versa. Several men tell us of making the disclosure to another person with great hesitation only to discover that that person was himself gay and a willing sexual partner. The steps of coming out are not clearly linear in their unfolding. Sometimes an individual may be in step three, not passing through step two until later. The last two steps also have considerable variety in their manifestations.

"We've been living together for almost fourteen years. Tom thinks the neighbors don't know about our relationship, but they always see us as a couple. But we're still in the closet to some and out mainly with other gays."

Although Tom and Jack think they are still in the closet, it seemed to us that it was true only in their attitudes about it and not in the reality of their everyday lives. The two men are seen by everyone as the couple they are.

Conclusion

Research has yet to identify all of the components important in relationship formation and development. A series of subtle, less obvious, and even controversial factors may underlie relationship formation. Unconscious motivations ranging from father–son and brother–brother to more primitive mother–child dependencies and need satisfactions have been postulated for gay and nongay couples alike. Hero worship, master–slave, and child–parent are only suggestive of a few combinations of individual intrapsychic dynamics that may be important in that first attraction, which may grow and culminate in the conception of a relationship.

We are also aware that the developing relationship that houses two individuals may be discovered to be inappropriate to the natural growth of one or both of those individuals. At those times separation from the relationship becomes necessary, if painful, lest the development of one or both persons be undermined. This runs contrary to the time-honored view that a couple should commit themselves to a relationship for life no matter what the outcome. We recognize that both individuals who constitute a couple have nature's mandate to grow or to stagnate and die. Only two growing individuals can form the vital couple that gives birth to a relationship.

CHAPTER 10

THE STUDY

This is a study of 156 male couples. We did not set out to support any particular hypothesis. We knew that there were male couples living together in relationships that had lasted for many years. Some of these couples were coming to us for counseling because their relationships were in distress. To respond to their questions with more knowledgeable answers and to increase our counseling skills, we needed to learn much more about how male couples who were not being seen in psychotherapy lived and managed their everyday lives together.

Developing the research design was a slow and arduous process. We recognized our need to know more about male couples but were unsure what questions to ask. We knew some of the questions ourselves, and we learned some questions from our patients. With these first questions we decided to interview a few sample couples who were not patients. We interviewed fifteen couples. We were later to identify those first fifteen as our pilot study. After each interview, we asked the couple what other questions we might have asked and what other information about them we missed. And so we learned more about the phenomenon of male coupling and much more about what areas to explore and what additional questions to ask. After each interview we added more questions, revised previous ones, and finally arrived at a list of questions that seemed satisfactory.

Definitions

Homosexual, Heterosexual, and Gay

Homosexuality, as we use the term today, came into existence in 1869.[1] Sexual behavior between persons of the same sex prior to that time was referred to as sodomy, pederasty, or buggery. Persons who engaged in same sex acts were therefore called sodomites, pederasts, or buggerers. There was no term to refer to persons who had affectional and erotic attractions to the same sex until they had engaged in behaviors that could be labeled by the terms of the behavior itself. There were no pseudobuggerers or latent sodomites, only buggerers and sodomites. The human condition that was eventually called homosexuality was first described by Karl Heinrich Ulrichs, a German lawyer and homosexual man. In an 1862 treatise Ulrichs coined the term *Uranian*, which he took from Plato's *Symposium*, to describe love between men.[2] The stimulus for his work was political. The multiple kingdoms and states of Germany were on the verge of uniting into the German Republic and thus coming under the Prussian penal code that made homosexual acts among males crimes. Many of the German states and kingdoms that would be united under Prussian law had adopted the Napoleonic Code, which treated homosexual acts just like heterosexual acts.

In his description of the condition of being erotically and affectionally attracted to persons of the same sex, Ulrichs argued that because the condition was inborn and not acquired, penalizing persons for this condition was unjust. The cause was taken up by a Hungarian journalist, Heinrich Benkert, who posed as a physician in order to command more attention. In an open letter to the Minister of Justice, Benkert argued for the legalization of acts between persons of the same sex and introduced the word *homosexuality* to describe the condition of sex and love between persons of the same sex.[3] Although his plea eventually fell upon deaf ears, the word *homosexual* was born.

A Viennese psychiatrist by the name of Krafft-Ebing recognized the importance of Benkert's and Ulrichs's concept of the condition of homosexuality, seeing the treatment of homosexual persons as new work for the young and developing medical specialty of psychiatry.[4] His belief that the condition of homosexuality was a pathological state amenable to some form of medical treatment would theoretically bolster the arguments for decriminalization of homosexual acts. From the early 1870s onward, persons with same-sex proclivities were not only considered criminals but were additionally labeled as sick and needing treatment.

Following the lead of John Boswell, we use the word *gay* to refer to "persons who are conscious of erotic inclinations toward their own gender as a distinguishing characteristic or, loosely, to things associated with such people, as 'gay poetry.'"[5] The word *homosexual* is used only as an adjective, as in "homosexual marriage." Homosexual behavior can be engaged in by a gay person or a nongay person. Marmor characterizes a homosexual person as one who is motivated in adult life by a definite, preferential erotic attraction to members of the same sex, and who usually (but not necessarily) engages in overt sexual relations with them.[6] The definition of homosexuality used in our study follows Marmor's characterization.

The word *heterosexual* is used as an adjective like *homosexual* in the same fashion as "heterosexual marriage" and to describe opposite-sex eroticism. Therefore, heterosexual behavior can be engaged in by a gay person, a homosexual person, or a heterosexual person.

Couples

Many kinds of coupling occur among gay men. (See chapter 1.) The clear identification of a male couple becomes problematic when the potential range of coupling arrangements is considered. Some couples live in separate homes, others have a series of partners lasting a few weeks or months. There are men who live in different cities—even on different coasts—who consider themselves a couple, as well as heterosexually married men in coupled relationships with other men. We chose to define a male couple in a conservative or traditional fashion so that the reader could make comparisons with traditionally recognized couples in a marriage. Also, our definition of a male couple would allow the reader to make comparisons with other traditional couples who are not married but living together in an ongoing committed relationship. We also were interested in examining the ways in which couples maintained their relationships and not simply how they developed them. We were not interested in short-term relationships, so we added a duration factor to our definition of couples.

These considerations led to the establishment of the following criteria for participants in this research:

1. Two gay men
2. Living together in the same home
3. For at least one year
4. And identifying themselves as a couple

This last criterion excluded men living together as roommates or friends.

We have established these narrow criteria in order to examine a kind of couple that would fit the image of traditional. There has been no established image of the traditional couple when discussing gay relationships, and it is needed for purposes of comparison if for no other reason.

As with gay couples, a wide variation of nongay couples exist. In contrast to homosexual couples, however, there *is* a clearcut image of the traditional heterosexual couple. Throughout the book we make frequent reference to nongay or heterosexual couples. Unless otherwise indicated the definition for such couples is:

1. A male and a female
2. Living together in the same home
3. For at least one year
4. And identifying themselves as a couple, usually in a marriage

Throughout the study *partner, lover,* and *mate* are used interchangeably to refer to one of the two males in a couple. *Lover* is the term most couples use to describe their partners.

We decided not to include female couples in our research for several reasons. We had a strong suspicion that male couples and female couples have so many distinct differences that mixing the two together would blur the focus. Also, gaining access to female couples would have been considerably more difficult. Finally, it was our bias that female investigators would be better equipped and more appropriate for a study of female couples.

Incidence—2.5 Million Male Couples

Today, most people, whether they live in large cities, small towns, or suburbs, know the two bachelors or the roommates who live together down the block, in the apartment across the hall, or in a cabin in the country. Their professions and jobs include plumbing, farming, teaching, medicine, zookeeping, and many others. Most people, however, are unaware that some of these bachelors and roommates are homosexual couples, living in a predominantly heterosexual society.

Our study does not measure the incidence of male homosexual coupling. Nonetheless, we asked ourselves how many such couples might live in the United States. Data from the Institute for Sex Research (Kinsey) indicate that approximately 14 percent of the adult American male population (11.6 million) have had an extensive homosexual experience.[7] In a letter to the National Gay Task Force, dated March 18, 1977, Paul Gebhard, Ph.D., Director of the Institute for Sex Research at the University of Indiana, indicated that 13.95 percent of adult American males have had extensive homosexual experience. These data exclude that portion of the original Kinsey sample taken from homophile groups. Assuming that close to 50 percent of the population is male and using 220 million as the population of the United States, there are 110 million males. Approximately 25 percent of this number are under age eighteen, leaving 82.5 million adult males. Fourteen percent of 82.5 million is 11.6 million males with extensive homosexual experience. The only data on the incidence of coupling among these men is derived from Bell and Weinberg, who report that 52 percent of white male homosexuals and 58 percent of black male homosexuals have lived with other men for from three months to more than five years.[8] By conservative extrapolation from the incidence of coupling data in several studies (Bell and Weinberg,[9] Jay and Young,[10] Spada[11]), we estimate that about 2.5 million male couples live in the United States. Not all couples would fit the criteria we established for this study, although many would. These couples live throughout the country, in large cities, in middle-American suburbs, on farms, in small villages, among the very wealthy, the middle class, and the very poor.

Study Design

We needed a research design that would allow us to collect reliable, reproducible data about the couples and, by our method of obtaining and reporting the data, to represent validly and accurately the couples being researched. We rejected the idea of handing out or mailing questionnaires to couples because we knew that we could learn more through personal interviews. For the same reason we similarly rejected the idea of having others, such as research assistants or graduate students, do the interviewing.

We used a general descriptive method and developed our own interview schedule after the pilot study. There were 185 questions requiring yes or no answers, brief specific facts, or multiple choice responses. However, this kind of descriptive information does not explain relationships, help make predictions, or allow investigators to seek meaning and implications. Therefore, we added sixty-three more questions that were more open-ended, allowing the participants the opportunity of explaining and describing their experiences and feelings. These questions added something more to the descriptions. In this portion of the interview we had the flexibility to probe for answers and to focus on capturing more elusive data that gave color and increased the accuracy of earlier responses. Analysis of the interviews and identification of recurrent, common themes in experiences, feelings, and interactions yielded data that enabled us, for example, to identify the stages of relationships.

The Data

We gathered three distinctly different kinds of information. Each added depth and dimension to our investigation.

1. *Objective facts and figures* that lent themselves to tabular presentation. These we called *data one*.
2. *Actual responses* offered by the couple of their behavior, thoughts, and feelings. These became *data two*.
3. *Our own observations and commentary* on data one and data two. These are *data three*.

These three types of data presented together give a more complete picture of the couples in our study.

Recognizing the complexity of any couple, we realized that the meanings participants gave to their experiences must be taken into account with respect. Any researcher involved in a field study knows that more happens in the interviews than is recorded. The complete picture of a couple that can be seen by the interviewers cannot be understood or presented with just the facts and figures. Therefore, we have chosen to include responses and observations that present these

male couples, rich with the nuances of meaning and feeling we ourselves experienced.

Participants

Researchers who work with invisible populations have difficulty
locating participants. Ideally, every research study seeks a representative sample of the population being investigated. We would be de-
lighted to report finding such a sample of male couples, but we have
not. The identification of enough couples to select a random sample
would be a formidable, probably impossible, task. We were interested
in interviewing couples who were not in treatment nor obtained
through gay organizations. We wanted to find the everyday, garden
variety men living together as couples. We wanted to examine their
relationships. We had met the couples we interviewed for the pilot
study in social situations. After each interview we asked the couple if
they knew other couples we might interview.

   This method of obtaining participants is often called the friendship network method because it relies on friends to recommend other
participants. After the pilot study we considered a variety of other
methods for obtaining couples, such as advertisements in newspapers
and periodicals; signs in gay bars, discos, and baths; or appeals to gay
organizations. We rejected each of these possible sources because the
friendship network assured us of access to couples not available in
other ways, such as older men, the less socially inclined couples, couples more in the closet, and those with limited contacts with other gay
people.

   Before making direct contact with a new couple, the referring
friend requested the new couple's permission for us to contact them.
Being contacted and reassured by friends first increased the probability
of participation by couples who otherwise would have been reluctant.
One of us would telephone the new couple and set up an appoint-
ment. In some cases it took as long as two to three years from the time
of our initial contact before a few of the couples agreed to participate.
Expressing reluctance, they declined at first and then agreed to be interviewed several years later. We interviewed every couple who
agreed, and over the five years only three couples said no and stuck to
it.

The sample represents a wide diversity of ages, educational backgrounds, employment, socioeconomic levels, and degrees of openness about homosexuality. The sample is predominantly white with a small representation of blacks, Mexican–Americans, and Asians. The average age of the men in the study is 37.5 years. (See tables 3 and 4 in chapter 11.) Ages ranged from 20 to 69 years with a median of slightly over 36 years. Bell and Weinberg report an average age of 37 years for their white male participants,[12] and Saghir and Robins report a mean age of 35 years with the median being 32.7 years for the homosexual men in their study.[13] Fifty-six and four-tenths percent (176) of the men in our study had one or more years of college education. (See table 5 in chapter 11.) This is a somewhat lower percentage than has been reported by other researchers. Saghir and Robins report 59 percent of their sample had graduated from or attended college.[14] Bell and Weinberg report 75 percent with some college or graduation from college among the white male participants in their San Francisco study.[15] Harry and DeVall indicate that 69 percent of their participants had at least some college education.[16]

The Interview

In reviewing the Kinsey interview strategy and rationale[17] and our own previous work,[18] we identified two interview methods that had distinct differences: the research interview and the clinical interview. The research type is intended to collect data that are reliable and reproducible and are available for tabular presentation and statistical manipulation. The clinical interview is useful in collecting both objective information and less tangible data about the thoughts, feelings, and interactional components in the respondents' lives.

Most interviews required four to six hours. Some couples were interviewed more than once over five years. More than 90 percent of the interviews took place in the couples' homes.

All of the interviews were done by us as a team. All interview visits were conducted similarly. We would sit down together with the couple and offer a brief explanation of our project. Then, each of us would interview one of the partners in separate rooms. At the end, we would meet together with the couple to clarify certain issues and problems, to make further inquiries, and to respond to questions they would ask.

Location

All couples in this study were from the Southern California area, the large majority being from San Diego. The County of San Diego has been our primary source of participants. It has a population of more than 1.8 million people. The population is ethnically and culturally diverse. About 24 percent of the people are of Hispanic background, about 6 percent are black, and about 2 percent are Asian. Less than 0.05 percent are American Indian.

During the course of this research, we have observed an increased political and economic visibility for the gay community in San Diego. In 1983, every major contender for mayor of San Diego sought the support of the gay community. A large organization of local businesspeople who are themselves gay or who cater to the gay community has developed. Increased visibility and respectability of discos, bars, and other places of entertainment for gay people have occurred since the mid-1970s; there now exist more than forty bars as well as restaurants, bath houses, and health spas that encourage a predominantly gay clientele.

The gay community now has its own newspapers, social service center, and religious organizations (including the Metropolitan Community Church; Dignity, an organization for gay Catholics; and Integrity, its Episcopalian counterpart). Similar growth seems to be occurring in most American cities of equal size. This may mean that a formerly invisible minority is succeeding in making itself visible.

Couples live throughout the city and county of San Diego, from the more affluent beach communities, the modern and modest tract home developments, and the older renewing neighborhoods, to the isolation of the nearby mountains or deserts. There are no special places where gay men live, as are found in the larger metropolises, such as San Francisco's Castro District or New York's Greenwich Village. There is wide dispersion of male couples throughout the larger community, depending upon socioeconomic level and individual taste. The majority of couples blend inconspicuously into the fabric of the neighborhoods in which they live.

CHAPTER 11

THE INDIVIDUALS

Each person in this study has a unique, interesting life story that began long before their current relationships. Information about the individuals sheds more light on the couples. Most of the facts and figures (data one) will be found in the text. We use actual responses (data two) and our own observations and commentary (data three) as was done in earlier chapters, to give life to our participants.

Age

(Tables 3 and 4)

The average age of the men in this study is 37.5 years, ranging from 20 to 69 years. The median age is 36 years, which means that half of the participants are younger than 36 and half are older. More than 82 percent of the participants (256 men) were between 25 and 50 at the time of our interviews.

Some of the men in this study had been living with the same partner for ten or more years already when men in the younger group were just beginning to crawl or walk. Before the younger men had seen the light of day, some of the older ones were fighting in the jungles of the South Pacific, the deserts of North Africa, or the valleys of France during World War II. Many of the older men knew about their homosexual attractions early but looked upon themselves as sick, while many of the younger participants found far easier acceptance of their homoeroticism as early as high school.

To see the difference age can make, compare the following two stories set fifty years apart.

"My father was a doughboy and never let me forget it. I was born in 1911 and my parents were farmers. I just barely remember when my father left for France. Mom always told me how scared we were that he

TABLE 3
AGE AT TIME OF INTERVIEW

Age	Number of Participants	Age	Number of Participants
20	1	46	3
21	2	47	9
22	2	48	9
23	4	49	2
24	8	50	6
25	5		
		51	8
26	11	52	2
27	13	53	1
28	19	54	0
29	20	55	0
30	12		
		56	1
31	12	57	4
32	10	58	4
33	4	59	4
34	10	60	3
35	8		
		61	0
36	21	62	2
37	10	63	0
38	11	64	1
39	16	65	1
40	12		
		66	1
41	12	67	0
42	8	68	0
43	6	69	1
44	9		
45	4		

Number of Participants = 312
Mean = 37.5 years
Median = 36 years

TABLE 4
AGE OF PARTICIPANTS BY FIVE-YEAR INTERVALS

Five-Year Intervals	Number of Participants	Percentage
20–25	17	5.4
25–30	68	21.8
30–35	48	15.4
35–40	66	21.2
40–45	47	15.1
45–50	27	8.7
50–55	17	5.4
55–60	13	4.2
60–65	6	1.9
65–70	3	.9
	312	100.0

Number of participants = 312
Ages 25–50 = 256 = 82% of total

wouldn't come back. When he did come home, I guess he didn't like the way I was jumping rope with the girls. He started trying to make a man out of me when I was ten. I remember how handsome he looked in his uniform when he came home, but I also remember feeling attracted to the boy next door who was about fifteen. Something was strange about me, even then. I hated myself for it. I wanted to be what my dad thought I would be. I struggled, I tried, I prayed."

A young man recalled: "I knew I was gay when I was seven, because I just wanted to be with other boys naked. Being in the city gave us lots of chances as kids to play sex games with each other. I started having sex with boys by the time I was nine. I never felt really bad about it, but knew by the time I was in junior high that not every guy was into it. Three of my best friends felt the same way I did, though, so we gave each other a lot of support. Nineteen-seventy was a good year to come out, at least to myself. I had heard and read about gays. I looked at myself as different but not bad."

These two examples highlight the difference fifty years can make in the experience of being a young gay man in the 1920s and the 1970s. We listened with great interest as men over fifty in our study discussed their current observations of the gay community and especially of younger gay men. Some observations are positive, stressing openness, availability of support systems, and organized gay activities. Some observations are negative, reflecting embarrassment about media representations of homosexual men in female clothing or the flaunting of outrageous behavior in public.

"Young gays have it far better now than when I was their age. They have supportive discussion groups with other men like themselves. Why, even the parents have their own groups, called Parents of Gays, where they share information and pride about their sons and daughters. Anyway, I sure am not leaving myself out now that times have changed. I joined the congregation of a gay church a few neighborhoods over, and once a month I go to a social meeting for gay senior citizens."

There is a distinctly more negative flavor in the next comment. "Most of the public queers scare me a little. I get embarrassed seeing pictures of men in dresses on TV. *Time* magazine has a cover story of a faggot soldier! And he says he's proud to be 'gay.' I don't even like that word. I don't want to be called 'gay.' All this public openness is showing homosexuals too much like they are, queer!"

The younger men in our study make observations about their older counterparts. They are interested in hearing about the existence of long-term homosexual relationships. "Where are these guys with long relationships?" or "I only know of one older couple who have been together a long time."

"I couldn't have imagined what it was like back in the fifties, but I talked to Phil and Jim—they've been together almost twenty-five years. They have loads of interesting stories and some great old porno movies. It's a lot easier for us nowadays."

And, on a more negative note: "I don't like to be around those old queens. They all seem to have such attitudes about everything, like the movie *Boys in the Band.*"

Frequently, men closer to middle age make observations about both ends of the spectrum. Men in their late thirties and forties continue to have a foot in the younger and more visible gay world, at the same time looking anxiously toward the more hidden world of the older groups.

Jim is forty-one: "Being together with Bob, who is five years younger, for the past six years has kept me right in the middle of things. I've come a long way since my days of shame and hiding about being homosexual. I'm almost to the point that I could march in a parade with a sign saying 'Gay and Proud.'"

Tom is forty-six: "I look ahead, but I really don't know many men older than me who are homosexuals. Whatever happens to the older gays? Do they change or just disappear? Most of the time I feel like I'm the oldest guy on the dance floor at the local gay disco."

Although age in and of itself is only a single variable, it is an important one. Recent research (Levinson,[1] Gould[2]) has demonstrated beyond any doubt that there are continuing developmental stages of adulthood that span a lifetime. As an individual gets older, he passes through different stages and undergoes changes just as the child does from infancy through adolescence. Our study has taken this theory of development one step further by applying it to coupled relationships as well.

Education

(Table 5)

All of our participants are high-school graduates. Often, although the individual we were interviewing has not been formally educated beyond high school, his vocabulary, breadth of interests, and wideranging knowledge led us to assume that he had a college education.

More than half of the men have some years of college and many have bachelor's degrees. A few have Master's degrees and a few more have doctorates in wide fields including medicine, dentistry, law, and the ministry. Others have technical training in specialized programs or trade schools, such as cosmetology, medical technology, plumbing, carpentry, and so forth.

For gay men there is usually some connection between education and issues of being homosexual. Some deal with the connections well, others not so well. Many of the men who earned college degrees report

TABLE 5
EDUCATION

Education Level (highest attainment)	Number of Participants	Percentage of Participants
High school	136	43.6
Technical school*	28	9.0
College(one or more years without baccalaureate)	79	25.3
Bachelor's degree	58	18.6
Master's degree	15	4.8
Doctorate	24	7.7
	340†	109.0†

*Technical school includes such training as cosmetology, real estate, trade jobs, nursing, laboratory, or X-ray technicians without bachelor's degrees.
†Twenty-eight individuals with technical school also are included in one other category, e.g., high school or college.

having immersed themselves in study in an attempt to avoid homo-erotic attraction to a roommate or classmate. Others reported male lovers during their years of study and found that sexual and affectional outlets enhanced their study efforts.

Mike is a thirty-seven-year-old Ph.D. physicist. "College was real work for me, but I loved it. It kept my mind off the guys who seemed to be available everywhere in the city. I stayed in at night and worked in the lab on weekends. Graduate school was even more immersion."

Another had a very different experience. "Being at Dartmouth it was an effort to get to Boston or New York. I was lucky, though, be-cause in my third year my new roommate and I started to masturbate together at night. From there it went to other kinds of sex play. We had it made then, because at least we had each other for relief and somebody to talk to. We kept each other sane in those days of compe-tition and study. We weren't really lovers, just sexual friends."

Some of the older participants tell us they had not pursued profes-sional careers because they believed and were told that homosexuality would be a serious obstacle.

At fifty-seven, Russ, who has had to contend with his blindness for the past three years, would be considered a successful man. He carries an unpleasant memory. "I saw a psychiatrist in 1950 because I didn't want to be queer but couldn't do anything about it. Some of my best friends were getting ready for med school and law school. I really wanted to be a doctor. That damned psychiatrist told me that homosexuals couldn't make the commitment to that kind of grueling study. I believed that doctor and even paid him for telling me that!"

Some of the men with high-school diplomas or some years in college attribute their lack of further schooling to issues related to sexual orientation. A few speak of a consuming interest in sexual pursuits. Some discuss heavy drug use for a period of their lives.

"I couldn't think of anything else. It was either masturbating until I got sore or cruising the park for someone to do it with. It became an obsession, and studying became impossible. All my nights were spent going from tearoom to tearoom (public toilets where men find sexual contacts). My grades fell. I was drinking, then smoking, trying everything there was to try. My dad finally said he wouldn't pay anymore, so I just dropped out and started to work in a bank."

Another said, "I think I would have gone further in school, but when I came out I really got caught up in the 'gay life.' It was so much fun. I was out every night with my newfound friends, getting to bed at four, five, or six each morning, having wonderful and wild sex, going to great parties. I was carried away by it all and couldn't see any reason to continue with school. I dropped out. Those guys at school were all just jocks. Drinking beer, talking about making it with girls, and watching football was the extent of their world. I tried but never fit. They hated my guts because I was different."

Coming out was an interruption in educational pursuits for some men, and others passed through this period of their lives and continued their education.

Employment

The jobs our respondents hold cover the entire socioeconomic scale, from janitor and rubbish collector to professor and business executive. The general public often assumes that gay men work at traditional female occupations, such as nursing, dancing, hairstyling, and interior design. Many do. However, in our study there are more men in traditional male occupations, such as gardeners, construction workers, and firemen. Also, there are numerous professionals, including doctors, lawyers, and ministers. The obvious and easiest cause of confusion for the general public is assuming that the men one knows, from family members to fellow workers, are heterosexual if they are masculine in demeanor and work in traditional male occupations.

More than 85 percent of the men consider their jobs to be important or meaningful parts of their lives. Fewer than 10 percent report discontentment in their work. Some who describe jobs as important see their work as a source of income that allows them time and energy to pursue other interests, such as travel, music, and reading. Some of those who describe their jobs as meaningful see them not only as sources of income but also as opportunities to help others, to make new discoveries, or to teach. Several men have made widely recognized contributions in writing, research, politics, or business. Discontentment with jobs is reported both by younger men with lower levels of employment and by older men experiencing restlessness or monotony in long-term employment.

There is a job discrimination problem for homosexual males. Some of our participants failed to get business or academic promotions because they were single. Upon closer inspection, for some the problem was rooted in the individual's anxiety about his homosexuality being discovered or a fear that the additional responsibilities would be too invasive of his lifestyle.

"I was up for the manager's position. There really wasn't anyone else as well prepared. When the job was given to someone else they told me it was because I didn't have a wife for all the social events the manager needs to attend. I figured it was because I was gay and not out of the closet, so I decided to leave well enough alone."

It is more difficult to determine the extent of actual discrimination against an invisible minority group such as homosexual males than it is against more recognizable groups like blacks or left-handed writers. Other researchers have looked closely at this problem. Harry and DeVall attribute much of the problem to the process of labeling deviants.[3] Homosexual labeling occurs when the individual identifies himself as homosexual or more virulently when gossip and rumor label him "faggot" or "queer" in the work place. No matter how accomplished or efficient he may be in his work, the labeling may well cause him to be overlooked or denied promotion in favor of others with fewer accomplishments and skills. Being labeled a member of a socially deviant group fosters isolation.

Many of the men in our study prefer to be self-employed rather than deal with the covert systems that penalize them for their sexual orientation under some other rubric. On the other side of that coin are those homosexual men who prefer to remain in their employment without the label by passing as nongay. Some have become very adept at leading a life in which their homosexuality is covert. They have learned to flirt with the female staff and laugh at the "fag" stories. They join the heterosexual majority outwardly rather than face the risks of clandestine labeling. Most of these men, of course, would rather have the situation neutralized so that their sexual orientation would not interfere.

Many men are openly gay in their employment and claim they have no difficulty whatsoever with the issues on the job. Some work in all-gay establishments; others work in industry, governmental agencies, or somewhere in the educational system. The level of employment satisfaction and the degree to which the individual is out of the closet and comfortable on the job does affect relationships.

Income

(Table 6)

Half of the participants have annual incomes of between $10,000 and $20,000, one-quarter less than $10,000, and the rest more than

TABLE 6
ANNUAL INCOME RANGE (INDIVIDUAL)

Amount of Income	Number of Participants	Percentage of Participants
0–5,000	43	13.8
5,000–10,000	43	13.8
10,000–15,000	69	22.2
15,000–20,000	87	27.8
20,000–25,000	18	5.7
Over 25,000	52	16.7

Number of participants = 312

$20,000. Remember, these data were collected between 1974 and 1979. Inflation has made a great change in income since that time. The poverty level was below $5,000 in 1974; in 1982 it was closer to $10,000. Some of the men in our study are millionaires while others are barely managing.

We find a wide variety of attitudes about money. Some individuals tell us they are not very concerned about money, and, indeed, their lifestyle and homes reflect as much. Some men are quite frank about how important their earnings are as symbols of success.

Larry, thirty-eight, leans back comfortably in a big leather chair in his plush living room, crossing his ankles and joining his fingers at the back of his neck so that both of his elbows are above his ears. "No, money really doesn't mean much to me. I wouldn't care if I had it or not. Of course, having enough makes life a lot easier." He admits, however, that he could not imagine giving up a single one of his opulent comforts, vacations in Europe, or his expensive hillside house.

"Damn right, money is important to me," says Al. "I've worked hard these past ten years to get where I am. So has Fred. We set out to make money and a lot of it. Both of us would sure like to make more, but until we do, we think we've done all right so far. What do you think?" He gestures toward the shimmering blue, forty-foot swimming pool in the elegantly landscaped backyard.

Gay men spend their money wisely and foolishly just like everyone else. Some have invested it; others buy clothes or furnish their homes comfortably. They spend a portion on entertainment and travel. For the most part, lacking the dependency of family, they have a relatively high level of expendable income.

Childhood

Data relating to childhood collected by most researchers are focused on the speculative etiology or predictors of homosexuality. Our interest in childhood was directed toward data that might shed light on current relationships.

Attitude
(Table 7)

We asked each man to select from five different adjectives the one that best described his overview of his childhood. Fifty-eight percent

TABLE 7
DESCRIPTION OF CHILDHOOD

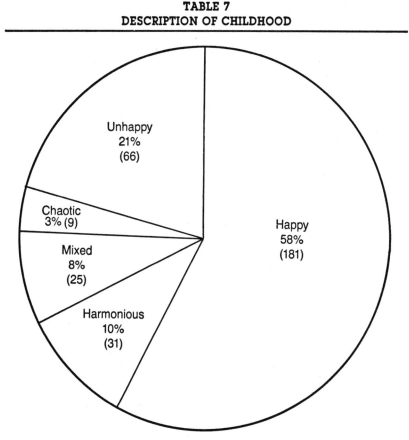

- Unhappy 21% (66)
- Chaotic 3% (9)
- Mixed 8% (25)
- Harmonious 10% (31)
- Happy 58% (181)

selected *happy,* while 21 percent selected *unhappy.* Three percent identified childhood as *chaotic,* 10 percent as *harmonious,* and 8 percent chose *mixed.* In explaining the selection those who chose *happy* often modified their responses with observations that everything about growing up could not be characterized by that adjective, but that generally their recollections are happy ones.

"The best parts were times when the whole family was together. Birthdays were big events for everybody. Planning things together, taking trips, feeling encouraged by them all at the least little success. They were happy days."

"When I was little, Sundays were 'together days.' Each of the children got to choose what the whole group would do sometimes.

There were occasional fights between us, but overall those were good times together."

"I remember my dad reading to me and Mom's being Cub Scout Den Mother. My parents always seemed to have fun with us."

Responses about unhappiness usually involved issues of feeling and being different or parental disharmony.

"I didn't know I was gay until I was seventeen. But I knew I was different from other boys even before the first grade. I learned how to pretend to be like them so I wouldn't always be left out. I led a double life without realizing it."

"Both my parents were alcoholics. Mother died of cirrhosis of the liver when I was in college. Dad had left before I got out of high school. I was the parent; they certainly weren't. I always worked. In the beginning nothing pleased them. Finally I began to realize they didn't matter. I was really unhappy in those days."

"I was always a sissy. It was terrible. The other kids teased and hounded me, and my dad was always picking at me. I could never please him."

Those choosing *harmonious* to describe their childhood usually explained their selection by using phrases such as "Things were always on an even keel," or "No one rocked the boat at home," or "There were no ups or downs. We were expected to follow the rules and do well—we all did."

Place of Growing Up
(Table 8)

Ten percent were born in and around the San Diego area, while others were born in various places from Munich and Tokyo to Hawaii and Alaska. All were U.S. citizens. More important than place of birth is the environment in which one is reared. Participants grew up in both small communities and large cities during their early years. Some families, especially those in the military service, moved every two or three years. Others have lived their whole lives in the same community. Some lived on farms, more grew up in small towns, and more than one-third grew up in cities.

TABLE 8
COMMUNITY WHERE PARTICIPANTS WERE REARED

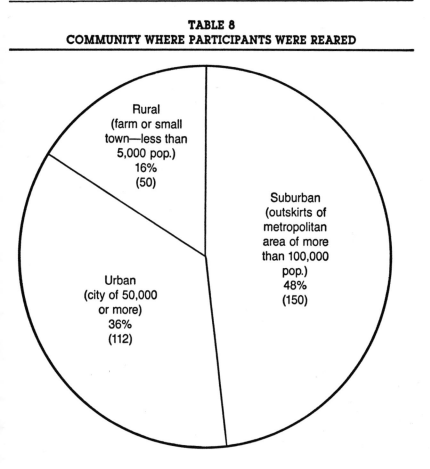

Rural
(farm or small
town—less than
5,000 pop.)
16%
(50)

Suburban
(outskirts of
metropolitan
area of more
than 100,000
pop.)
48%
(150)

Urban
(city of 50,000
or more)
36%
(112)

Socioeconomics of Family
(Table 9)

Socioeconomic levels for most were identified as middle-middle-class. Participants reared in the suburbs generally came from the middle or higher socioeconomic levels. Those identifying their families' socioeconomic class as upper-middle, upper, or lower were usually reared either in a rural or urban setting.

"Economically, I'd have to say my family was really rich. My family are mega-farmers and make millions every year. Socially, however, my family is definitely middle-class or less."

TABLE 9
SOCIOECONOMIC STATUS OF FAMILY

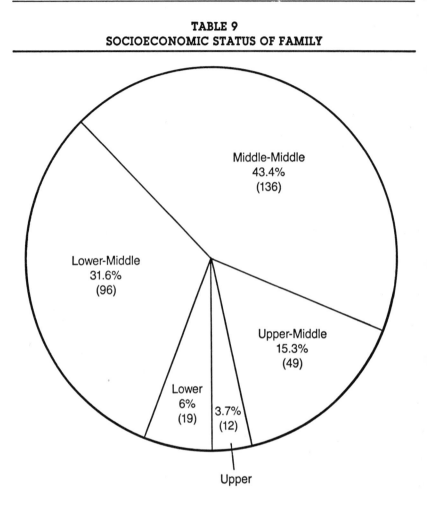

"Always the right clothes, the right schools, the right parties, etc. Money and culture, mixed with quiet and hostile elegance, was where I came from."

"Typical Long Island suburbs, Levitt housing, front lawn, and church on Sunday. We had color TV, first on the block. I'd get my brother's hand-me-downs, which tried to keep me in my place— second class."

"Both my parents were teachers, Des Moines, nice old clapboard house, hollyhocks in the spring garden, canning in the late summer, trips to the river or the lakes in Minnesota. It was a good life, but knowing I was gay made it tough after a while."

"Poor, poor, poor. We were 'white trash,' that's all there was to it. Welfare checks got used to buy beer for Dad. I got out of there as fast as I could."

"Mother taught school. I tried to be the best little boy in the world. She'd never deny me anything. My grandparents always had us for the summer. Granddad was a doctor and Grandma was the proper doctor's wife."

Parents

(Table 10)

More than 80 percent of participants lived with their parents until age sixteen. The other 20 percent lived with a single parent (through divorce or death of one parent) or were reared by others (including grandparent, aunt, or orphanage). The majority of parents were alive at least until the participants had reached age sixteen. Some parents divorced or died during the first sixteen years. In no instances did both parents die before any participants were sixteen. In two instances boys were reared in orphanages or multiple foster homes. In three cases boys were reared by grandmothers or aunts.

Divorce
(Table 11)

The divorce of parents took place before age sixteen in nineteen of the families. The responses they give us to questions about this experience fall into three basic categories. First, almost a third of the nineteen discuss the shock and sadness they had felt with parental separation. Several talk about the loss of fathers. Second, another third of the nineteen talk about the parental divorce being a tremendous relief to them. Their parents had been constantly fighting and arguing, making the home a place of tension and unhappiness. Third, almost one-third claim that they do not recall any serious disruptions occurring with the divorce. They continued to see both parents at various times but remained somewhat aloof from the situation.

As usual among heterosexual offspring in divorced families, the participants in every instance lived with their mothers, at least for

TABLE 10
STATUS OF PARENTS

	Up to Age 16		At Time of Interview		
	Alive	Divorced/Separated by Death	Alive	Divorced/Separated by Death	Remarried
Father	284 (91.0%)	19 (6.7%)/9 (3.2%)	119 (38.1%)	30 (9.6%)	26 (8.3%)
Mother	303 (97.0%)	19 (6.3%)/28 (9.2%)	134 (43.0%)	30 (9.6%)	19 (6.1%)

There were no instances where both parents died before age 16.

256 parents together to age 16 (82.05%).

89 parents alive and together at time of interview.

TABLE 11
DIVORCE OF PARENTS

No parental divorce prior to participants' leaving home	250	80%
Divorced or separated prior to participants' leaving home	62	20%
Prior to age 16	12	3.8% of Total (19.4% of 62)
Prior to age 10	7	2.2% of Total (11.3% of 62)

Number of participants = 312

some period of time. Five of the participants never knew their fathers until later in their lives because the divorces had occurred prior to their memory. In these cases stepfathers assumed the father-surrogate position.

Relationship Between Parents

Most participants report their families as unremarkable, just like parents of others they grew up with. They got along well for the most part, with the usual ups and downs. The majority see their parents as mutually caring and supportive. About a third tell us that they never saw their parents touch or display affection toward each other. The other two-thirds came from families with various degrees and ways of showing affection. Some tell us their homes were scenes of constant tensions between parents who fought over every issue. Several of these men left home during their teenage years as a consequence. Almost one-third report that their parents were always polite and considerate but did not encourage expressing feelings. Some men tell us their parents were among the happiest couples they had ever known.

"Fights were the rule in our house, peaceful coexistence the exception. Why those two ever stayed together so many years is still a mystery to my sister and me."

"Italians yell and shout at each other, like everyone is hard of hearing. I think loud voices had deeper meanings in our home. Mom would complain to me about Dad. Dad would complain to me about Mom. More than not, I was in the middle and the thumbscrews were on, and I mean on."

"'Don't shake the boat, you might find the floorboards are loose. That's how it was for us. 'Nice people don't disagree.' My mother never seemed to accept the fact that she had to put her pants on one leg at a time like everyone else. She always said, 'Don't cry, don't be sad, don't be too funny or too happy. Keep everything on an even keel.'"

"My folks were always each other's best friend, and they still are at sixty-five. They've supported my life, my career, and my homosexuality. I think I've probably got the best parents in the whole world."

"I learned how to take care of Tom from knowing those two. They really have each other down pat. They know what pleases each other and are never afraid or ashamed to show it. In some ways I still see them like newlyweds."

Relationship With Parents
(Table 12)

More than three-quarters of the men remember beng closer to their mothers, while less than 5 percent say fathers. The remaining claim they did not feel closer to either parent. The influence of closeness to one parent or the other on the quality of their current relationships is very difficult to assess. It is easier to see, however, that in those men who claim closeness to neither parent the potential for influence on the relationship is more obvious.

"My memories of childhood are still really vague. Maybe I just don't want to remember, but I look back on it and think I was just an 'it' for my parents. Meals, clothes, spending money, but closeness? What's that?"

"From my very earliest memories I think I was an independent little cuss. Mother would try to hug me and I'd pull away. Dad wasn't around that much—he's just a shadow in my memory. I remember falling off my bike at eight or nine and really scraping my knees badly. I

TABLE 12
RELATIONSHIP WITH PARENTS

	Mother	Father	Neither
Parent closer to preadolescent	256 (82%)	12 (4%)	44 (14%)
Parent closer to adolescent	237 (76%)	16 (5%)	59 (19%)

didn't want to cry; I didn't want to go home. Something inside me told me there wasn't any sympathy there."

"Mom was too busy with her social world, and Dad was working or at the country club. I had a black nanny named Beatrice. She was everything to me, my whole world. I could go to Bea with the simplest little thing, and she'd drop everything to be there for me. I must have been her whole world, too, as I look back. She's dead now, but I sure wish I could have a long talk with her."

In male couples where one or both partners give this response more frequently we find increased difficulty with conflict resolution, less evidence of intimacy as estimated by the partners' ability to be vulnerable to each other, and more instances of a discrepancy in having affectional needs satisfied by each other. Although there are numerous other influential variables in addition to closeness with parents, one of the above-mentioned examples was present in more than half of the couples where one or both partners denied closeness with either parent.

There is a shift away from closeness to either parent during adolescence, with mothers losing the most ground during this period. The decline in parental closeness may well be related to the adolescent stage itself, but for most boys wrestling with same-sex proclivities there is a higher all-around incidence of withdrawal not only from parents but also from peers and siblings.

Physical Contact With Parents
(Table 13)

Participants report more physical contact with mothers than with fathers. There was a much higher frequency of affectionate touching than physical discipline. During childhood mothers are usually around more than fathers and provide the most affection. We find this to be the case for most men. There seem to be strong feelings expressed by those men who remember punishment by their fathers. Fathers were more responsible for physical punishment than were mothers.

"I remember Mom telling me to just wait until Dad got home because I was going to get it. I knew that meant I was going to get spanked."

Other types of physical punishment included pulling hair,

TABLE 13
PHYSICAL CONTACT WITH PARENTS

	During Childhood		During Adolescence	
	Yes	No	Yes	No
Father	69—22%	243—78%	34—11%	278—89%
Mother	284—91%	28—9%	69—22%	243—78%

			Type of Physical Contact		
	Yes	No		Yes	No
Father	51	18	Hugging and kissing	2	32
	69	0	Lapsitting and holding	4	30
	41	28	Wrestling and jostling	21	13
	43	26	Spanking	30	4
	53	16	Other physical punish-ment	26	8
	Yes	No		Yes	No
Mother	282	2	Hugging and kissing	56	13
	284	0	Lapsitting and holding	3	66
	2	282	Wrestling and jostling	2	67
	206	78	Spanking	5	64
			Other physical punish-ment	21	48

pinching, and face slaps. Mothers had a greater tendency to use these alternative types of physical punishment during adolescence.

"By the time I was fourteen spankings were out. Mom would slap me in the face. What a humiliation that was! Boy, I'd do almost anything to stop her."

Participants remember some wrestling and jostling with fathers during preadolescence, but many of them report negative feelings about the behavior. Some men recall that they were manifesting some effeminate characteristics that their fathers would try to eliminate by roughhousing with them.

"Dad would pin me down to the floor and I'd feel panicky. The more I'd scream or cry, the tighter he'd hold me down. 'You're gonna learn to fight back if it's the last thing I do.' Those words of his still ring in my ears."

"I'd jump on his back, then he'd roll over and tickle me. I used to love it when he'd rub his bearded chin on my belly. I still like that when Jay does it to me."

"I never saw my dad as a jock either, but Mom was always trying to get us to wrestle. She didn't like the way I walked—too much like a sissy. I guess she thought a few tumbles with Dad would make me different. Was she ever wrong!"

For some this type of behavior continued into adolescence and was the only source of contact with fathers. There is a sharp decline in contact with both parents during adolescence that seems to occur for almost everyone. Several participants tell us about how they would try to obtain affectionate responses from their fathers during early adolescence. They recount experiencing their fathers' embarrassment or clumsiness.

"Having a twelve- or fourteen-year-old crawl up into his lap was more than Dad could handle. I just wanted him to hug me and kiss me like in the old days. He'd do it, but I always felt like I must have smelled bad to him."

Several men report that close physical contact with both parents—including hugging, lip kissing, and other affectionate interchanges—have continued throughout their lives.

"The whole family were great touchers. We hugged, we kissed—everyone, not just my parents. I remember watching my father hug and kiss my grandfather when I was about fifteen. I always kiss my father on the mouth. If I don't he's always saying, 'Hey mister big shot, where's my kiss?' That's the Jewishness in him that I love so much."

"You know, we Latins kiss and hug everyone. I'm not sure why, but our blood seems to cry out for touching. Everyone kisses and hugs everyone else. Maybe that's what makes it so easy and acceptable."

The twenty-eight men who report no physical contact with either parent during childhood usually agreed that there must have been some touching, but even with probing during the interview they are unable to recall it. Male couples who report more childhood and adolescent affectionate contact with parents also report a high degree of that same behavior with their lovers. When partners come from families with large differences in the expression of affection, problems can easily arise.

Father–Son Relationships

More than half have childhood memories of pleasant and supportive relationships with their fathers. If they were not close to their fathers, they had mutual respect that generally continued into adulthood.

Some participants describe their relationships with their fathers in terms that have been popularized by psychoanalytic influence. These include words such as *distant, absent, indifferent, unresponsive, detached, hostile,* and *oppressive.* All of our participants seem somewhat aware of these psychoanalytic beliefs about homosexuality being partially traced to relationships with parents. More often than not these men simply fit themselves into the descriptions they had read or heard without evaluation. Most have experienced some period in their lives when they wanted to explain their homosexuality to themselves or to blame it on someone or something. For some the general acceptance of the psychoanalytic explanations have served this purpose.

Some of the men tell us about being distanced from their fathers. Often they had created the distance rather than their fathers rejecting them. Typically, the father would attempt to share some pleasing activity with his son, but the son would find he did not enjoy it or could not do it.

"Dad spent hours and weeks trying to teach me how to throw a ball. I must have been about five. I guess I just couldn't learn, so he left me alone after that. He gave a lot more attention to my older brother Tom, who was a natural athlete."

"I can remember my dad gettng so impatient with me, even before I was four or five, for not 'acting like a boy.' I don't think I wanted to please him, so after that he left me alone."

"I could never please him no matter how hard I tried. I guess our interests were so different. I didn't want to go fishing with him or work with him in the repair shop in the garage. He didn't like that and finally gave up on me and basically ignored me growing up."

Some men use words like *close, caring, loving, dependable,* and *fun* to describe their relationships with their fathers.

"Dad was always around. We did everything together until he got sick after I started high school."

"Some of my happiest memories of childhood are afternoons in a little rowboat on the lake with my dad. We'd talk about everything under the sun. He was so patient with me, even with my dumb questions."

"I always thought my dad was the handsomest man in the whole world. He had broad shoulders, big hands, and classic features. He was always fair with us. I knew he loved me and I still do."

With some couples we find clear evidence of the influence of father–son relationships.

"Sometimes I feel like Jay is really like the father I loved as a kid, even though he's only two years older than me. Jay is so dependable, loving, and kind, like I remember Dad."

"He's the dad I really never had but always wanted. I'm not saying that all our relationship is like he's the father and I'm the son, but sometimes we know that's happening between us, and I really like it."

"Jack is sixteen years older than me, and it seems that folks always think of us as father and son until they get to know us a little while. Sure, there are some examples of those features between us, like I look to him for advice sometimes because he has more experience than me. But he leans on me sometimes, too, and I seem to become the daddy."

"Bob is so stubborn. Once he makes up his mind there's no changing it. He's just like my dad in that way. It drives me crazy at times."

Mother–Son Relationships

The majority of men report their mothers as loving, caring, and important in their lives. As with fathers, most are familiar with the psychoanalytic theory about gay men's overattachment to stereotypical close-binding mothers, and a few describe their mothers accordingly. On close examination, though, few mothers fit the stereotype.

"Although she's been dead for almost six years now I still miss her a lot. She was the kindest and gentlest woman I've ever known, but that doesn't mean she was wishy-washy. She was strong and firm but understood so easily. I got a lot of my own patience and gentleness from her."

"She influenced my life more than anyone else. She encouraged me to go on to school even when the others were telling me it was time to stop. She taught me so many things—how to accept other people's ideas, how I had to use my own brain and make my own decisions. We still talk to each other at least once a week."

"I remember when I told her I was gay. It was hard at first because she thought it was her fault. She called me the next day and said she had sat up all night thinking about it and that she still knew I was as all right as she thought before I told her."

Not all descriptions of relationships with mothers are as glowing. A few men report strong negativity in their relationships with mothers.

"She caused me endless troubles. Her drinking was at the root of it most of the time. I could never bring friends home because, sure enough, if I did she'd be dead drunk. When we were alone she'd sometimes curse and tell me how terrible my father was."

"Mother was always afraid I'd get hurt. I couldn't play football because, 'Really now, you're just too little to play rough with those big boys.' Actually, I was just as big as the rest of them, but I bought what she told me. I have always been afraid of getting hurt by physical contact."

"With the constant bickering and fighting between my parents I would far too often find myself square in the middle, Mother demanding that I protect her and Dad telling me to get out of the way. Sometimes she'd hold on to me just like I was a shield from my father."

Often during our interviews, while we are discussing other issues, couples inadvertently give us information about their partner's relationship with his mother.

"Phil would never admit it but he's still very influenced by what his mom thinks and says to him. I think he's still too connected to her."

"Bob has so many of his mother's characteristics about him. He likes the same things she does, like green vegetables at every meal and a tablecloth at dinner."

"Stan even talks like his mom sometimes. I really like her so it doesn't bother me. In fact, it's usually at those times that he makes the most sense."

Besides these examples in our own observations of couples and in some of their mutual teasing, we witness a certain campy talk and behavior that involves mothers.

"Oh, you're such a sweet mother," when the partner brings in the coffee and sets it on the table.

"Ted is so much a mother to me at times. He worries about my catching cold, he insists that I take my vitamins every day, and he reminds me to send birthday cards."

On the more serious side, when one or the other is in some crisis we hear evidence of tenderness described as maternal.

"When I got sick last year Bruce took care of me like a child. I was really sick, and he nursed me back to health just like a mother would."

"It might sound a little corny but there really have been moments when I've felt depressed and defeated, and he shows just the right touches of caring and concern, sort of like a mother would."

Only Child

In addition to twenty-six men without siblings, a few others feel they were reared as only children because their brothers or sisters were nine or more years older.

"When I was really small I guess I never gave it much thought, but as I started school I remember wishing that I had a little brother to play with."

"I loved being the only chick in the nest. I got attention from both my parents. I remember getting pretty much everything I wanted from them."

"I hated it. In fact, I'm still angry with my parents for having only me."

"It meant I never had to share. That became a problem in school and later on, too. Steve still calls me on my selfishness at times. I think it's because I was an only child."

Brothers and Sisters

(Tables 14 and 15)

There is a wide range of attitudes toward siblings, and we do not find any clear-cut distinctions between those with one rather than several siblings. How a person thinks and feels toward brothers and sisters while growing up and how he might feel and think about them as an adult can be quite different. In asking our participants to describe their retrospective feelings from childhood, the range of responses fit four general categories. Although they are not mutually exclusive, these categories come close to representing the responses:

1. I was usually close with one brother or sister (20 percent).
2. I was never very open or comfortable with them. I guess I felt different (25 percent).

TABLE 14
NUMBER OF SIBLINGS

Number of Siblings	Number of Participants	Percentage of Participants
0	26	8.3
1	119	38.1
2	102	32.7
3	41	13.1
4	9	2.9
5	6	2.0
6	9	2.9

3. Other than the usual fights and teasing between us, we were glad to have each other (18 percent).

4. I always had mixed feelings about them. Sometimes I'd really like them; at other times I'd wish they weren't around (37 percent).

Even those with the most negative reactions to siblings recall family times together warmly, especially memories of holidays and vacations.

"I do remember holidays like Christmas when everything was upbeat, happy, like a storybook family. I love to remember those times."

"Sometimes Mom and Dad would take all of us camping. I can just remember those wonderful campfire meals, all of us singing together at night, roasting marshmallows, snuggling into our sleeping bags with no limits on how long we talked."

"I remember how proud we all were of my brother's high-school championship. He was four years older than me. I even got into the excitement of having a real hero in the house. He was great to me in those days."

Attitudes and feelings about their relationship to brothers and sisters in the adult years are strongly influenced by their homosexuality. Almost all of the men in our study tell us that their sexual orientation is such a core part of themselves that their ability to achieve closeness with others depends upon the other person knowing about and accepting it. We have often heard the story of our participants experiencing new intimacy and closeness with brothers and sisters when they have shared their sexual orientation with them. The inti-

TABLE 15
NUMBER OF BROTHERS AND NUMBER OF SISTERS

		Number of Brothers				Number of Sisters	
1 Sibling	119	86 (72%)				33 (28%)	
2 Siblings	102	1 Brother/1 Sister 38 (37.5%)	2 Brothers 38 (37.5%)			2 Sisters 26 (25%)	
3 Siblings	41	3 Brothers 14 (33.5%)	2 Brothers/1 Sister 14 (33.5%)	2 Sisters/1 Brother 13 (33.0%)		3 Sisters 0	
4 Siblings	9	4 Brothers 2 (22.2%)	2 Sisters/2 Brothers 4 (44.4%)	3 Brothers/1 Sister 3 (33.3%)	3 Sisters/1 Brother 1 (11.1%)	4 Sisters 0	
5 Siblings	6	5 Brothers 0	4 Brothers/1 Sister 3 (50%)	4 Sisters/1 Brother 0	3 Brothers/2 Sisters 2 (33%)	3 Sisters/2 Brothers 1 (17%)	5 Sisters 0
6 Siblings	9	6 Brothers 0	5 Brothers/1 Sister 2 (22.2%)	4 Brothers/2 Sisters 3 (33.3%)	4 Sisters/2 Brothers 3 (33.3%)	3 Brothers/3 Sisters 1 (11.1%)	6 Sisters 0

Total Siblings 566
Brothers 350
Sisters 216
Ratio Sisters/Brothers 0.62

mate nature of this disclosure frequently rejuvenates former feelings of warmth and trust in both. This experience takes their relationship to a new level of responsiveness. The process of coming out includes coming out to families. It is frequently initiated through a sibling as a direct response to the rejuvenated relationship. With those men who have found sibling acceptance and understanding of their sexual orientation, we also find strong family ties. Men who have continued to remain distant and estranged from their siblings and parents either have been unable to share their sexual orientation or have experienced some form of rejection because of it.

Gay Brothers and Sisters
(Table 16)

Eight men have a brother or sister known to them as gay—three sisters and five brothers.

"I always thought my sister and I had more in common than our parents. She's been living with her female lover for the past six years. It wasn't until two Christmases ago that the four of us got together and really came out to each other. They live in Kansas City, but we talk to them at least every week."

"Tim, my younger brother by three years, is gay. He lives in New York City. I don't think he really likes me. He still has scars from childhood when I used to make fun of him. My hope is that we'll get it together one of these years. We need each other, but he hasn't found that out yet."

"I knew he was gay. He's been living with another guy for the past eight years. We just never talked about it until I went to visit him six months ago. He's so much in the closet that even when I told him about myself he wouldn't say much. His lover and I talked all night once. That was great."

TABLE 16
NUMBER OF SIBLINGS KNOWN TO BE HOMOSEXUAL

Sisters	—	3
Brothers	—	5

TABLE 17
BIRTH ORDER

NUMBER OF SIBLINGS	ORDINAL RANK						
	1	2	3	4	5	6	7
1	65	54					
2	13	25	64				
3	10	11	10	10			
4	1	1	3	2	2		
5	1		1	2	·	2	
6	2	1	2	1	1		2
	92	92	80	15	3	2	2
	32.1%	32.1%	28.0%	5.2%	1.0%	0.7%	0.7%

Other Issues with Brothers and Sisters (Table 17)

Past investigations (Slater,[4] Bieber et al.,[5] Saghir and Robins[6]) have reported data on brothers and sisters, birth order, and ratios of brothers and sisters to support old illness theories. We have found them unremarkable in themselves.[7]

Our general impression is that men in relationships lasting longer than ten years have more brothers and sisters. This is an impression about longevity but does not include the question of relationship quality. We believe that the influence of siblings on relationship quality is much more closely correlated to the quality of interaction with brothers and sisters during the developmental stages of growing up.

Religious Background

(Table 18)

More than half of the men grew up as Protestants while more than a quarter were Roman Catholic. About 15 percent were reared in Judaism and a small number in other religious traditions or as atheists. Almost all of the men grew up with some religious tradition and participated as children in all that went with it.

TABLE 18
RELIGIOUS BACKGROUND OF PARTICIPANTS

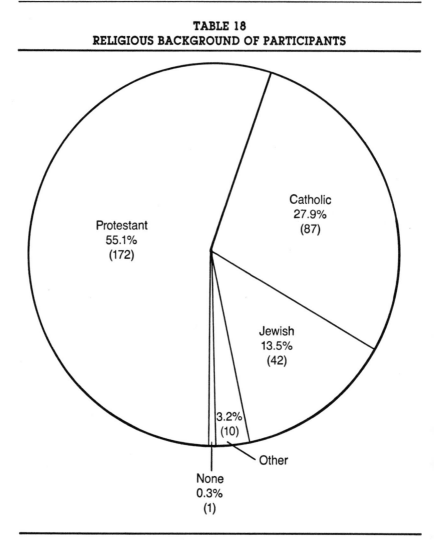

"Are you kidding? With my father being a Baptist preacher we had to go to church. He died when I was in college. By then I knew I was homosexual. It was a relief to think I'd never have to face him with that fact. If he's up there listening to me now, I'm sure he'd understand, but he sure wouldn't have when I was nineteen!"

"Mom used to say it was important for us to have some religious roots, being Americans and all that, so she'd pack us off to Sunday school. I think that's how they used to get time to have sex on Sunday mornings, when all the kids were at church."

"Church was a way of life for us. We had real community there. It was more than worshipping together—the church suppers and socials, the teen club, the sports activities. Most of it I really enjoyed. My troubles with religion started when I began to face my homosexuality."

Among Catholics there were two distinct groups: those who attended church intermittently and those who attended church regularly and were educated in Catholic schools. Many of the more devout childhood Catholics had some flirtation with the priesthood, either giving it serious consideration at some point in their lives or actually joining a seminary or religious order.

"My whole life seemed to be my Catholicism. Mass, the family rosary, the liturgical seasons, there was such harmony and peace with the rituals and traditions. All of the rituals helped keep my sex repressed for a long time. It worked then, but when I got older it was nearly impossible to reconcile my sexual urges and my religion."

"Yep, I went the whole route. Parochial school, Jesuit high, then four years in a major seminary before I could face up to what I was and wanted. Actually, it was a priest who helped me face myself. I'd like to be a practicing Catholic again if only the Church would change. Maybe some day. I do go to meetings of Dignity, a gay Catholic group, now and then."

Of the forty-two men who identify themselves as Jewish, some grew up adhering to strict religious orthodoxy while others claim a more ethnic connection to Judaism.

"Bar mitzvah was the high point of my life in those days. I worked so hard in 'schul' that I started to dream in Hebrew. In our house being a religious Jew was more important than anything else in life. Keeping kosher, saying prayers, following every ritual was a way of life for us. We still celebrate Chanukah and Passover here, and we celebrate the Christian holidays, too. Al and I love the traditions of both. We've gotten over our guilt trips about religion."

"Going to synagogue was only for the High Holy Days. Mom and Dad paid for temple membership but it was more because we were Jews, not from interest in Judaism. The roots, culture, and history were the most important. Actually, I think my father was an atheist."

By mid-adolescence almost all of our participants knew of religious prohibitions against homosexuality and were aware of their awakening homoerotic attractions. Among the more devout, internal conflict was an inevitable result.

"I knew it was wrong, the Bible said so, but nothing I could do would change me. I wanted men. I felt nothing for the girls. It was turmoil four plus."

"To have stayed in good graces I would have had to go to confession three times a week. Too much masturbation! But when I told the priest I had 'dirty thoughts' about boys, I thought he'd jump right out of the confessional at me!"

"I believed I was doomed to hell when I found out how bad it was to be 'one of those kind.' I prayed, I went to every tent meeting that came around. I joined Youth for Christ. I sang in the traveling choir. On one of those trips the minister crawled into bed with me. Then I really didn't know what to do. I suffered the torments of hell longer than you'd ever imagine. What a pity. When will things ever change?"

"I heard them say it was wrong, but I never really applied it to me. I loved Bobby in those days and he loved me. We played around a little, that's all. We figured that it was love, and they kept telling us God was love. It all made incredible sense to us. Actually, it still does."

Current Religion

When asked if they consider themselves to be religious, more than three out of five respond affirmatively. Of these men, one in four is a churchgoer. Those who attend traditional churches report comfortable accommodations to the antihomosexual beliefs. The remainder, who continue to feel alienated by the traditional antihomosexual belief, attend the Metropolitan Community Church, Dignity, or Integrity, where religious services are held.

Those who consider themselves religious and do not attend church practice religion in their own special way. Mark and Nick have combined their Christian beliefs with their deep feelings about Eastern philosophy. They meditate together, which gives them a sense of religious experience. One couple, who were both reared as Catholics, talk about their participation in a Eucharistic service with friends in their home. The majority of these nonchurchgoers do not have explicit religious observances or rituals but explain the importance of religious values in their daily lives and relationships.

Ten couples tell us that one of the main reasons they were attracted to each other was the similarity of interest and feeling about religion. In an additional small number of couples we find the differences in their individual religious backgrounds contributed to increased tension in their relationships.

School and Athletics

(Tables 19 and 20)

Most men in our study report their performance in elementary and high school as average. The high-school years show a drop to below-average performance for a few but an increase to above-average or outstanding for many more. Some admit that they began to work harder in high school because they were different from the majority of their peers, who were successfully participating in athletics and dating, as mentioned earlier.

A higher percentage of these men played some sports in childhood than in adolescence. One explanation for this discrepancy is that those who were unable to develop some degree of proficiency before adolescence stopped playing sports altogether. In addition more played noncontact team sports as adolescents than as children (e.g., tennis, track, and gymnastics). Approximately one out of four scorned participation in any sports.

Homosexual Awareness

(Tables 21 and 22)

A majority of these men were aware of their attraction to boys or men before age ten (Table 21). First homosexual experiences are reported in chapter 14. Many responses are qualified by statements like "I didn't know that was homosexual," or "I thought everybody felt the

TABLE 19
ACADEMIC PERFORMANCE

(a) Elementary School

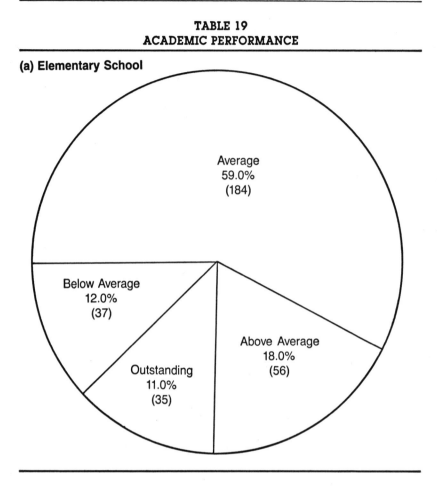

Average
59.0%
(184)

Below Average
12.0%
(37)

Above Average
18.0%
(56)

Outstanding
11.0%
(35)

same as I did." Some were not aware of their same-sex attraction until age sixteen or even twenty-five. Every man had some knowledge about his attraction to men by age twenty-five. Not all acted upon that awareness in the same way. Some sought help for their homosexuality. In fact, at one time or another almost one in four received medical, religious, or psychological counseling for their homosexual inclinations.

Many of these men have not experienced serious difficulties in their awareness and acceptance of homosexuality. Although each person struggled with his differences from siblings and peers at one time

TABLE 19, cont.
ACADEMIC PERFORMANCE

(b) High School

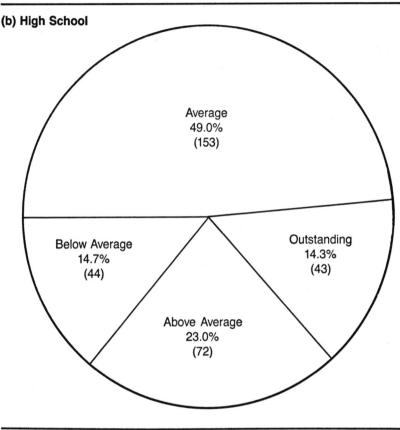

Average
49.0%
(153)

Below Average
14.7%
(44)

Outstanding
14.3%
(43)

Above Average
23.0%
(72)

or another, the large majority eventually adapted to their homosexuality. Among the sixty-eight men who had consultations, counseling, or treatment for homoeroticism, we find a wide range of responses. Some were sent by their parents for evaluation or treatment during early or mid-adolescence when they themselves requested it or when they were discovered in a homoerotic situation by the family. Others sought counseling or therapy while in college or had talks with their ministers or priests. Some found that talking with professionals was an effective way to get assistance in adjusting to their same-sex orientation.

When asked their beliefs about the origins of homosexuality (Ta-

TABLE 20
PARTICIPATION IN ATHLETICS

Preadolescent Sports	Yes	No
	239—76.5%	73—23.5%
	Number of Participants	Percentage of Participants
Team sports, contact	129	54
Team sports, noncontact	62	26
Individual sports, contact	29	12
Individual sports, noncontact	19	8
	239	100
Adolescent Participation	**Yes**	**No**
	198–63.4%	114–36.6%
	Number of Participants	Percentage of Participants
Team sports, contact	55	28
Team sports, noncontact	73	37
Individual sports, contact	22	11
Individual sports, noncontact	48	24
	198	100

ble 22), a few cite genetic and biological predisposition. Some think it is learned from early childhood. A few choose psychological predisposition. The largest number choose a combination of these factors. No one proposes any additional possibilities. In response to the question "Do you consider homosexuality an illness or aberration?" 98.7 percent answer no. Four participants answer yes. Even though living in committed relationships with other men, four of our respondents nevertheless view themselves and others around them as ill solely on the basis of their homosexuality.

Coming Out

The process of coming out was described and explained in chapter 9. Gay men usually are not able to give a precise time for coming out because it is a process. They do remember things like their first visit to

TABLE 21
AGE OF AWARENESS OF HOMOSEXUALITY

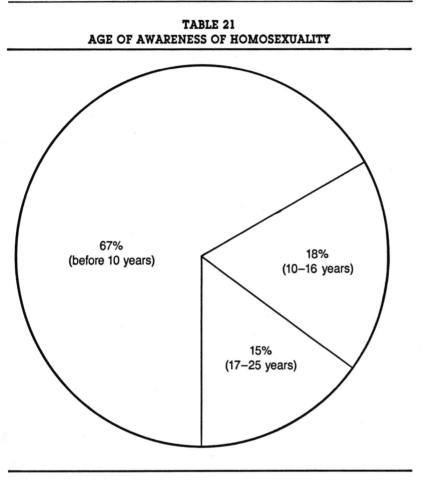

67%
(before 10 years)

18%
(10–16 years)

15%
(17–25 years)

a gay bar or their first sexual encounter with another man. Important milestones in the process of coming out include disclosure to friends, family, employers, and others.

All of the men have reached at least the fourth step—they have established their own identity as a gay person. And many have been at the fifth step—full integration and acceptance of their gayness and complete openness about it—for a long time. Three out of four are out with their nongay friends and almost half are out to their employers. More feel that their employers know about their sexual orientation and are unconcerned.

TABLE 22
BELIEFS ABOUT ORIGINS OF HOMOSEXUALITY

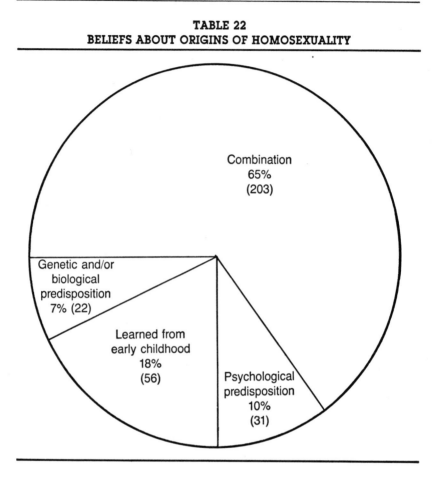

Combination
65%
(203)

Genetic and/or
biological
predisposition
7% (22)

Learned from
early childhood
18%
(56)

Psychological
predisposition
10%
(31)

More than half have discussed their homosexuality with parents, brothers and sisters, or other close relatives. Of those who have not discussed it with family approximately one in five claim that their families are well aware of their sexual orientation. A small number have experienced open or covert rejection by parents or other family members because they are homosexual. On the other hand, two out of five have varying degrees of family acceptance and support.

Relationship History

Table 23

Most of these men dated and socialized with women between early adolescence and age twenty-five. The small number reporting no important relationships with women either were never in conflict about their attraction to men or consciously avoided intimacy with others because of what seemed to be developmental personality problems. Among those with histories of association with women, some discuss high-school dating as going through the motions without feeling attracted or attached. Others report genuine affectionate bonding with women, and still others tell of sexual attraction and fulfillment that led to commitment and marriage.

Heterosexual Relationships

Forty-seven men were married at least once. The length of these marriages was from three months to twenty-one years. In addition to those men who were married, fifty-one have lived with women in a relationship for longer than three months at some time in their lives from their late teens or early twenties to much later. Almost one-third have been married or have lived with a female lover. Retrospective reasons for these relationships include lack of full awareness of their homosexuality, a desire to cure or change themselves, the desire to have chil-

TABLE 23
HETEROSEXUAL RELATIONSHIPS

Previously married	47
Range of duration of marriages	3 months to 21 years
Mean	3.4 years
Number of children	52
Age range of children	3 to 28
Sex of children	25 males, 27 females

dren, a need to explore heterosexual interests, and affectionate and sexual attraction to women. Some men discuss their earlier heterosexual relationships as false starts in their exploration of coupling. They found benefits such as affection and companionship or friendship and sharing of common interests, but vague dissatisfaction lingered. By falling in love with another man they eventually discovered that they could not find full satisfaction or fulfillment except with a male partner.

Previous heterosexual relationships reportedly exert different influences on current homosexual relationships.

"When we were starting out together I tried to treat Jim like I had my wife Diane. It was almost a disaster. Jim finally got me to see that being in a gay relationship is different from being in a heterosexual marriage."

"We had all those romantic ideas about marriage, just like heterosexuals, but got into lots of trouble with the butch–fem kind of stuff. Since I had been married I just assumed Ted would do what my wife had. What a mistake that was!"

"I thought the relationship with Sharon was an equal one. Boy, did I have a lot to learn when Bob and I were together for a while! We both think we have a relationship based on equality now, but for months I had trouble realizing that he was just the same as me, that I didn't always have to be the leader, the doer, the starter."

Children

Twenty-six men are fathers, with a total of 52 children: twenty-five boys and twenty-seven girls. (See Table 23.) These children are from previous marriages. Two fathers have children living with them at the time of our interviews. (See chapter 13 for further information on children.)

Homosexual Relationships
(Table 24)

Nearly three-quarters of the men have had previous relationships with a man in which they lived together as lovers for three months or longer. Of these, more than half have had only one previous relation-

TABLE 24
PREVIOUS MALE RELATIONSHIPS
(Living Together)

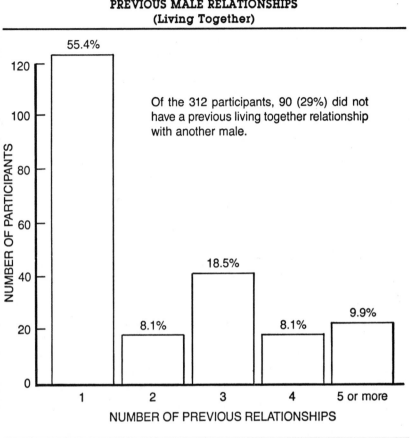

Of the 312 participants, 90 (29%) did not have a previous living together relationship with another male.

ship with a male. A small number have had five or more. The length of these relationships ranged from three months to sixteen years.

"It took me a while to learn that there was much more to relationships than just sex. With my first lover sex was number one, and when we both started looking at other guys it was too much for the relationship to bear because there wasn't much else there."

"I guess I was just in love with being in love. Not willing to take much responsibility for keeping things together. I just thought love would take care of everything."

"We were so different. I learned that I needed a lover who liked the same things I did."

"I just always believed that gay relationships couldn't last until I met Frank. With eight years behind us he's got me forever."

More often than not men claim they have learned about themselves and what they want from previous relationships. Some think that their own process of maturation occurred with the help of other relationships. Others feel that previous breakups were failures on their part though sometimes they blame it on their former partners. A surprisingly large number maintain close contacts with former male lovers. A few even consider them among their closest friends.

The Military

(Table 25)

More than half of these men served in the armed forces of the United States. The length of time in the military ranged from six months to twenty-four years with an average of 3.6 years. Sixty-one served as officers, 104 were enlisted. All branches of the service are represented. Four were discharged on the basis of their homosexuality.

No men in our study were on active military duty before the beginning of World War II. Of the thirty-nine men over fifty, thirty-three served during World War II and afterward.

"I was a good flyer and I loved the Air Force. The service taught me a lot, got me away from home, and showed me the world. I'm better because of it."

"I joined the Navy to see the world and overcome being gay! Can't imagine that now, but back in those days I believed I'd get rid of being homosexual that way. The Navy was real good for me, at least I really came out and found myself."

Another said: "My military career was my life for so long that it's hard to believe. I was in the top third of my graduating class at the Naval Academy. Got married, had kids, went to sea, got promoted. Divorced, retired finally after twenty-three years as a commander. That's pretty bad for an Annapolis graduate. I had my problems in the Navy. Got passed over twice because of drinking."

"The Army was the pits from the very instant I got inducted. I didn't want Vietnam, just like everyone else, but sure enough I was

TABLE 25
MILITARY SERVICE

Number of Participants with Military Service = 165—52.9%

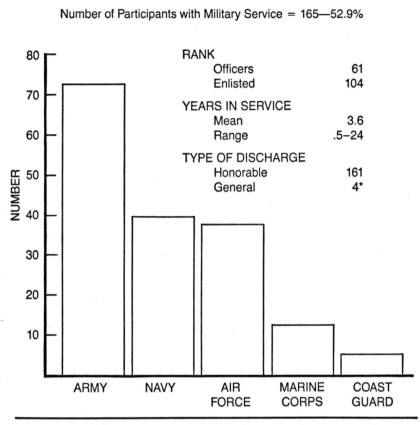

RANK
| Officers | 61 |
| Enlisted | 104 |

YEARS IN SERVICE
| Mean | 3.6 |
| Range | .5–24 |

TYPE OF DISCHARGE
| Honorable | 161 |
| General | 4* |

*All four discharged for homosexuality.

lucky enough to go. I got it in the leg from mine shrapnel, went to Japan for two months in the hospital, then right back to that godawful Nam. Hit again in the shoulder got me a second Purple Heart and a trip home for good. We should never have been there."

The high percentage of participants with past military experience can be explained partially by the fact that many had passed through or been stationed in California, especially the San Diego area, and returned to live there.

TABLE 26
POLITICAL IDENTIFICATION

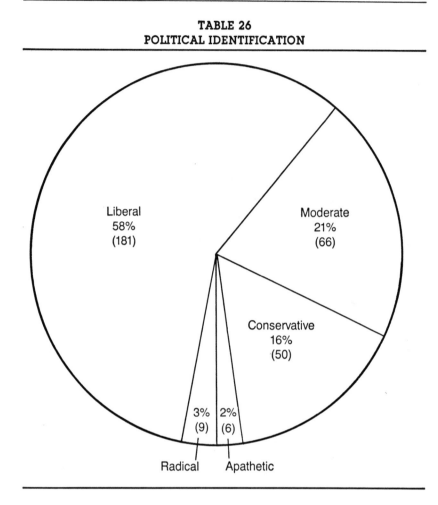

Politics

(Table 26)

We assumed that, as a social minority, homosexuals would tend to rate themselves as liberals. The majority do just that but not for the reason we had assumed. Political attitudes are more strongly linked to socioeconomic status than to minority status. It would be inaccurate to label all of the wealthy participants as conservative or all the lower-income couples as liberal, but there is a trend in that direction.

Over the five years of data collection we witnessed changes in the attitudes of participants and changes in the political climate regarding homosexuality in San Diego. The growing political awareness among all people has prompted many more gay people to be concerend about where candidates stand on gay issues.

The Person

This chapter has presented some major factors about the 312 men in our sample. Each is an individual, but we have told you only about the characteristics of the group as a whole. In conclusion we introduce four individuals as a reminder of the diversity of these men.

Chris

Chris is tall, with black hair, fair skin, and blue eyes. His gaze has a certain penetrating quality about it. Strikingly handsome, his sharp, suntanned features complement his maturely developed, lithesome body. He is thirty-eight and an attorney with an active general legal practice. He has lived in this community for nine years, having moved here from Chicago where he first started his law practice after graduating from a well-known Midwestern law school.

He was born and reared in central Indiana, the second of three children. His father and mother had a family business which they operated together in a town of 60,000. Chris was always a churchgoer along with the rest of his family, attending Presbyterian services and Sunday school until he left for college at age seventeen. His grades in elementary school were slightly above average, but he zoomed into the outstanding group in high school and was offered several scholarships to good universities.

His childhood was unremarkable, and the exchange of affection in his family was limited and controlled. He was not close to either his brother or his sister and confided more in his mother than his father. He tried some athletics when he was younger but failed to master the skills that other boys had and was always chosen last when teams were decided. He was a scholastic star in high school, which earned him family and peer praise as well as his college scholarship.

Chris's first awareness about homoerotic interests occurred in the Boy Scouts when he was eleven. He had a few sexual contacts with others then but felt badly about them. He dated in high school but only for events like proms and big church dances. He tried to deny his attraction to other boys. He never remembered being called a sissy and never thought of himself as such.

Away from home at college, he was a leader from the start. Girls were attracted to him, and he started dating one girl steadily in his second year. At that same time he had his first ongoing sexual experience with another male. He also had his first sexual experience with a woman, not the same one he was dating. With this sexual success and excitement he found reassurance, companionship, and affection. Consequently, Chris decided he was not homosexual. Graduating from college at twenty-one, he immediately began law school. During his third year he met the woman he married a year later.

"From all appearances we were the storybook happy couple, but something was missing. After two years I began finding occasional homosexual contacts. I knew the marriage wouldn't last. I wasn't finding fulfillment, and my wife was never going to get everything she really needed from me."

Admitting the mistake and getting a divorce was a painful but necessary step. Chris moved to Chicago, where he had ample opportunity to explore his homosexuality and come out. During this time he took a vacation in California and visited San Diego. During the next year he moved here.

Steve

Steve is of medium build, with blond hair that has an impish way of falling over his green eyes. Although not handsome in the classical sense, at thirty-three years old he still has evidence of his earlier boyish comeliness. He is now the manager of a large printing shop and has held a series of sundry jobs until this one, which he started more than four years ago. He was born and reared in the San Diego suburbs, where his father was a factory foreman and his mother a licensed vocational nurse. His one older brother joined the Navy when Steve was ten.

In retrospect Steve feels he grew up on his own. Occasional Sunday mornings were spent at a Baptist church, but he never became involved. At school he got passing grades but was more interested in adventures that got him into trouble with his parents, such as playing hooky or stealing apples from the local supermarket. He began his homosexual activities with neighborhood boys when he was five and says he always knew he was gay. Athletics came easily to him. He was coordinated and good at sports, but admits his interest was mainly in his teammates. He was a laid-back surfer, hitching rides to the beach with other boys, finding many opportunities for exciting sexual activities with the other surfers.

Steve never dated girls. He liked marijuana and alcohol. He got through high school by eighteen without really giving it much thought. During three years in the Navy he visited many ports in the Orient that stimulated a multitude of interests. Finding buddies for sex was easy for him, so his energy was focused on reading and learning. During his last few months in the Navy, he was stationed in San Diego. After the Navy he found a job as an electronics technician, then as an office manager at several different places before taking his present job. In his first year out of the Navy he met a man a year older than himself. They moved in together after the first week. During their year together Steve believed that their relationship revolved more around drugs and alcohol than each other. They split up, and within a month Steve was living with another lover. That, too, lasted a year. Steve claims they fell out of love.

Alan

His feet never seem to touch the ground. He talks fast, he moves fast, and he is effective. At fifty-seven he looks more like a young forty. There's gray in his sideburns, but the rest looks Vanquished out, or maybe it was never gray. As we walk through the doorway into the next huge room, his white-sleeved arm points to a series of magnificent woodcarvings. He begins to tell me about them. I wonder if he'll sit still for an interview. He does.

Born and reared in Boston, Al was the son of a railroad conductor—"in the days when that meant something," he is quick to add. He recalls proudly boarding the elegant train with his father, who presided over the crew and passengers on the overnight runs to exotic places like New York City, Washington, D.C., and Atlanta. Alan was not a college graduate. He's proud to call himself a self-made man.

Alan left home at nineteen, worked a while in the garment district in New York, and then got drafted. Three years in World War II saw him move from a buck private to a field-promoted captain in North Africa in 1944. "I was a damned good soldier in those days." Back from the war, he met a Boston debutante who married him. Within five years he fathered two children, started sexual activity with young men, began a very profitable restaurant business, divorced, and moved to California. By the time he was twenty-nine Alan was living in San Diego. He started as a representative for a small new company making computers. He was given stock in that company before he went into his own business. His business acumen has gotten him to a point in life where everything he touches makes money. He collects artwork, rebuilds old cars, and runs three miles every day. He travels extensively. Politically, Alan is very conservative. He has little or nothing to do with other homosexual men or women. He is charming, engaging, and confident. He likes living in the house he built. Although he does not have frequent contact with his children, he supported his son through medical school. When he speaks of his children, there's a touch of sadness in his otherwise even and enthusiastic voice, as if those relationships are an unfinished piece of his life.

Ken

"I was born the same year that Hoover became president. My father used to say the crash of '29 happened to celebrate my first birthday. Isn't that a hell of a thing to tell a kid?"

Ken is fifty, tall, a little beefy around the middle, with thinning gray hair combed forward from the back in an amateurish attempt to cover the bald spots. We couldn't help but look, even stare, at his beautiful hands, the nails carefully trimmed and buffed, the slender fingers long and tapering. You can almost see them moving on their own against a black velvet backdrop, telling his whole story in sign language. We learn that Ken has played the piano since he was eight. He grew up in Milwaukee where his father was a foreman for one of the big brewing companies. The Great Depression had little impact on him, he recalls; he and his two sisters always had meals on time and clothes to wear. Two years of college came after he spent six months in the Army right at the end of the war. Childhood was middle-class, maybe lower-middle, he can't say for sure. His dad was a boozer; Ken says most brewery workers were in those days. Ken knew he was homosexual by the time he was ten but says he'd never even heard the word until he was in school in Madison in 1946. He started having sex with other men then and he hasn't stopped since.

"I struggled with it for a long time in my mind but never enough to keep me from doing it.

"After the war, California was the place to head for. I went to L.A. and got a job selling ladies' shoes for one of those inexpensive shoestore chains. I was good at it but hated every minute that I had to push the handbags, push the polish, push the hose to make the extra commission. I was twenty-three when I came to San Diego. I worked for a bank for a while before I saw where their money was coming in from. Business, something of my own, was really what I wanted." Ken takes a deep breath and moves out to the edge of the sofa. "I really wanted to make enough to buy myself a grand piano." He's been very successful. But more about Ken in chapter 12.

CHAPTER 12

THE COUPLES

The typical male couple does not exist. Although we hoped we would find such a couple, all hope vanished by the time we finished the interviews. As we have said before, our very earliest question was, "What keeps them together?" What we did find as a partial answer was not a simple formula, but rather the stages of their relationships. What gets them together in the first year is different from what keeps them together in the fifth, the tenth, or the thirtieth year. They do share a mutual love that also undergoes change as time passes. The same ongoing love is just as important for heterosexual couples, and they have a whole system to support that love. However, if we learned one thing from this entire study, it is that love alone will not ensure that a relationship will survive. To put the question of staying together in sharper focus, let us look at the following two couples, one heterosexual and the other homosexual.

Alan, age forty-eight, and Susan, age forty-six, have been married for twenty-five years. They are both college graduates. Alan is a hard-driving engineer, having risen from apprentice to a high position in management with an annual income of more than $70,000. Susan gave up her early career plans to marry Alan. They have three children, all in their early twenties, beginning new families of their own, and frequently visiting home. Alan and Susan are regular churchgoers, active in politics and in social organizations. Susan's mother has lived with them for the past five years. The couple owns an expensive home, shares in Alan's corporation, and other income-generating properties.

What keeps Alan and Susan together as a couple? They have a legally and religiously institutionalized marriage. They have three children, a live-in relative, and considerable financial holdings. They have many friends who recognize their long-standing relationship. Alan's corporate advances have been based partially on his stable family life. Alan's wife assists with corporate-related social functions, and she handles his home life, freeing his full attention for his professional work. Their assumptions of ongoing love for each other were implicit in the religious vows they took, "for richer or poorer, in sickness and in health."

Let us now look at a male couple.

Carl, age forty-four, and Keith, age forty-two, have been living together for twenty-three years. They met in college while Carl was a junior and Keith was a freshman, and they started living together the following year. They graduated and started a small business together. After five years of hard work it developed into a large financial success. They shared common goals of attaining financial security early in their lives, which assured them of more freedom and time to explore outside interests as they grew older. Both men have contributed to their parents' retirement and have extensive property holdings in common. They are not openly gay beyond a small circle of friends.

What has kept this couple in a relationship for twenty-three years? Although they have none of the obvious binding ingredients shared by Alan and Susan, Carl and Keith are just as much a couple as are the other 155 couples in this study. The stages of relationships offer many answers to the riddle of their relationship's cohesiveness and duration. This chapter provides some of the data that assisted us in uncovering and understanding those stages.

Length of Time in Relationships

(Table 27)

Although durability is not the most telling indicator of satisfaction in the history of a relationship, the very fact that many human beings stay together for long periods of time is important to note. Slightly less than a third of our male couples have been together longer than ten years; just less than a third have been together between five and ten years; and slightly more than a third have been together between one and five years. Before this current relationship most of the men had at least one previous relationship—male or female. Most lived in some coupled situation for a considerable portion of their lives after eighteen. Most had begun some experimenting with relationships in high school or even earlier.

TABLE 27
LENGTH OF TIME IN RELATIONSHIP

Years	Number of Couples
1–2	21
2–3	16
3–4	12
4–5	12
5–10	46
10–15	17
15–20	12
20–25	6
25–30	6
30–35	5
35–40	3

Number of Couples = 156
Mean 8.9 years
Median 5.0 years

Some men report a series of short-term relationships that usually ended with the passing of limerence. Jack is a case in point.

"It was a new guy every night for weeks, then suddenly Mr. Right-Guy was in my bed, and I was in love all over again. 'This is it,' I'd think to myself but after three months he was off with someone else, or maybe I was. Then another Mr. Right would be there next to me again, and the cycle would repeat itself. I really was believing that love doesn't last with gays. Then I met Bill. He wasn't Mr. Right the same as all the others. After knowing him for three months it was just there—really feeling secure and stable for the first time." Jack and Bill have been together almost five years.

Many of the men in our study started their current relationships at a time when neither partner was seeking a lasting lover. On the other hand, most admit that they always viewed settling down with a long-term partner as the ideal. Most men did not couple with the partner they had conceptualized as their ideal man. On the contrary, the partner selected usually had qualities that were far more fulfilling and sustaining than some of their preconceived ideals.

"When we first met I thought Tom was just a cute kid." David is fifteen years older than Tom. Tom's comments about David are, "He was so much older than me, not particularly attractive, but as we got together more frequently I found myself yearning to be with him more of the time." Tom and David have been together more than eight years.

"John wasn't as sexy as most of the other guys I had been with. In fact, the first time we made love, I thought he was a real dud. To start with, I liked the way he lived and the things he talked about. There were some things about him that made me look twice at being with him, but those worries disappeared after the first few months."

Although some couples did begin their relationships with exciting sexual attractions to each other, very few offer sex as the ultimate reason for the relationship. Most agree that exciting sex is available with a large selection of partners. But finding other attractive features, such as mutual interests, sensitivity, and caring, carries far greater weight.

"Talk about banjos and bells! When Wayne touched me I would get aroused like you wouldn't believe. I could always find good sex. Every fourth or fifth guy I'd make it with would find the right buttons to push. But Wayne had more than just sex appeal. He was classy, but mostly he just had his head together."

Where They Live

Aside from a few couples interviewed during the pilot phase of this study, all of the couples live in San Diego, California, either within the city limits or in the county. A few live on ranches or farms; some live in remote cabins or cottages in the mountains or desert. Most live throughout the city and county of San Diego, from the more affluent beach areas, the modern and modest tract home developments, and the older renewing neighborhoods, to the suburbs and smaller towns nearby.

Places where couples live and the frequency of moving appear to be most closely associated with their economic status. Men together less than five years move more often, usually to apartments, condos, or houses indicative of their increasing individual or combined incomes.

More than half of the couples have lived in the same home for more than three years, a quarter have moved at least once in the year preceding the interviews, and approximately a quarter have moved within the preceding three years. Many men in the sample have lived their entire lives in San Diego.

Interviewing the couples in their homes gave us insights into the lifestyles they have forged for themselves. Half of the couples live in homes owned jointly or by either partner. All of the men together longer than fifteen years own their own homes. Approximately 20 percent of the couples live in environments similar to the very first home we visited.

Russ and Bruce live in a quiet, upper-middle-class neighborhood with tennis courts, swimming pools, tree-lined streets, and six-foot redwood fences that surround new condominiums. A tall gate is opened by Russ, leading into a central garden courtyard filled with blooming cymbidiums and fuschias. The home itself is decorator perfect: leather and chrome furniture, modern sculpture, interesting artifacts, and a dining room mural painted by Bruce. Three bedrooms and two baths, carefully and thoughtfully furnished, with a downstairs family room used as a study with long bookshelves crowded with books, records, and a stereo system, and a fully equipped kitchen complete their home.

Another 10 to 15 percent of our couples have small living quarters that are masterpieces of quality and thoughtfulness, not necessarily expensive. "Nesting" was a word that always came to mind. If you have ever watched hummingbirds build their nest, you know the exactitude they demand. Every scrap of material is carefully selected and blended into the individual masterpiece each tiny nest becomes. Jim and Phil live in such a home. They are both waiters living in a rented two-bedroom 1940s stucco house in a lower-middle-class neighborhood. They have been living there for two years and have been lovers for seven years. Their home is meticulously tended both inside and out. The furnishings represent a thoughtful assortment of pieces collected over the years, some built by the couple, some antiques, but all functional and comfortable. The kitchen walls are covered with beautiful utensils. The couple shares cooking as a special hobby. Behind the house they are growing a wide variety of edibles in an attractive vegetable garden.

Ed and Wes have lived in San Diego for only three years, but they have been together as a couple for twenty-three years. They bought a two-bedroom house in a lower-middle-class neighborhood at the same time they bought their now failing business. Their home is clean but sparsely furnished, lacking any signs of being homey. Inexpensive but durable furniture is in the living room and small dining area off the kitchen. Ed shows us the freshly painted bathroom while Wes complains that Ed had stolen the time from their business to paint it. This home lacks a sense of being theirs. Their business is their real home. We can find no evidence of nesting. This seems more like the resting place of magpies who take over the abandoned nests of other birds, regardless of their quality. A small percentage of our couples live in this kind of environment.

Tom and Richard inhabit an old, somewhat ramshackled bungalow in a beach community. The sink is piled high with dishes. The dog has shed hair everywhere. The main furnishings are large pillows scattered about the small living room. Orchid plants hang in the windows, and others have found spots on shelves and countertops. The atmosphere is warm and intimate but much less fastidiously manicured than many. Richard's artwork abounds throughout the house. They have a beautiful garden with hanging baskets of flowers and exotic plants. This couple is definitely nesting, like sparrows who use any material available to make a home. This home represents another 20 percent of homes in the sample.

Ospreys build their beautiful, large nests in high places. Peter and David did just that. Their home, perched high on the cliffs overlooking the Pacific, is large and rambling, filled with original oil paintings and carefully selected antiques. The huge formal dining room has a table that seats twelve easily, and there is a full-time, live-in employee. We move from the Chippendale room to the cozy warmth of a modern and tastefully decorated den with a cheerful fire blazing in the fireplace. Close to 10 percent of the couples live in similar surroundings.

The other approximately 30 percent of couples live in many different places. Some are in walk-up furnished apartments. Others live in large apartment complexes where dozens of apartments open onto the same long corridor. As mentioned above, some live in mountain cabins or cottages, and some are in desert hideaways.

How They Met

Gay men frequently say they cannot find a prospective lover in the steam baths, discos, bars, and other places such as gay beaches. Yet, more than half of the couples met in one or another of these places.

Their first contacts usually were sexual. They tricked with each other and then began to talk. The talk usually led to another meeting, then dinners, movies, parties, and so forth. One would spend more time at the other's home, especially nights sleeping together before the decision to move in was reached.

"It's a little embarrassing," Hank answers, "but I want to tell you how it was. In those days I was spending half my time in tearooms, you know, public toilets, hunting for quick thrills. Twice in one week I did it with the same guy. At first I thought he was a cop until he made the first move. After the second time he was waiting outside in the park when I came out. He asked me for a light and then offered to buy me drink." That's how Hank describes meeting Jack, his lover of twenty-three years.

The two Bills tell a different story. "We were introduced in a bar. I really wanted to take him home with me, but I didn't think he was interested. That same night we ran into each other in a different bar, and I was able to get him home for a fast tumble. Afterward we talked. He invited me to a party later that week. Gradually we were spending more and more time together. I'd sleep at his place; he'd sleep at mine. We talked about living together. It took us almost six months to make that decision."

The other couples met in other ways. Some were introduced by friends at parties, met in class, or started talking on a bus, train, or airplane. One couple met many years earlier when one of the partners was in his late teens and working as a male hustler. A few met through professional contacts. A few worked together and met on the job. Some were fellow students. A few were professor and student. One couple met in the laundromat. Some met in the military, on active duty, on ships, or at other military installations. Two met while in combat and recall the events of twenty-five years earlier with vivid detail.

"I hated every minute of Korea until I met Dan. It was ugly, cold, and lonely out there. It was downright scary, never knowing whether or not you'd get hit. I was in a foxhole alone, just after the sun had set. I was laying back, smoking a cigarette, when this blond Adonis jumps in next to me and says, 'Want to make out?' Me, private first class, United States Army, in a foxhole close to the front lines, kissing the most beautiful man I'd ever seen. It wasn't a dream, either. Things just got better from there. And that was twenty-five years ago now."

Ken and Peter have been together for seven years. Ken is nine years older than Peter and is a professor at a large university. Ken reminisces, "I always knew it was taboo trying to make it with a student. The straight professors could get away with murder with those coeds, but being a homosexual made the game all different. Peter sat in the back row of my 10 A.M. lecture on Tuesdays and Thursdays. I remember it well. I'd watch him walk into the back of the room so I could get a good look at him. One day after class he was waiting outside the building for me. Said he had a problem with an assignment. I suggested that he call me at home."

Over the past ten years more recreational, social, and political organizations have developed in the gay community, making more places available for individuals to meet. Sexual orientation is the main common factor bringing them together in these places, so those available for pairing can and do represent extreme divergence in backgrounds, occupations, educational levels, and socioeconomic status. The pairing of the physician and the stevedore, or the fireman and the priest, become more easily understood among gay men because their first meetings occur on territory neutral to class and social status.

How the Relationship Started

We asked how soon after the first meeting couples moved in together. The shortest time was one day, and the longest was four years. Although a number of couples started living together after a courtship of less than a month, the majority moved in together after that first month. In many cases both partners continued to maintain separate living places despite the fact that they were always together at one place.

"He kept his apartment, I kept my house. We were never separated after the first month because we always stayed at one place or the other. Having our own places was sort of like having security blankets. That situation went on for over a year."

Such arrangements offer the opportunity for distancing between partners in at least a symbolic way. The intensity of Stage One blending in the first year is modified potentially by each having his own independent living space available.

Not all of the relationships started smoothly. Some started, then stopped, then started again. In a few instances couples describe being initially fearful of the intensity of their feelings and backing away. Arguments and disagreements over trifling concerns would keep them apart for long periods of time. In a few cases one sought the other out a long time after their first meeting or brief previous encounter.

"A year after I met him I was still thinking about him. I hadn't seen him in months, but something kept telling me that he was the guy I really loved. I went after him."

Age at the Start of the Relationship

(Tables 28 and 29)

The average age at the start of the relationship for our entire sample was 28.4 years. The range was from sixteen to forty-five years old. Two-thirds of the men are the same age as their partners or within three years of the same age. The age difference for the other third is from four to twenty-two years, with the largest clustering between four and eight years. Of the eight couples together longer than thirty years one has an age difference of four years, two have a seven- and eight-year difference, and the last two have a sixteen- and seventeen-year difference.

Sixteen couples have an age difference of ten years or more. Eight of these couples are still in the first five years of their relationship, while the other eight have been together between five and thirty years. The eight of these couples together the shortest time talk more about their relationships as having father–son, mentor–student, or guru–follower qualities. Although couples do not use these exact phrases to discuss it there are clear elements of such relationships when one of the partners is under twenty-five.

"Alex is a mature twenty-one-year-old man. He knows what he wants and he's out to get it," says Vince, his forty-one-year-old lover of one year. "It just makes things easier for him when I'm here to give him advice. He learns really fast. I sure wish I had had someone like me around when I was twenty-one."

The older the men, the less significant the age differences. For example, though Pat is forty-two and Kent is twenty-nine, a difference of thirteen years, neither man attaches importance to their age difference. In couples with more than ten years' age difference who have been together for more than five years, the age difference is usually of

TABLE 28
AVERAGE AGE AT START OF RELATIONSHIP

Number of Years in Relationship	Average Age at Start
1	29.6
2	27.9
3	28.5
4	28.0
5	30.0
6	29.4
7	28.6
8	29.8
9	28.3
10	26.9
11	26.3
12	30.0
13	33.3
14	28.7
15	23.5
16	26.3
17	27.8
19	27.4
20	24.0
21	24.2
23	19.5
24	26.5
25	25.5
26	22.0
27	26.5
28	21.0
29	19.0
30	25.3
31	34.8
33	26.5
35	26.8
37	25.0

more concern to the older partner than to the younger man. These couples talk of the complementarity they find in each other. They learn from each other, with the older partner providing direction and stability for the younger. These couples do express more elements of sexual disharmony than others, however.

TABLE 29
DIFFERENCES IN AGES

Number of Years Difference in Age	Number of Couples
0	28
1	33
2	24
3	18
4	6
5	8
6	4
7	9
8	6
9	3
10	3
11	2
12	1
13	2
14	1
15	1
16	3
17	2
18	0
19	0
20	0
21	0
22	2
Number of Couples = 156	

Those closer in age share positive and negative attitudes about their age similarities. Many feel competitive feelings are a problem or had been in the past. Others feel that the opportunity to learn and to grow together is connected to their age. Still others report that past relationships have taught them to find a partner closer to their own age who shares the same interests and feelings.

The fact that the two couples who have been together for thirty years have a sixteen- and seventeen-year age difference and the two couples together thirty-five and thirty-seven years have a seven- and eight-year difference indicates that in some of these May–December couplings relationship longevity is greater.

Incomes

(Tables 30 and 31)

More than three-quarters of the couples have combined annual incomes of $20,000 to $50,000. These couples rank in the top 20 percent of the general population of this nation.

Because it is a general rule in male relationships that both partners contribute to their mutual support, almost all couples have two salaries. In those five instances where one member remains at home by couple agreement, the unemployed partner usually has some income during the year from short-term jobs or investments.

Five couples have income discrepancies in excess of $10,000 though this is sometimes masked by income in addition to salary. As an example we interview Rod and Brian at their second home in the desert. It is baronial in its style and appointments. It has been Rod's for many years, long before he and Brian met. Rod has vast real estate holdings. Both men report earnings in excess of $25,000 annually. While Brian's salary as bank manager exceeds $25,000, it does not approach Rod's wealth or income.

TABLE 30
ANNUAL COMBINED INCOME OF COUPLES

Amount of Income ($5,000 intervals)	Number of Couples	Percentage of Sample
$ 5,000–10,000	6	3.8
10,000–15,000	12	7.7
15,000–20,000	9	5.8
20,000–25,000	37	23.8
25,000–30,000	20	12.8
30,000–35,000	8	5.1
35,000–40,000	19	12.2
40,000–45,000	18	11.5
45,000–50,000	9	5.8
Over 50,000	18	11.5
	156	100

TABLE 31
ANNUAL INCOME DIFFERENCES WITHIN COUPLES

Difference (by $5,000 increments)	Number of Couples	Percentage of Samples
Same	55	35.3
Within $5,000 of each other	46	29.4
Within $10,000 of each other	50	32.1
Over $10,000 difference	5	3.2

Number of couples = 156

Although some individuals in the study are not employed and stay at home to manage housemaking, several of these men have incomes from other investments.

There is further limitation to this data. Since we did not obtain income data over $25,000 annually, in some cases one partner may have an annual income of $25,000 while his partner may have income in excess of $100,000.

Another couple exemplifies this same situation. "He makes a lot more money than I do. Doctors just make more than civil servants. Sometimes I'm really bothered by that fact, but most of the time I just lay back and enjoy it. That's how Scott wants me to take it. If I can't afford to do it, I just tell him. If he says he really wants to go and will foot the bill, I usually take him up on it. We've made a couple of investments together where we both contribute the same amount. Those babies are going to pay off soon and give me a nice hunk of cash to make more with. Scott's helping me catch up."

Income differences or similarities have minimal effects upon couples in their early years together. Their experiences of Stage One merging, high limerence, and high sexual activity tend to minimize their socioeconomic differences. In later years, when wide income discrepancies are present, the more affluent partner may feel annoyed or the less affluent one may feel inadequate. Earning power can become a competitive device or a means of dominant–submissive struggle between men, especially in Stages Three and Four. Also, in Stages Four and Five couples with near equal incomes at the lower end of the scale can join forces to increase their mutual incomes. And a wealthier partner can assist the other in increasing his income. As demonstrated earlier, couples do forge creative commingling money styles for the good of the mateship.

Employment

Another distinct feature of male couples is the expectation that both partners will be employed. With the exception of those who are re- tired, only in five couples did one partner not work outside the home. However, even among these men, each earned some income through occasional jobs, management of joint financial holdings, and so forth.

Because both men have been socially scripted to give priority to work, each usually understands how the other feels about his career. This works to the couple's mutual advantage not only when decisions about jobs have to be made but also on a day-to-day basis. Couples report that they frequently talk over decisions about their interests and compatibility. Two dentists, two real estate agents, or two bankers share much in common. Their most frequent complaint is "too much shop-talk," but neither seems serious about it. One couple, both wait- ers at different restaurants, laugh together uproariously about their ex- periences with customers. One frequently fills in for the other at his job in case of sickness or other reasons for being absent.

Seventeen couples have the same occupations. Eleven work to- gether in the same business, either owning it together or with others. In seven couples one partner is retired, and in two couples both are retired for a total of eleven men. Five other men remain at home by mutual consent of the partners to manage homemaking activities. Two of these five also manage other business affairs of the couple, such as apartment houses, but do not make a salary for this work. One cou- ple made this arrangement from the start of their relationship.

"I had a college degree and had been working as an eligibility worker for the welfare department when I met Craig." Erik is describing how they decided he would not work.

Craig says, "My life as a company executive takes more energy than I sometimes have to give. I wanted to have a home life where I could find peace. I didn't want to have to work when I got here. Erik wanted to take care of me like that, and I'm really happy to pay the bills."

Erik adds, "But I do make money every now and then by selling and buying old cars, and I have a little income from a family trust."

Couples working together in their own business or with others offer mixed commentaries. A few believe that working together has made them more compatible by supplementing or complementing each other's skills and attitudes.

"We work together very well if we keep our territories straight. I do the books and ordering. Doug is the upfront man."

"Before we started the business we hardly saw each other. Now at least we get time to talk and plan. It's been really marvelous for us."

One couple tells us that their work together has broadened their range of mutual friends and interests to the point that they say they will always work together. Others express vacillating feelings about having too much togetherness to the exclusion of all else in their lives.

"We're together too much, no time for friends, no time for fun away from work. Maybe we can change all that by next year at this time."

"We disagree so much more than we used to. We seem to fight over every little decision, more like competitors than partners."

Interestingly enough, the eleven couples working together have been in their relationships more than five years. This also represents a characteristic of Stage Four—increasing productivity. Working together on the job may be more feasible as individuals become more compatible.

Couples with similar professions or jobs who do not work together generally like their similarity of employment as well as the separateness of their jobs.

"It would just be too hard to work together. We'd hassle over everything. But getting advice from him and knowing what he's talking about is great."

"We've thought about opening our own business, but after the initial excitement we both get depressed. We read that as a bad sign for working together."

Most couples have different jobs, more white-collar than blue but usually within the same socioeconomic boundaries. Even with job differences they tend to have similar educational levels and developmental backgrounds. It is far more common to find a lawyer and a dentist, or a mechanic and a bank clerk, or a hairstylist and a printer together than a mixture of these. The similarity in the social class status of their jobs tends to but does not always dictate the level of their social lives as well.

Exceptions to social class similarities in work do exist. Sixteen couples have wide discrepancies, both in education and employment.

Keith is a university professor. He and Todd live in a comfortably furnished condominium with the living room lined with bookshelves holding a wide assortment of fiction, history, philosophy, and science. One room is identified as the study and contains a record collection running the gamut from classical to popular. The conversation is lively and entertaining. Todd's range of interests and the depth of his knowledge are impressive. He has a high-school diploma and is employed as a construction foreman.

In some such instances a Pygmalion effect may be responsible for apparent compatibility. In most of these sixteen couples it is high complementarity that carries the relationship past the earlier years.

The retired participants give mixed reviews about their current lives. One such couple, together for thirty-one years, retired at the same time ten years ago. They had planned to enjoy what they had accumulated after years of hard work. Both express feelings of restlessness and boredom in the absence of new challenges. Other retired men find their time completely occupied with interests and activities, such as gardening or collecting antiques. Some travel extensively with or without their partners. One retired participant is frequently recalled to temporary consulting jobs because of his unique expertise. All retired participants are financially secure.

Possessions

(Table 32)

The longer couples are together, the greater the amount and the more mutual are their possessions. Combining of possessions, however, is related to the stage of the relationship and it comes best in time. There has been consistency in this finding. Couples who tend to combine their financial resources too rapidly or too early in their relationship can encounter special problems as a consequence of not recognizing the symbolic nature of the economic merger.

Although couples in this study have combined their financial means after ten years, there are a number of circumstances where complete merger probably would not occur. Couples with wide age and

TABLE 32
POSSESSIONS

	1–5 Years	5–10 years	10–37 years	Total
Owning House or Condo	18	21	43	82 (52.6%)
with only one partner owner	14	6	0	20
with joint ownership	4	15	43	62
Home furnishings owned by one partner	8	—	—	8
Home furnishings owned 50–50	30	9	—	39
Home furnishings jointly	23	37	49	109
Automobiles* (one partner)	61	39	11	111
Automobiles* (jointly)	0	7	38	45
Other investments (independently)†	9	11	6	26
Other investments (jointly)	3	15	29	47

*All couples have at least one car.
†A total of 73 couples report other investments.

wealth differences, couples with broad-ranging income discrepancies, or couples with particular characterological and personality differences can find total economic equality unacceptable and undesirable.

Of all possessions the last to be jointly owned are automobiles. Again, even though couples consider their cars as joint property, the cars still were designated clearly as "mine" or "his." Automobiles seem to be among the most personal of belongings for these men. All of the couples had at least one car; some had several.

Wills

In many ways making wills parallels the slow process of financial merger, and for many it becomes a further symbol of commitment to the relationship, especially in late Stage Four and early Stage Five. Including partners in the distribution of property after death has the implication of an expectation of a lifetime duration of the relationship. More than a third of the couples have wills. In every instance provisions are made for the partner either as executor and principal beneficiary or as recipient of a substantial portion of the other's estate.

Separations

The potential for easy separation in the male couple led us to think that temporary separation of partners would be a frequent occurrence. The findings are surprisingly contradictory to that expectation. Defining separation as one continuous month apart for whatever reason, just under a third of the couples report separations. One-third of these attribute their separations to problems within the relationships.

Couples offer numerous examples of separation for a day, a few days, or even a whole week because of frustration, anger, disappointment, or boredom with partners. Getting back together after brief separations often leads to clarification of needs and expectations. As couples develop ways of dealing with conflict, especially in Stage Three, they report fewer separations.

Job changes, company transfers, military commitments, school, family problems, and vacations are a few of the causes the other thirty-five couples report for their separations. For many of the couples separations forced by outside circumstances produced problems in their relationships.

"We had been together three years at the time Tim left for L.A. and graduate school. We knew that we'd be separated for at least six months, since my job in New York wasn't over till the summer," comments Ray.

"We talked a lot on the phone and wrote letters," says Tim, "but both of us got interested in other people at the start. Once we got back together that summer it was hell getting acquainted again."

Ostensibly these separations arose from circumstances outside the relationships. On the other hand some couples explain that long business trips, job transfers, or vacations apart occurred during periods of tension. The separations precipitated letter writing, time alone or with others including dating, and a consolidation of feelings that often resulted in renewal of the relationship. On closer scrutiny the separations seemed to occur when partners needed distancing or individualizing or when long periods of monotony were present.

The intense blending of male partners during Stage One easily promotes emotional fatigue. With the least sign of discord, such emotional fatigue can result in the partners separating. Other research (Saghir and Robins,[1] Bell and Weinberg[2]) reports permanent separations occurring with the greatest frequency during the first year and before the end of the third year.

Expectation of Durability

Every individual was asked how long he thought his relationship would last. Four choices of response were offered: (1) it will last forever, (2) it will last for a long time, (3) it will last for a while, and (4) gay relationships seldom last. Again, responses tend to be related to existing age of the relationship. Couples in Stages Five and Six more frequently select "for a while," couples in Stages Three and Four select "it will last for a long time," and couples in the earlier stages select "forever." None select the fourth response.

While couples together more than twenty years select the "for a while" answer, it appears to represent some understatement and is almost always accompanied by a smile of enigmatic wisdom. On the other hand, in newer relationships manifesting continual high rapport and blending, there is both the expectation of long or forever mateships and the belief that their relationship is special and different from all others.

"We know you have been interviewing other couples, but we think our relationship is probably different from the others."

Relationship Quality

Quality can be evaluated by the application of societal standards of what a good relationship is supposed to be. Western society evaluates quality based on the criteria of mutual trust, caring and sharing, love, complementarity, and compatibility. Couples in our study were asked to report their individual levels of satisfaction based on their own subjective criteria of relationship quality. In some instances, as outside observers, we saw couples with *Who's Afraid of Virginia Woolf* qualities. These same Virginia Woolf couples report high degrees of satisfaction with their relationships. Most couples report ups and downs in their degree of satisfaction over the years together. Hardly anyone says their relationship is always satisfying.

Stage Five and Six couples recite many of the satisfaction themes found among those in the early years. In addition they seem to find great satisfaction in their common history and reminiscences and talk about dependability and companionship, often identifying their partner as their best and oldest friend. Some express satisfaction in the assurance that they will be together until death.

There is danger in viewing relationships as the static, totally fulfilling "Ozzie and Harriet" fantasy. Couples who adopt this popularized standard see themselves and their relationship as flawed when in actuality the shift in values and the fluctuation in satisfaction levels are predictable components of their individual and relationship growth as they pass through the successive stages.

Couples with consistently high levels of satisfaction are the ones who report the highest levels of compatibility in most areas of their lives.

Affection and Romance

Almost all mention varying degrees of being guarded at times in the public expression of affection. They talk about a lack of affectional spontaneity when they were with certain relatives, and their young children. Light kisses on the cheek or a brief touching of hands is consciously avoided while in the supermarket or walking along on the beach. Even among the most open and comfortable, some degree of caution is exercised in openly exchanging affection in circumstances where it would be acceptable and even expected of heterosexual pairs. A few men are very uncomfortable with giving to and receiving from their lovers any form of affection. Demonstrations of caring and loving are made in other ways. These individuals tend to be older and make comments like the following:

"When we started our relationship twenty-four years ago, we had to make sure that no one knew about our being homosexual, to say nothing about our being a couple. We were very careful to come across in public and with our families as casual friends who were living together for the convenience of the arrangement. Of course, any signs of affection would have raised doubts in their minds, so we were careful not to show anything with each other. Maybe those concerns are reasons for our not being more naturally affectionate with each other even in private."

On the other hand, a twenty-six-year-old in his first male relationship believes his own family, which showed no form of affection for one another, was the reason he felt awkward in expressing affection with his lover.

Stage One couples understandably are very physical with each other. "I couldn't keep my hands off him" is an often-heard response of couples recalling their first year together. Kissing, hugging, and hand holding are the usual expressions. During sexual play, lengthy exploration and caressing of the partner's body are common. When in public or at parties, they stay close together. Frequent eye contact—brief or prolonged—is remembered to be like touching each other.

During Stages Two and Three the frequency and intensity of physical contact decrease somewhat. As each gets to know the other better the couple becomes more attuned to certain forms of affection that each enjoys and the times when he enjoys it most.

Many Stage One and Two couples express affection openly and frequently almost regardless of where they are. This is especially true, however, when they are with other gay people. Couples tell us over and over again how important affection is in their relationships. However, the frequency and forms of affection change with the length of time in the relationship.

During Stages Four, Five, and Six, additional forms of affectional responses are added to the couple's repertoire. Some believe that their most valued expressions of affection are in things they do for the other which he likes. Bringing his coffee to bed or leaving fresh toothpaste on his brush at the right time are examples of such affectionate attention. Sometimes affection gets communicated though attention to the details of a relationship, which enhances those qualities usually labeled as romantic.

Some men seem truly puzzled by our questions about romantic elements in their relationship. Others start answering before the question is completely out: "Candlelight dinners with a favorite food, a nice wine, and classical music in the background."

"Remembering, at the same time, some special moment from the past."

"A few special places that we go back to."

"Watching the sunset while sitting close together."

Unexpected and surprise gift-giving, bringing home flowers or a special wine, are reported with frequency. Couples who have been together the shortest times are the ones most likely to report their entire relationship as a continuing romance. Couples together longer talk about doing things they know would elicit romantic feelings in their partner. Some talk about using this as a means of breaking tension caused by disagreements.

We observe some romantic or affection-seeking activities that occur with the couples together for twenty to thirty years. When we ask about affection and romance we usually learn that they have experienced some renewal of tenderness toward each other.

Not all of the couples have high affection or romance. But those who deny being affectionate or romantic seem to have other ways of showing it. Some joke with each other in ways that are clearly affectionate. One might embarrass the other by bringing up a past memory, but the embarrassment seems to be more over the attention from his lover than from the memory itself. Sometimes their tenderness and affection take other forms, like slapping each other on the buttocks or giving a gentle shove.

What Do They Call Each Other?

Married couples use specific, well-established terms to refer to each other, such as *husband, wife,* and *spouse.* For male couples no such words exist. We asked couples what they call each other and gave them the following list to choose from: (1) lover, (2) partner, (3) companion, (4) spouse, (5) roommate, (6) friend, and (7) other. Although they all admit to referring to the other by one of those terms at some time or other, the term *lover* is used most often. Most men qualify the use of the term, however, claiming their partner to be much more than a lover but also a friend, companion, and so on. More

would use the term *spouse* but think that term is more exclusively heterosexual and refers to partners in a marriage. A few participants want
to invent new terms and provide neologisms like *wiband* or *husife*. Until a better term comes along use of *lover* probably will continue.

Pets

Thirty-five percent of the couples have a pet living with them, most
often cats and dogs, though one couple has hamsters, another has
horses, and some have birds or fish. Some are totally dedicated to their
pets' well-being, while others seem merely to tolerate them.

Political Attitudes

When we asked the couples about their political views we found a
high level of attitudinal compatibility. Eighty-five percent see their
own and their partner's political views as being very similar or the
same. Only 5 percent have extremely different political opinions,
while 10 percent see eye to eye on the majority of issues.
    Conservatives tend to pair with conservatives and liberals with
liberals. Attitudes about gay liberation and gay activism are more divergent. Twelve men have strongly negative or at least neutral feelings about gay liberation. Approximately 20 percent report a discrepancy between themselves and partners over their willingness to
support gay activism. Close to 40 percent of the couples do not read a
gay publication with any regularity, but about 60 percent do. Forty-
three percent have attended a gay political or fund-raising event at
some time in their lives, while 57 percent have not. Several of the
older men report a positive change in their own attitudes about the
gay movement in the past few years.

The Couple

At the end of the last chapter we introduced four individuals. We now
present the same four men as the two male couples they are.

Chris and Steve

Chris and Steve were introduced to each other by a mutual friend at a gay bar one evening more than eight and a half years ago. Chris was then twenty-nine, Steve twenty-four. Steve recalls really liking what he saw and feeling eager to "get it on." While Chris had similar feelings he was far more cautious and less expressive. Steve remembers buying two or three drinks for him before Chris agreed to go home with him. Chris remembers the event as unusual; he rarely went home with anyone, preferring to take them to his place instead. Chris spent the night and both remember the sex being great. Steve started pressing for a relationship almost from that moment on. His feelings for Chris were intense, but Chris was much slower in accepting his own feelings for Steve. It was six months before Chris agreed to moving in together; in retrospect, Steve thinks he was right about that.

This all happened more than eight years ago. Over that time Chris and Steve have passed through Stages One, Two, and Three. Chris expected sexual exclusivity, and the thought never entered Steve's mind. It was easy for Steve in the beginning, but after five or six months he would make occasional visits to the baths. Chris would detect the evidence somehow or other, and then they would fight. On more than one occasion each felt the relationship was over. Gradually, Chris came around as far as Steve was concerned. One of the things Chris likes most about Steve is his ease with his own homosexuality. Chris says Steve taught him a lot about that. Steve likes Chris's thoughtfulness. Steve admits that he has lived by his impulse, while Chris has been living by his wit. Combining the two has made a good team, they feel. They now own their own home, have a dog and a cat, and view themselves pretty much as an old married couple. They have a sailboat, and both enjoy their outings alone or with friends. They entertain other couples, both homosexual and heterosexual. Both families have been to visit, but Chris's father continues to refuse to accept the situation.

Ken and Alan

They met in mid-1950, when Alan was twenty-nine and Ken was twenty-three. They are planning a trip to Brazil to celebrate their twenty-seventh anniversary together. "I met Ken at the train station in Del Mar; you know, the one down by the beach. He was coming down to the Del Mar races, and I was meeting another guy at the train. When I saw him I was in love! Six-foot-two, muscular, light brown hair, with a white suit and a panama hat! The friend I was meeting had sat with him on the ride down, so he asked if we could take Ken to the race track."

Ken tells his side. "Ted, Alan's friend that I met on the train, told me that Alan was quite an operator. He hadn't exaggerated. I wondered from the start of my conversation with Ted if he was homosexual. When I saw him and Alan hug each other, I was pretty sure. It didn't take Alan long to invite me home. At any rate, I moved to San Diego a month later. We didn't start living together until May 1951."

"Alan had some pretty set ideas about how we should live together in the beginning," Ken says. "But I stood up to him really strong. He thought he was going to be the boss and that was that."

In 1952, they started a distributorship for high-fidelity sound equipment and opened a series of retail outlets. Their business boomed beyond their wildest dreams. By early 1960 they were already very wealthy men.

"Around that time we started talking to each other about getting out of business altogether. We made an agreement to work until 1970. Regardless of where things in the business were, we'd sell out and retire," Alan says. That's what they did. We have no way of knowing the extent of their wealth, but they are definitely affluent.

Their lives are very busy. Both are involved in civic and cultural affairs. They belong to a variety of organizations. The majority of their friends are heterosexual couples with whom they travel, play bridge, and otherwise entertain. Alan is an active collector of artwork; Ken collects pre-Christian artifacts. They have a few gay friends in San Francisco and New York, but on the whole have no interest in the politics or social world of other gay men.

CHAPTER 13

EVERYDAY LIVES, FAMILY, FRIENDS, AND SOCIAL LIFE

This chapter places the couples in the context of dealing with each other around the ordinary activities of day-to-day living—household chores, finances, jobs and professions, home environment, disagreement and conflict, leisure time together, and their everyday interaction with others in their lives, such as families and friends.

Household Chores and Roles

Near the top of the list of old beliefs about male couples is that one of the partners is more masculine while the other has more feminine characteristics. Next on the list is the belief that one plays the husband and assumes the manly duties while the other becomes the wife and functions accordingly. This stereotypical notion is held by many in the general public and was reinforced by numerous writers in the past (Cory,[1][2] Bergler,[3] Bieber,[4] Ellis[5]). Our couples manifested very little evidence of stereotypical behavior. A few of the older couples do seem to represent the more stereotypical idea of gay coupling, but it is rarely found in couples who have been together less than twenty years. Perhaps the older couples have assumed the gender-related patterns as a consequence of their upbringing. Even in these couples, however, the partner identifiable as more feminine might also be the mechanic, carpenter, or handyman around the house. The more masculine partner might have developed sewing skills and may even do needlework as a hobby.

If male couples do not assume the traditional gender-related divisions of labor, who does what, and how do the chores of managing a household get accomplished? Handling the tasks of daily living vary according to the stage of the relationship. For example, couples who report to us about Stage One tell us how they did everything together

231

during that first year. They find a great deal of intimacy and fun in sharing these tasks. At times there is a certain play quality to it, as if they are playing at housekeeping. Couples in Stage Two usually develop a division of tasks as each person gradually assumes responsibility for those he prefers. More often than not, each functions in those tasks he is best at performing, like cooking or cleaning. When neither partner particularly likes or wants to do the task, both assume responsibility for it, or the partners alternate.

Stage Three couples usually are experiencing some changes in the way they deal with household chores. As they deal with reappearance of the individual, frequently there is a disruption in their daily routines.

"In the beginning we used to do everything together. Then after a year or so everything fell into a neat routine. Steve would cook and shop. I'd clean up. Housekeeping we continued to do together. After being together four years I decided I was going to learn to cook, too, and Steve wanted to learn how to manage the bills. We made an exchange."

Stage Four couples trade chores or substitute for each other with great ease. Also, because they know each other's shortcomings and accept them with greater ease, they tend to do those chores they know the other avoids or does poorly. Although both partners participate actively in household affairs, one usually predominates in management.

The longer couples have been together, the higher the probability that each partner has certain clearcut household duties. Couples in Stages Five and Six are much more likely to have relatively fixed tasks.

The assignment of daily chores does not always parallel individual likes or dislikes. Sometimes the division depends on the partners' particular skills or work schedule. Couples almost always tell us that they both feel the division of tasks is equitable. This may be another one of the advantages of entering the relationship as equals, without the traditional gender-related role expectations that the other will do certain things for him. Often the division of labor in a relationship is similar to the division in previous relationships. Sometimes men are attracted to each other by their style of living. We did not find very many men who were strong opposites in how they wanted their home managed.

These men find no threat to their masculine egos in doing house-hold duties that are traditionally feminine. In fact, in more cases than not, each cherishes the opportunity to function in one or more of the usually feminine-identified roles of cooking, washing, or cleaning. With very few exceptions we discover fluidity and flexibility in their attitudes and functions.

The most interesting factor in all of this is that the men them-selves have rarely—if ever—given the whole business of everyday liv-ing much thought. They have fallen into their patterns without discussion or reference to what married couples or other male couples do. They have developed patterns that work for them without consid-eration for what others think or do.

Finances

Male couples, especially in the first few years of a relationship, differ significantly from heterosexual couples in understanding and manage-ment of finances. At the time of a marriage, finances are blended to-gether for heterosexual couples, and it traditionally is assumed that the husband will be the financial provider. Often a joint decision is made that the wife will work outside the home, but the issue of the husband's working is taken for granted. As mentioned earlier, when two men begin their relationship there is an assumption that each will contribute financially. Among our entire group of couples—retired, students, temporarily unemployed, as well as those who are generating incomes—the unspoken understanding of joint financial responsibility is implied from the very outset of the relationship.

During Stage One, couples who have similar earning power evenly split the day-to-day costs of living. Generally, these are the younger couples and couples with comparable job experiences or levels of training. One of several different methods of money handling is used:

1. Some couples draw up a careful budget from the start, with each contributing equally or an amount proportionate to in-come earned. Sometimes one person pays all of the bills through his personal checking account, and the other gives him that portion which is his contribution.

2. Some split the bills from the start. "He pays the rent. I buy the groceries and pay the phone bill unless he's made too many long-distance calls." In these instances, money for individual needs comes from individual salaries or incomes.

3. Some couples alternate months, with one paying the bills one month and the other paying them the next.

4. Some put equal amounts of money into a central fund each month, and all of their joint bills are paid from it. Should more money be necessary, each partner contributes.

Among those couples in Stage One whose members have significantly different earning power, verbal arrangements are reached about who pays how much and for what. Generally, these are couples with wide age differences and couples with dissimilar job experiences or levels of training. Usually, each contributes a proportionate amount of money according to his income. Methods of handling money are similar to those outlined above.

Beginning with Stage Two some couples move away from these formulas and schedules of payment. In addition couples report that the gradual merging of finances is a reflection of their developing commitment to each other and to the relationship.

Some couples have existed for long periods on one income. The partners support each other in times of unemployment, studying, or illness. The partner making the money usually says that if the tables were turned he is certain his partner would support him financially, too.

Another interesting feature in these financial arrangements is the fact that both partners usually have some portion of money that each considers his own. This gives each person some degree of financial independence and some mad money to be spent as he sees fit. Difficulties can arise when one partner has considerably more free money to spend than the other. Sometimes this is the result of differing attitudes toward money. These differences generally are the cause for relationship failure but may precipitate long periods of tension that affect other areas of the couple's life together.

As reported in chapter 7, couples in Stage Five generally achieve complete financial merger of money and possessions. This merger appears significant enough to be the important indicator of the partners' commitment to the relationship. Which partner handles the money, how they reach agreement about expenditures and investments, and other financial questions infrequently appear to be serious problems for couples in either Stage Five or Six. Some couples find their relationship a fiscal disaster area when both live considerably above their means and find themselves deeply in debt. Other couples have been so frugal that over the period of one or two decades together they have amassed a fortune.

By and large the majority fall somewhere between these two extremes. With average or slightly above-average incomes they live a very comfortable middle-class existence, watching their color TVs, laundering their clothes in their automatic washer, and cooking in microwave ovens.

Leisure Time

Stage One couples do almost everything possible together. Stage Two couples continue to do a lot together. As would be suspected, in Stage Three, with reappearance of the individual, there are many things they begin doing separately. Some resume old leisure activities that were dropped. Stage Four couples are much more variable in time together. One of the functions leisure activities serve is helping to establish independence. Stage Five couples seem to spend the least time together with some leisure activities apart. Stage Six couples come back together and once again spend most of their time together.

More than half of the men participate in physical fitness activity, such as jogging, swimming, or going to a gym or health club. Some play games like racquetball or tennis. Others are on volleyball, baseball, or football teams that play together weekly or more frequently. Athletic participation is not seemingly stage-related either, but associated more with the age of the individuals.

At home they watch TV, listen to music, play cards, play musical instruments, garden, cook, tend to their various collections, and entertain friends at dinner parties.

Outside the home they go to the beach, fish, and sail. Some are antique car enthusiasts who attend car shows. They attend various gay community events, go to theme bars at specific times, and many are avid moviegoers.

Being Out as a Couple

There is a direct connection between the quantity and quality of relationships with family and friends and the extent of a couple's social activities on the one hand, and the degree to which the couple is open about its sexual orientation on the other.

In chapter 9 we reviewed the steps of individual coming out. Where each partner finds himself in the process of coming out affects the relationships. In some cases both partners may be completely out before the relationship begins. In these instances their relationship is equally out of the closet from the beginning. These couples usually have a history of sharing their relationship with close friends and family members from the start.

For an individual to enter into a coupled relationship he must be out of the closet to the extent that he has acknowledged his homosexuality, has explored sex with another man, probably has visited places where gay men meet, and has decided to live with another man as his lover.

The degree of a couple's participation in activities, whether with family or friends, is usually determined by how open each partner is about his homosexuality. If one is more in the closet than the other, their gay activities together are limited by that fact. Once a gay person is out, there are various levels of openness:

1. Out to gay friends and participating in a gay lifestyle
2. Out to nongay friends, both individuals and couples
3. Out to some or all family members
4. Out to employers, colleagues, and other professionals
5. Out to everyone without worry

In many instances partners may find themselves to be out with the same groups of people, or there may be variations between the partners about to whom they are open. As an example one partner may be open with his nongay friends, family, and coworkers, while the other partner may not.

Levels of openness seem to be linked more frequently with the age or the era of growing up for men rather than with the various stages of the relationship. Again, older men together the longest have a tendency to be more closeted, while the younger men in relationships of shorter duration are more open. These various levels of openness can become quite complicated for the couples themselves as well as for their families, friends, and social life. Their social lives are limited to the lowest level of openness.

Ted and David are in their mid-fifties and have been together for twenty-eight years. Both could be categorized easily as "old school gentlemen," always formal, extremely polite, usually with starched white shirts and ties. Ted's parents lived in the house next door for the first twenty years the men were together. They were elderly and ill for the last ten years, and the two men cared for them devotedly. Never once was the subject of homosexuality discussed. Ted and David spend most of their social time with heterosexual couples in their own age group and belong to bridge clubs, travel groups, and book clubs. They always seem to be considered merely as another couple by their friends. The subject of homosexuality is never raised.

A sharply contrasting example is Doug and Mike. These twenty-eight-year-old men have been together more than four years. They started a very profitable business that serves the gay community. Both of their families invested generously in their carefully financed venture, which has paid off handsomely. The couple has a broad social life with both gay and nongay friends. Their general attitudes are stated simply: "If they reject us on the basis of our homosexuality, it's really their loss, not ours."

Families

Most couples have formed extended families including other gay couples, close friends, and other family members. This is a phenomenon that develops everywhere, especially in the absence of families of origin. Bruce Voeller, founder and former codirector of the National Gay Task Force, believes that much of the work of the first decade of the gay rights movement has resulted in the creation of surrogate families composed of other gay persons for mutual support.[6]

Again, when men in our study have come out to their families the usual method has been through siblings. Although many made their sexual orientation known through parents, usually mothers, they first discussed the subject with the brother or sister to whom they were closest.

Many of the men say they tried as teenagers to broach the subject with parents, who either ignored or halted any attempt at discussion. Gay men often wait until they have been in a relationship with their lover for several years before they approach their families. This is easier for many to do within the context of a loving and caring relationship rather than in the abstract form of discussing homosexuality in general.

Talking with the family may be easy for some but is generally a time of high stress for all concerned.[7] Close to 45 percent of our participants have talked with all or some family members about their homosexuality and their relationship. For some this has meant a complete rupture in the relationship with parents for many years. In other cases it has been the event that has opened the door to increased closeness, sharing, and intimacy with parents, which had never existed before.

Many families still live in and around the San Diego area. The gay family member generally says he has avoided family get-togethers, mainly because he has felt his partner would not be welcomed. Most acknowledge that their families need time to work out their own feelings about having a gay son. Interestingly enough, many families hear the news, accept the partner, and then proceed to deny the significance of the relationship, sometimes for years. Some couples report spending considerable amounts of time with the parents of one partner or the other, yet homosexuality is never discussed. The family treats the couple as a pair when invited to dinners and parties but often does not introduce them to others as a couple unless they work together, share a business, or have some other socially acceptable connection.

Families frequently have neither a social nor a psychological context in which to understand their son's homosexuality. Parents and siblings generally harbor the old notions and myths about homosexuality. They often respond, "But you've always been so normal." The gay son often fails to understand his family's denial or guilt; he forgets that he has been dealing with the issue within himself for years. He did not reach his current level of self-acceptance until he passed through all of the difficult steps his family must take to reintegrate him into their daily lives.

Rejection by families has been painful for some. Being denied access to the comfort and warmth of family acceptance often can be the beginning of a depression or a serious relationship setback. At the same time it may also be a very solidifying and unifying experience for a couple, especially in those instances where the partner supports his lover's need for increased attentiveness and understanding.

One of the couples in our study tells of a mother's eventual response to their relationship. One partner had five brothers and sisters, all of whom were in marriages or heterosexual relationships. His mother in particular had some difficulty in accepting the fact that her son had settled down with a man and, indeed, was living a prosperous and professionally contributing life. That mother finally came around and in a moment of closeness admitted that in her opinion he had the best relationship in the family.

Gay men in our study seem to have closer relationships during their adult years with their sisters. A larger number report sisters and brothers-in-law as being more accepting and understanding than their heterosexual brothers. Our sample is really not large enough nor did we explore this question fully enough to do more than make this simple observation about it.

Some of our couples have become the focal points of their families, though this situation is not common. The couples describe annual get-togethers that are traditionally sponsored by the gay couple for the two families. The mothers and fathers are friendly with each other apart from the couple themselves and may even be close social friends. In these instances the families are accepting and supportive. In fact, a few couples even tell us how their parents worry about them when they learn their son and "son-in-law" are having a disagreement.

A few couples actually have a family member living with them, either at the time of our interview or at some time in the past. The age-old problems with in-laws usually hold sway in these cases. It is the rare couple who is able to live with other family members for any extended period.

A few couples carry the primary responsibility for the care and supervision of aging parents in retirement communities or nursing home facilities. We are certain that there is no difference in the experience of these men and that of other couples who do the same things.

The majority of our participants do not enjoy full family support or participation. Many have a warm relationship with one set of parents and no relationship with the other. In other cases the families are unaware of or disregard their son's sexual orientation. These men return to their respective homes at holiday times and on other occasions of family celebrations without their partners.

For a few men parental deaths have been times of deep loss and mourning. The loss of fathers or mothers has been equally devastating for some, particularly when these deaths occurred at times when the men had just begun to make new emotional openings with their parents.

Relationships With Former Spouses

The possibility for relationships with at least forty-seven former wives exists in this group. We say "at least" because a few men had been married more than once. Those who continue to maintain ongoing contact with children younger than mid-to-late adolescence generally have contact with their former wives. We did not investigate the number who are paying alimony or child support.

Only ten men report any significant ongoing contact with a former wife. Two of the wives have come out themselves and, according to their former husbands' reports, are living satisfactory and fulfilled existences with other women. A very large percentage are remarried and have no further contact with the men in this study. In those cases where contact has been maintained the wife knew about her husband's homosexual interests before their marriage. Typically, she expected her husband to deny his homosexuality for the sake of their marriage, as indeed he himself usually intended. As time passed he usually discovered that his basic attraction to other men could not be denied. Some couples dissolved their marriages after working out their differences in some form of counseling or psychotherapy. Others who have maintained contact had a friendly relationship that allowed each to grow and be open with the other. The men who give this latter history report the same openness in their homosexual relationships.

More often than not, men relate stories of painful divorces in which both they and their wives suffered anguish and anger. Sometimes they report bitter court battles that finally resolved when the husbands relinquished the majority of their community property to their wives. Although the homosexuality of the men is often cited as a major contributor to the divorces, many other relationship problems, such as personality incompatibility, divergence of value systems, or lack of intimacy share the responsibility equally.

Relationships With Children

With increasing frequency, in our clinical practice we are asked by homosexual fathers about their children. The recent literature (Green,[8] Kirkpatrick[9]) about homosexual parents has focused more on lesbian mothers than on homosexual fathers. Miller's recently published articles on the subject of gay fathers have begun to open the topic for discussion.[10] Our study includes twenty-six fathers with fifty-two children. We have not had the opportunity to investigate the lives or responses of the children themselves.

Some men got married because they wanted to be fathers, even though they knew of their same-sex orientation. Others knew about their homosexuality but married in an attempt to cure themselves, or at least with the hope that marriage would control their homosexuality. Most now admit they misjudged but are extremely grateful to have children.

One important question that always arises in any discussion about children of homosexual parents is the effect that the parent's sexual orientation will have on the children. In the research work cited above there is no evidence to support the old notion that parent's orientation has any influence whatsoever on children's eventual orientation. We are always mindful that all of the gay persons themselves have grown up within the context of heterosexual relationships. In fact, Ellis used the point that despite the pressure of parents, peers, and social mores to be heterosexual, a certain percentage of persons develop as homosexual, to argue that all homosexuals were psychotic.[11] Absurd as that notion now appears, for some uninformed segments of the community parental orientation is still an issue. In fact, three of the fathers in our study still express concern about it.

Often enough, a gay father's choice of a partner is partially dependent upon the other man's interest and response to his children. We suspect that this is no different from similar circumstances among opposite-sex oriented men and women with children.

As mentioned earlier, some couples actually have reared children or are in the process of doing so. These couples are the exceptions. One such couple, together for four years, has had custody of the younger man's seven-year-old son from the start of their relationship. In this case both fathers say they feel equal responsibility for their son. The boy visits his mother for a month each year; she lives at a great distance. The routine child care is provided by the stepfather more than the biological father because the stepfather is employed in a job that keeps him at home most of the time. This arrangement was worked out by the couple for the benefit of the child.

The couple admits that their own lives are constricted to a certain degree by the boy's presence, but each feels they receive such enrichment from the experience that the rewards are well worth the sacrifices. The boy's father came from a disrupted family background, while his partner came from a very traditional nuclear family. The father is eager to supply stability and continuity for the child. The couple views routines, dependability, and traditions as important features of being together.

When the child entered school, the couple had some difficulties in situations where a parent's presence was expected and necessary. The boy understands that the two men love each other and live together like other children's parents even though they are both men. The couple reports no difficulty with the school or other parents up to the present. Each has functioned as a parent in the school setting, with the stepfather parenting more frequently than the father.

Expressions of affection and tenderness are exchanged freely among the three. It would be a very interesting study to follow the growth and development of this boy and this couple. The couple has a lot of common sense and thoughtfulness about rearing the boy.

Another couple has two children with them, a boy and a girl, both in early adolescence, who chose to stay with their father after an angry divorce. The children actually lived with the male couple intermittently over the succeeding seven or eight years, visiting their mother frequently, but they basically considered their father and his lover's house as home. The couple explains that because the partner who is not the father is so young he can hardly function as the stepparent. He is seen by the two children more like an older brother and friend. The father tells us he assumed the major parental responsibilities, including the discipline and financial support. He told both children about his homosexuality when he started living with his lover. He tells us he talked with them each individually. His son had already known from his own observations but was very happy to hear about it from his father. The daughter was most accepting, telling her father that her love for him did not depend upon whom he loved. Besides, both of these children really love and respect their father's lover. We learned that they loved the couple's lifestyle, the flow of interesting friends they have, their work, and their home. Both children are away at college but return home for holidays and vacations. They bring their friends home with great frequency, but only after sounding them out for negative attitudes about homosexuality. At some point before bringing the friends home they explicitly tell them the situation. The friends themselves usually became friends of the couple and return for visits even without the children.

"Hey, Dad, can we go skating in the park this afternoon?" ten-year-old Billy shouts down the hall to his father, who is sitting in the living room with his lover of six years, talking about life as a gay parent. Although Billy doesn't live with Don and Richard full-time, he usually visits on weekends and is an active and full participant in their lifestyle.

"How has Billy dealt with the issues of homosexuality?" we ask.

"He's never really known or remembers me being any other way than with Richard. He knows men can love men and women can love women. He really likes our friends and talks about wanting to be gay himself. Actually, he looks pretty heterosexual to me at this time," Don explains, and continues, "Richard and I find that the more open we are about being gay, the easier our lives become and the more fun we have. We know some couples who stay at home and refuse to socialize except with a few other uptight gays. We just couldn't do that."

"Learning to be a stepparent, and a gay one at that, was one of the hardest things I've ever done." Jeff is talking about his relationship with Steve's fourteen-year-old son and twelve-year-old daughter. "But the effort has been worth it in terms of the return I get from the kids now." Although the children did not live with the two men at the beginning of their now seven-year relationship there have been long periods of time when they have lived with the two men.

Many men with children spend weekends and extended vacations with them. For some couples these can be difficult times, but the majority report that time with the children is fun and exciting.

In many cases the couples focus their entire time around the children's visits. The children's weekends are planned in advance so that some activity is always available. In this group are twelve couples who have regular contact with the children.

These couples have many of the same problems as any divorced father living with a new partner. Though homosexuality can become an issue, it is usually minor compared to other difficulties that arise. Children of divorced parents sometimes have problems of their own that are side effects of the parental breakup. One couple talks extensively about their need to deal with the severe emotional disturbance of two of the father's three children.

Other cases are more humorous but just as poignant. When two gay men are confronted by a ten-year-old son about their relationship the response can become quite intense. One couple tells us that their nine-year-old daughter refers to her father's lover as her guardian. Other couples do everything they can to withhold information about their gayness from children—usually because they themselves do not know how to handle telling them. Some go so far as to pretend they are roommates by sleeping in separate bedrooms when the children are around.

For some couples the presence of children in their lives has been a binding, sobering, and joyful experience; for others a painful and dissonant one. The majority of men with children claim they are grateful to have had the opportunity of being fathers.

What is clear from the couples we observed is that whenever the father accepts and feels good about his sexuality and his love relationship, he can carry out the duties of parenting in a way that enriches his own life and that of his children.

Friends

Most people choose friends because they offer support, validation, companionship, fun, and entertainment, among other things. The very same things are true with the couples in this study.

Our data indicate that the vast majority of our participants consider their closest friends to be other gay people. One hundred percent have gay friends. About two-thirds report that they spend almost all of their time with other gay men. Another third report spending most but not all of their free time with other gays. A few spend half of their free time with gay friends, and a few spend more than half of their time with nongay friends. Those couples most in the closet have the fewest gay friends. Typical comments are "We had some fellows over for dinner once and one of them made a pass at Jim," or "Most of them are only interested in sex," or "They seemed silly to us," or "We just aren't interested because we haven't found any like ourselves." These couples form a very small minority of our sample.

Stage One couples are more inclined to have fewer friends around who also are gay. Stage Two and Three couples may develop entire new sets of friends, either other couples like themselves or nongay couples they feel are more like themselves. Stage Three couples have more individual friends who are identified as "his" or "mine." This same circumstance is even more true for Stage Four couples if individualization has occurred. Stage Five and Six couples have the most friends identified as "ours" rather than "his" or "mine," including a higher percentage of heterosexual couples.

Many couples report that nongay couples and individuals validate their relationship more than many of their gay friends. In fact, a number of men indicate to us that their closest friends are heterosexual women. Both the gay man and the straight woman can be affectionate without expecting sex, and they can interact on an intimate, emotional level. Neither of their partners is jealous of the relationship because it involves no sex.[12]

Many couples report that heterosexual males are among their closest friends. It is important to recognize that couples who give us these data represent a combined 12 percent of the sample, by no means a majority.

The rest of the men choose other gays as close friends. Except for that small group who have intimate ties with lesbian couples or individuals, our participants identify other male couples or individuals as their friends. The small percentage who list lesbian women as close friends state that they find their best rapport with them.

Social Lives

Diversity reigns supreme in the social lives of our participants. As mentioned earlier the only limiting factor is how out of the closet a couple is. Social lives also have definite connections to the developmental stage of the relationship. Stage One couples have less active social lives with others because their major interest is in each other. The exceptions are couples who may be older and those with a history of several previous relationships. Couples in Stages Two and Three have more diversity. They visit bars, restaurants, and discos with the greatest frequency. Stage Four couples socialize at home more and continue to go out with less frequency but with regularity. In Stage Five more socializing occurs at home with couples, and Stage Six couples do the least amount of socializing outside their own homes.

The social activity most couples like best is entertaining at home. Reasons couples give for this preference include the intimacy they can share with others over a meal, the opportunity to have others see their home and enjoy it, the ease they feel in being able to control situations at home, and their mutual interest in cooking and serving a meal or hosting a party. Home entertaining runs the gamut from large, formal dinner parties to having another couple over for beer, popcorn, and a TV show. Several couples say that they entertain at home several nights a week, with dinner, cocktails, dessert, or late coffee with friends. Part of the entertainment may be business-connected, some just for pleasure and fun.

The higher the level of social participation, the more elegant and extravagant the social events. Since there are no social clubs that cater to gay patrons, gay men form their own social groups. Some participate in bowling leagues, reading clubs, or political activities. The growing political power of the gay community means that some of our couples spend part of their social lives in political circles.

An interesting social group we encountered during the course of this research is a hidden community of mostly blue-collar workers who meet to drink beer, share stories, and watch sports events on TV. If they go to bars at all they frequent nongay ones where they encounter their fellow workers, be they telephone linesmen, construction workers, or firemen.

Many of our couples travel extensively. Some spend large portions of the year in Mexico, Europe, or the Orient. Others travel to San Francisco, Los Angeles, Las Vegas, or Palm Springs to meet other friends and participate in a wider selection of activities directed at the gay community. Most couples vacation together, though a small percentage do plan separate holidays. A more common phenomenon among couples together between five and twenty years is for partners to take occasional weekends away without each other. These jaunts usually include plans for sexual activities of one kind or another and are generally supported by both partners.

Many couples plan short getaways especially to be with each other. Living in Southern California they have a wide selection of relatively inexpensive places to visit. Those who take these times away seem to value them greatly as times for themselves when they can talk and find quiet time relaxing with each other.

About 20 percent of our couples report going to the beach as an important social event. The beaches are readily accessible to most of our couples. There are various beach areas where homosexuals tend to meet, from remote "swimsuit optional" beaches for nude swimming and sunbathing to the more easily accessible beaches on the inner bays where gay men play volleyball and softball.

More than 80 percent of the participants have been in a gay bar or disco in the month preceding our interviews. The social life of some centers around bars and discos most of the time. A few couples visit the baths together but most go alone. Gay bath houses are generally recognized as places for outside recreational sexual activity. Gay gyms and health spas provide a new social meeting place.

Some couples have found comfortable social settings with church groups. Some spend a great deal of time at the cinema. Others soak up every available cultural event, such as operas, plays, touring company shows, ballets, and local specialties like the Shakespeare Theater. Some never miss a rock or jazz concert. Others have season tickets to football, basketball, or baseball games.

Some take courses through local college and university extensions. Others have hobbies in groups with a social focus, such as photography enthusiasts, antique car buffs, and skiers. Antique collectors, auction followers, and swapmeet buffs are beginning to take on their own genre of socializing. Some men meet to share their latest pornography selections, usually in home movies or video cassettes. Other couples have swimming pools, jacuzzis, or hot tubs that serve as a focus for social interaction as well as sex with other couples or individuals.

For most of our couples, alcohol is a great catalyst for socializing. As mentioned elsewhere we did not specifically determine the extent of drug usage but consider that the majority of couples and individuals in this study have used one of the more socially accepted drugs as part of their social lives. Extensive use and availability of marijuana at the majority of social gatherings was a part of gay subculture long before it found its way into the majority of nongay social lives. The widespread availability and use of drugs among gay men is usually socially accepted. As a consequence, a higher incidence of substance abuse and alcoholism has been recognized among gay men. In recent times many such persons have acknowledged their problems and formed successful support groups and organizations to encourage and maintain sobriety. They often see themselves as socially different from the start, which actually gives some carte blanche to other unorthodox activities less ubiquitous among the majority society.

The social lives of many couples are filled with examples of play. Many tell us that they had not really learned to play before their partners introduced them to the varieties of ways it could be accomplished. When we began to look at this play behavior, both of us thought of the ego-psychology phrase "regression in the service of the ego."[13] Sometimes, in allowing the child that is in each of us to take over, couples find release from tension. Social situations with mutually trusting friends where anything goes are part of the social lives of a few couples. Again, couples with these avenues of play open to them in their social lives represent more out of the closet, more comfortable, and more fulfilled lives and relationships.

Not all couples appear to have rich social lives. Some couples admit that they feel perfectly content to be together, to work, and to stay at home. They may not reach out to others but report that they have a string of friends who drop by to talk, watch TV, listen to music, or just find peace and quiet. Some couples complain that they do spend the majority of their time alone together but know no way acceptable to them to make social contact with others.

Some couples participate in dual social lives. A few have women friends who make social appearances with them in their efforts to maintain a heterosexual or at least bisexual front. They find this necessary for business and professional reasons.

Conclusion

There is so much diversity in the lives of these men that it is impossible to identify a specific lifestyle. The reality of their lives represents many different lifestyles. They have families, or they create new ones. Some are fathers and cherish that role. They participate in every imaginable recreation and make a few new ones. They play and sometimes live out their fantasies as they enrich their own lives and often those of their friends.

CHAPTER 14

SEXUALITY

"He was standing in the pulpit, preaching his Sunday sermon. I knew I wanted him then and there." Albert smiles as he recalls seeing Jacob for the first time. "There was only one problem I was sixteen and he was thirty-one." It took Al about two months to get Jacob alone in a room at the downtown YMCA. "He was lying on the bed, and I was sitting next to him hardly able to keep my eyes or hands off him. He was the picture of innocence—acting like he had no idea what was happening."

"I really wasn't sure what was happening," Jacob chimes in in self-defense, "but when that beautiful boy started making love to me I was hooked for life." That was in 1940, and they overcame many obstacles to live together, including Jake's leaving his beloved ministry and Al's leaving his comfortable home. In 1941 they moved from the Midwest to San Diego to live together. Both got drafted the following year and were separated for more than three years. Al was fighting with the Allies in Italy, and Jake was a Navy officer in the South Pacific.

"Those three years were the hardest times of our lives," Al says. "When Jake put me on the train in L.A. that hot May afternoon in 1942, he told me to have a good time with the freedom I was getting. What he meant was that it was OK to have sex with other men while we were separated. The idea revolted me at the time. I never had sex with anyone else during the entire war."

"Well, I wasn't so virtuous." Jacob picks up the story. "I had sex with lots of guys. I was so lonely for Albert that I'd crawl into bed at night hurting with the anguish of it all. Then the next day I'd treat myself to a little party and would feel better. I'd write him long letters—some he got, others never reached their destination. All the mail was censored in those days so we had to use code words to tell each other how we felt. Remember that, Al?" Jacob turns to his lover of thirty-six years, waiting for him to tell his side of the story. It seems as if they speak almost as one person.

Albert adds his comments. "Yes, you know those were hard days for gay men. I missed Jacob so much that I almost went crazy in the beginning. Then I wrote lots of letters to him. Some I never mailed, but it did help. I'd masturbate thinking about him, hoping he was thinking about me. When it was time to go home again, I was so eager you wouldn't believe it. He was back in San Diego in January of 1946, and I wasn't due in until June. I told him I wanted the same apartment with the same furniture and fresh flowers. I wanted everything the same again, including him."

"When he got off the train at the Santa Fe depot I didn't recognize him. It was over three years, and he was fifty pounds heavier and two inches taller with a beard! I'd sent a boy off to war, and he came back a great big, strapping man." Jacob sits on the edge of his chair excitedly recalling the events.

"He looked pretty much the same to me—beautiful, shining green eyes, that marvelous smile and his ever-intriguing physique," Albert says about that meeting. "He took me back to the apartment—not the same one as before, but almost. He had flowers, all our furniture, even the pictures on the wall were in the same places I had remembered. We cried a lot as we went about looking at each treasure together. Then I finally got him on the bed and took out all my sexual frustrations by making love to my man again."

The readjustment for this couple was not so easy. It took them months to get reacquainted. Albert had come close to a nervous collapse after his first few encounters with killing in the war. Even to this day, more than thirty years later, his eyes glaze over and he gets a faraway look on his face when the subject is broached.

"I had always expected sexual fidelity from Jacob. My parents were faithful to each other, and I expected us to be the same," Albert says. "Then Jacob's eyes started wandering even toward the end of our first year here in San Diego. There were so many gorgeous sailors walking around downtown, he couldn't resist. I remember once he told me he was going out with this other man. At first I ranted and raved, carried on like a wounded virgin, and he didn't go out. Then it happened again after a few months. I remember it so well, do you?" he turns to Jacob quizzically.

"Do I? How could I forget it? I did go out with the guy after Albert told me I had to do what I had to do. I sneaked in that evening about 9 P.M. and found Albert waiting up with a dozen red roses for me. He could have done anything else, hit me, cried, screamed, been angry, but when he gave me the roses and a big hug I got his message in big neon lights," Jacob recounts.

"I figured he was bound to be doing it again and again and that I had just better get with it or else I might lose him. I sure didn't want to come across as the possessive wife. Anyway, he didn't go out with anyone else for almost six months after that. Then we talked about having a three-way. We always refer to having sex as having a little party, you know, our way of asking each other. Well, we started picking up sailors and having little three-way parties. I loved them, and it made the sex with Jake a lot hotter in those days. In fact, we've never expected monogamy ever since. You know, outside sex has been part of our relationship since around 1950, isn't that right, Jake?" Albert asks.

"Heaven knows, there have been lots of times when we'd go for years without having sex with other guys. We were too busy and we were living too far out in the country or whatever the reasons were. It also saved us from getting jealous. Jealousy was always our worst enemy in these outside sexual adventures. I guess that's one of the reasons why three-way sex was always better. After Al gave me those roses, he didn't have so much trouble with jealous feelings. It was me who got so jealous the first time he got involved outside. Man, I almost went nuts, fearing that he'd leave me for the other person," Jake fills in the missing pieces.

"You haven't asked us about our sex lives nowadays," Albert interjects after we'd asked hundreds of questions about the past. "We sleep in separate bedrooms now, but we usually start out in the same bed together every night. Jake likes to read late, and I get to sleep early so I can be on the job early. We still have sex together about once a week."

"I have more trouble getting hard now than I used to, but I sometimes get it up in the shower and come out and wave it at Al around the corner of the door. He's always there in a flash." Jacob blushes a little.

"He has the world's most beautiful body and I still worship it," responds Albert. "We also have parties at other times. It's comfortable together."

"There are a couple of long-time friends who call every month or so and come over for a little three-way party. One fellow is even a grandfather and married, yet he's been having sex with us for over twenty-five years," Jacob reports.

Fidelity Without Sexual Exclusivity

(Tables 33 and 34)

Sexual exclusivity among these couples is infrequent, yet their expectations of fidelity are high. Fidelity is not defined in terms of sexual behavior but rather by their emotional commitment to each other. Ninety-five percent of the couples have an arrangement whereby the partners may have sexual activity with others at some time under certain conditions. Only seven couples have a totally exclusive sexual relationship, and these men all have been together for less than five years. Stated in another way, all couples with a relationship lasting more than five years have incorporated some provision for outside sexual activity in their relationships. Many of the couples have started their relationship with either explicit agreements or implicit assumptions about sexual exclusivity, which they have modified over time, finding emotional fidelity more enduring.

Our culture has defined faithfulness in couples always to include or be synonymous with sexual fidelity, so it is little wonder that relationships begin with that assumption. It is only through time that the symbolic nature of sexual exclusivity translates into the real issues of faithfulness. When that happens, the substantive, emotional dependability of the partner, not sex, becomes the real measure of faithfulness.

TABLE 33
SEXUAL EXCLUSIVITY

At Start of Relationship		Explicit Agreement	Implied Assumption
Exclusivity	114 (73.1%)	92 (80.7% of 114)	22 (19.3% of 114)
Nonexclusivity	26 (16.7%)	11 (42.3% of 26)	15 (57.7% of 26)
Nonagreement	16 (10.2%)		
Inapplicable	16		

TABLE 34
CHANGE TO NONEXCLUSIVITY BY LENGTH OF TIME IN RELATIONSHIP

Years in Relationship	0–1	1–2	2–3	3–4	4–5	Over 5
Number of Couples Undecided	3	5	6	2		
Number of Couples Decided	8	13	31	36	14	5
Number of Couples Maintaining Exclusivity		3	1	2	1	

Couples who lacked agreement at the start of the relationship all moved toward nonexclusivity by the fifth year.

Each man grew up feeling that being sexually exclusive was an issue of morality. In addition, they grew up believing that heterosexuality had intrinsic moral value while homosexuality was basically immoral. To arrive at the acceptance of being gay and of extrarelational sex, each of these men has had to alter his own value systems. Because gay men are automatically placed outside mainstream values anyway, some find it easier to explore nontraditional sexual patterns.

When we ask the men in this study why they want sex outside the relationship, their answers include the following responses:

1. "All my sexual needs are not met by my partner. Sex together gets boring at times, and I need new material for my fantasies."

2. "My partner is not really my sexual type. I still like to have sex with a certain type of man."

3. "It's fun and adventure. The more variety and number of partners, the more adventure and fun."

4. "I have some kinky sexual interests that my partner doesn't share."

5. "We have found that having sex with others often enhances our sex together afterward."

6. "Sometimes I do it with another guy because I'm so angry at my lover."

7. "At times I get scared with how emotionally tied to each other we are. Having outside sex at times gives me a temporary distance I feel I need to have from my lover."

Other reasons include the nonavailability of a partner because of physical separations, illness, and temporary lack of sexual interest. The diminished frequency or absence of sex together as time passes are other reasons.

Sexual expression is seen by most men to have lots of different meanings. "I see sex with Peter on a whole bunch of levels. At times it's been the most important way we say how much we love each other. Sometimes we've made love in anger and then again to relieve our urges for sex. We've never felt that either of us should be sexual only with the other. From the beginning that was absurd. He knew as well as I that we would trick out, so why start our relationship by making rules and denying that probability? We do lots of things alone together, and we share those same activities with others. We have pleasant meals with others. We dance and party with others. And we have sex with others. Sex can be like a recreational sport and still maintain its specialness for us between ourselves. Our relationship is maintained by our love and willingness to make it work, not what we do with others in bed."

Ralph says it differently: "I did start my relationship with Brad with the intention of not having sex with others. Although a wide variety of sexual partners was part of my lifestyle, I was willing to give that up for a partner like Brad. Fortunately, Brad felt the same way about it. At first we had some mutual assumptions that we would be monogamous. Then when things got a little shaky between us, we made a verbal agreement to be sexually faithful."

As mentioned in Stage One, most couples experience sexual exclusivity early in the relationship. It is the natural outcome of limerence and with the decline in limerence, exclusivity sometimes remains an important ingredient in relationship stabilty.

Nearly three-quarters of the couples report that sexual exclusivity was either explicitly agreed upon or that they each had an implied assumption about it when they started living together. Explicit agreement means that the couple talked about it and both partners accepted sexual exclusivity as one of the bases of their coupling. Implied assumption means that the issue may or may not have been discussed but that both partners accepted the principle at some level from the outset.

Almost 17 percent of the couples had explicit or implied assumptions of nonexclusivity from the start. Another 10 percent had some level of nonagreement from the start. In most instances the partner who was not in favor of exclusivity gave only temporary assent to exclusivity. In two instances the partner who wanted sexual exclusivity agreed to experiment with having sex with others, even though he felt negatively about it.

Once they began having sex with others, most couples did not return to a permanently exclusive sexual relationship. However, in actual practice, a number of these couples report years of sexual exclusivity. Others agree to temporary periods of sexual exclusivity.

The biggest difficulty we uncovered in the discussion on this issue was the intellectual and emotional dichotomy the couples experience in putting sexual nonexclusivity into practice. In principle most accept the idea of sex play with others, but when their partner exercises the option, feelings of jealousy, fear of loss and abandonment, or just plain anger frequently erupt. In some instances the men are unaware that their partner's outside sexual contacts have been precipitated by their own irrational responses. This invariably set the stage for a disagreement, fight, or withdrawal. Many men say they recognize their double standard. "It's OK for me to have sex with someone else because I know how I feel about you, but it's not OK for you to do the same thing." The undelivered communication in these cases is, "because I can't or don't really trust you." It is a heritage of male training in our culture.

Many couples in the earliest years together linked faithfulness with sexual exclusivity, while couples with a longer history think faithfulness has little or nothing to do with sex. This difference is understood more easily when our participants speak for themselves.

"Although I didn't start living with Jim just for his sex appeal, I did want him only for myself. If he even looked at another guy I would be jealous and irritable. Then we started looking at other guys together. I learned that being sexually attracted to another person didn't diminish my feelings for Jim, but they did change. He was always careful of my feelings, thoughtful about me to the point that no one else had ever been. When I was depressed or disappointed he was there. When I was angry and headstrong he talked to me. When I was childish and irrational he let me cool off, but he didn't leave. After awhile, I began to see that his presence, dependability and responsiveness were the real issues of faithfulness and not whom he played with sexually, as long as I wasn't left out."

The culture does not provide for same-sex relationships. As a consequence men in younger relationships sometimes mimic culturally accepted norms, one of which is that partners in a relationship are the property of each other. Although two gay men enter the relationship as equals, the subtle, underlying assumption of mutual ownership creeps in. The deep human need to possess and be possessed may have its roots in our separation from mother, which once and for all establishes our total individuality, or it might be the human attempt to escape the inescapable fact of our existential isolation. The need to possess the partner, however, focuses most acutely on sexual fidelity, which symbolizes commitment to the relationship. If the partner violates or wants to violate that symbol of coupling, the threat to the relationship can be overwhelming.

As a result of this study, we believe that the single most important factor that keeps couples together past the ten-year mark is the lack of possessiveness they feel. Many couples learn very early in their relationship that ownership of each other sexually can become the greatest internal threat to their staying together.

Although most of the couples have some degree of sexual nonexclusivity, they have not reached these arrangements by the same routes, nor has it been easy for many of them. In fact, more than 85 percent of the couples report that their greatest relationship problems center on outside relationships, sexual and nonsexual.

The easiest couples to account for are those who began relationships with some sort of sexual nonexclusivity. Men in this group arrived at the agreement as a consequence of (1) experience from previous relationships, (2) knowledge of themselves that contradicted exclusivity, or (3) their partner's insistence on other options. Only one-sixth of our sample (twenty-six couples) are in this group. Yet by the end of the fifth year of relationship more than 95 percent are in this group. Bell and Weinberg warn:

> Moreover, it should be recognized that what has survival value in a heterosexual context may be destructive in a homosexual context, and vice versa. Life-enhancing mechanisms used by hetero-

sexual men and women should not necessarily be used as the standard by which to judge the degree of homosexuals' adjustment.[1]

Those men who start their relationships with high levels of limerence find that sexual exclusivity—either explicit or assumed—is not challenged until one partner finds these feelings on the wane. As we have discussed elsewhere, a decrease of enthrallment often brings about thoughts of ending the relationship. We speculate that this decreasing limerence and accompanying renewed sexual interest in others is the cause of the separation of many male couples in their first year. Couples who have survived this phase frequently have had surreptitious sexual contacts. Sometimes both partners had occasional sex contacts with others and withheld that fact. This situation can cause extraordinary tension that finally erupts in self-accusatory confessions or painful confrontations. Once the issue is out in the open, however, the couple has several methods of dealing with it.

1. They agree tentatively to a time-limited trial experiment with extrarelational sex. They might agree not to discuss these sexual contacts operating on the principle of "what I don't know won't hurt me."

2. They drop the issue for discussion, but each continues to think about it and fears losing his partner. Emotional estrangement can last for weeks or months until either the offended or the offender makes some counter-move that forces a discussion of the issue.

3. They discuss the issue but come to no conclusions. At this time the usual course of action is for one or the other to talk about it with friends and gain support for his position.

4. They discuss it and agree not to have sex with others. With these couples the issue comes up again and again, usually from the partner who did not have sex outside previously either because he now wants it, or because he wants reassurance that it has ceased.

5. They discuss it and decide to try sex with others within some limited framework. For example, both go to the baths together, or they have sex together with a third person.

Although couples develop trial ground rules using different combinations of the above approaches, they move toward permitting sex with others, often with clearly outlined rules about the recreational nature of that sex and a mutual promise to avoid emotional entanglements with sex partners.

Anticipating jealous feelings and threats to the relationship from sexual contacts with others, some couples are surprised to discover that the partner's sexual adventures not only are exciting to hear about, but also enhance their own sexual interactions. They remember intial efforts to carefully avoid discussing these sexual exploits, and later agree upon the importance and benefits of being honest and straightforward with each other.

In some cases one partner simply announces to the other his intentions of having sex with others. Sometimes this is put up as a trial balloon to test the partner. At other times the partner simply does what he said he was going to do and accepts the consequences. This method is one of the most disruptive. The offended partner is usually shocked, hurt, and then angry. Sometimes he goes so far as to move out for a time or force the other to move.

Some couples who start their relationship with implicit assumptions of exclusivity discover later that the assumptions they had made were incorrect. Neither really expected sexual exclusivity for himself, but thought the other did and had therefore followed those assumed rules.

Outlining the ways in which couples arrive at agreements for having sex with others does not convey the anguish, pain, hurt, and heartache that often accompanies such change. Nevertheless, developing a set of ground rules was reported to be very helpful.

The following is a list of some of the ground rules for sex with others our participants shared with us. It is not meant to be exhaustive or complete, but to provide the reader with a flavor of the diversity of approaches. Though some couples said they had no agreements at all about sexual partners, deeper probing usually revealed unspoken expectations.

1. Sex is allowed at such places as the baths, where having a brief sexual interchange is a mutual and unspoken understanding.
2. No sex with mutual friends.

3. Sexual encounters must not interfere with the couple's customary or planned time together.

4. Sex is permissible only when one is out of town.

5. Sexual encounters are always verbally shared with the lover.

6. Talking about it is expected, but it must be at least 48 hours after the sex took place.

7. Outside sex is allowed only with advance agreement of one's lover.

8. No emotional involvement with sex partners is allowed.

9. Outside sex is permissible in three-ways or group sex only.

10. Outside sex is permissible, but never discuss it.

11. Outside sex is not permissible at home or if it is permitted at home, not while partner is there alone.

12. Outside sex is permitted at home in the partner's absence, but not in certain places, such as in the couple's bedroom.

13. Secondary emotional relationships with sexual friends are allowed, but the lover is not to be excluded.

Many of these rules appear alone or in some combination. At times they may change, be dropped, or be replaced by new ones. The important point here is that, generally speaking, some framework is set for sex with others. Our observations lead us to think that these rules are attempts at control in an area that continues to be an elusive source of anxiety and fear for most couples. They feel that the sexual monster inside of each of us needs bridling. We do not trust it in our partners, and least of all in ourselves.

Sex by Stages

In Stage One there is an intense sexual excitement usually mutual and uninhibited. Couples recall frequent and often lengthy lovemaking that is highly passionate at some times, low-keyed at others. Total body exploration is remembered to be a sensual, adventuresome, and highly gratifying aspect of lovemaking. Eager to please their partners and be pleasured in return, they frankly and directly share with each other their sexual fantasies, desires, and feelings. Both verbally and nonverbally, each man in turn communicates to his partner his own sexual and sensual turn-ons—touches, pressures, positions, tastes, sounds, and sights. With sexually inexperienced men, the more practiced partner guides his lover in learning more about himself. Again, high levels of enthrallment in the first year dampen the desire for extrarelational sex, and most couples find themselves sexually exclusive. A sharp decline in masturbation without the partner is experienced. Toward the end of this stage the most common form of additional sexual involvement occurs by occasionally bringing another man into their sex together (a three-way).

In Stage Two there is a gradual decline in the frequency of sex, from daily to a few times per week. Couples talk about an increased knowledge and attentiveness to their partners' likes and dislikes in lovemaking. The amount of time during lovemaking and sexual play is not as long as it was in their first year and continues to include nongenital and nonerogenous body exploration and stimulation. There is more expression of affection, such as holding, cuddling, and caressing. Couples often begin to have sexual experiences outside the relationship if they were sexually exclusive at the outset. If they have not paired with a man who meets or approximates their physical or sexual ideal or both, they experience a renewed interest in seeking fantasy types in extrarelational sexual activities. An interest in masturbation without the partner also returns if it diminished in Stage One.

Depending upon how they are dealing with conflict and handling reappearance of the individuals, Stage Three couples can experience a continuation of tenderness and open affection. At the same time, however, each partner experiences confusion over individual or mutual decline in intense sexual attraction to the other. They experience a greater desire for a variety of sexual partners and for sexual novelty, especially for those sexual activities that the partner dislikes or finds difficult to gratify. Competition for sexual partners can increase, especially in men closer in age. By the end of the first five years, all couples in this study have moved past any agreement to a permanent monogamous relationship they might have had, though they might have long periods of sexual exclusivity.

After five or more years together there is a thoughtful reappraisal of the relationship among Stage Four couples. Reappraisal about sexuality also occurs at this time. With the decline in jealousy, more effective communication develops around sex with others. Talking about it usually progresses to the establishment of new ground rules like those mentioned above, and frequently precipitates some rejuvenation in the couple's sexual lives together. They try new behaviors with each other that have not been present in their previous sexual repertoires. They have greater security about outside sexual partners because they feel more secure in the relationship and its history.

When Stage Five begins there is a decline in the frequency of sex together, but, almost paradoxically, couples report that the quality of their lovemaking is higher at this time. There is a decline in the urgency of orgasmic release, with a consequent increase in cuddling, holding, and caressing. Many describe changes in their individual sexual interests or in their fantasy types or behaviors. We find a greater acceptance of each other's more exotic sexual desires, which goes hand in hand with easier communication. Although this period may be accentuated by some degree of partner competitiveness over sexual escapades with others, the couple shares these partners more freely.

Near the end of Stage Five there is a marked decrease in sexual frequency or even long periods of abstinence with each other. There is decline in intensity and desire for most couples. There are more frequent complaints about changes in one's own and the partner's body, more difficulty in finding outside sexual partners, and an even greater intensity in competitiveness over them. Most couples in this phase use some words that translate into boredom with their sexual routine together.

In Stage Six relationships there usually is an overall relationship renewal. For many couples there is a renewal of interest and enjoyment with each other and a return to more affection and tenderness. Sometimes this is translated to sex and sometimes not. There is a considerable decline in sexual activity outside the relationship if such has not already occurred.

After three decades together the usual male couple reaches its highest level of peace and contentment. These qualities are reflected in sexual expression. Most of the couples report satisfaction with their sex together but also experience a marked decline in frequency. In fact, most of our couples minimize the importance of sex at this time but emphasize their continuing needs for affection, tenderness, and closeness.

This brief outline of sexual attitude and behavior change presents the usual features we found in the development of male couples. The wide variations that can and do exist with couples were not addressed. These variations are related to ages, age differences, social backgrounds, previous relationships, and many other factors.

Importance of Sex

Seventeen men in this study tell us that sex is always important to the relationship. These seventeen respondents all have been in their relationships from one to five years, usually in the first three years, which highlights the probability that sexual expression during this high-romance period is more important than later in the relationship. Two hundred and ninety-five respondents agree that sex is sometimes important, more for some than for others, but not a single subject indicates that sex is never important. Many couples also mention that their mutual freedom to express their sexuality with others is one of the most important factors that maintains their bonding. The remainder of this chapter focuses on the individual's sexual development, past experiences, and, finally, special features of the sexuality of the relationships in this study.

Learning About Sex

(Table 35)

More than 83 percent of the men in this group learned about sex mainly on their own, usually from boys their own age or slightly older. By the age of seven most report knowing that babies somehow or other came from mothers. Attaching this bit of information to sexual coitus came later for most, between the ages of ten and fourteen; a few did not really understand the fact until they were fifteen or older. Only 3 percent of the men remember having parental instruction about sex. This was provided by mothers in six instances and by fathers in three. The nine men who report acquiring the information from their parents have vague memories about it but generally admit that they were either unbelieving or indifferent about the knowledge at the time. Twenty-eight participants learned the facts of life from a sibling or

TABLE 35
HOW THEY LEARNED ABOUT SEX

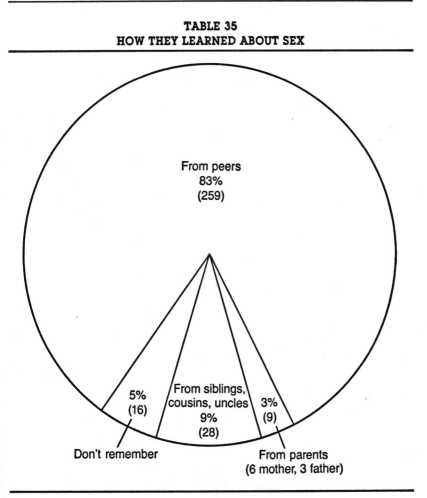

From peers
83%
(259)

5%
(16)

From siblings,
cousins, uncles
9%
(28)

3%
(9)

Don't remember

From parents
(6 mother, 3 father)

some other close relative like an uncle or cousin. A small percentage do not remember how they acquired information about sex.

Prepubertal Sex Play

(Table 36)

Nearly two-thirds of these men recall sex play before the onset of adolescence. This childhood behavior usually took the form of games like playing doctor or nurse, playing house, or simply swapping looks at each other. These sex rehearsal activities occurred between the ages of five and ten, with the highest number recalling ages six and seven as the exact time of the activities. More than three-quarters of our sample had their first such play with other boys their own age or somewhat older. A small number of men with prepubertal homosexual play report their first experiences were with boys who themselves were postpubertal, around fourteen or fifteen. Slightly more men had a sexual experience in adolescence with older men. These older men were family, friends, relatives, or sometimes youth or church leaders. About the same number of men recall sex play or exploration with a brother or sister during this period.

Less than one in five remembers being discovered by parents or other adults during their childhood sex play and being punished or scolded for it. Most recall feelings of guilt or recognizing that sex play was something of which their parents would disapprove. A very few report high levels of sexual activity during their childhood years with both boys and girls.

The wide variety of activities that constitute the prepubertal sex play most often includes looking at and touching the genitals of the other. In addition to these activities a number recall mounting attempts, oral–genital play, mutual body rubbing, and, more frequently among boys, observing and competing with each other how far or how high they could urinate. Two men in our study were penetrated anally before age ten.

Age of First Orgasm

A few men recall experiencing orgasm without ejaculation between the ages of nine and twelve. The remainder associate their first orgasm with ejaculation, which occurred either through direct genital manipulation or nocturnal emission. More than half of the men cannot recall with any certainty when their first orgasm occurred.

One man experienced his first ejaculation after age sixteen. The other 311 report their first ejaculations occurring between eleven and fifteen, with the highest frequency occurring at age thirteen. Almost a quarter of the men report their first ejaculations as nocturnal emissions. A number tell how thrilled and frightened they were by the ex-

TABLE 36
PREPUBERTAL SEX PLAY

	Number of Participants	Percentage of Participants
Some prepubertal play	200	64.2
Remember first play with boys	150	75
First with another boy around 14–15	23	11.5
Experience with older men	23	11.5
Play with siblings	31	15.5

perience. Fear of being detected by parents is mentioned often. Some tell of feeling that there was something wrong with them.

Masturbation

(Tables 37, 38, 39 and 40)

Forty-two percent of the group learned about autoeroticism through self-discovery. Some say they had read about it, others discovered it while stroking or fondling their own penises in the shower, bathtub, or bed. Fifty percent of the men learned about it from peers or older boys while only a few learned about it from older men. Eight men began regular masturbation at age nine but by age fourteen almost all of the participants had begun masturbation. All of the men have masturbated; most still do.

TABLE 37
HOW LEARNED ABOUT MASTURBATION

	Number of Participants	Percentage of Participants
Self-discovery	131	42.0
Sibling	15	4.8
Peers	122	39.0
Older boy	34	11.0
Man	10	3.2

TABLE 38
AGE OF BEGINNING OF MASTURBATION

	Number of Participants	Percentage of Participants
9	8	2.6
10	12	3.8
11	32	10.3
12	63	20.2
13	107	34.3
14	85	27.2
15	4	1.3
16	1	0.3

We asked for information on solitary masturbation practices in the month preceding the interview. Most (84 percent) of the respondents had masturbated at least once per week up to more than once daily during this time period. Eleven percent had not masturbated at all during that month.

We asked them the method of masturbation they had used in the beginning. Ninety-two percent used their hands, nineteen rubbed their penises against the bedclothes, a towel, or carpet; and six employed some method of penile insertion into toilet paper rolls, vacuum cleaner hoses, or other improvised receptacles.

The information given about attitudes and feelings toward masturbation is most informative. Some of the younger men in this study have never experienced any negative feelings about self-pleasuring. These represent a small minority of the sample. Most of the men experienced periods of intense guilt and shame around their earliest masturbation. Some of the older men remember well the admonitions they heard in childhood about the "wicked evil of self-abuse." Most of them laugh about it now, especially when they learn that masturba-

TABLE 39
METHOD OF MASTURBATION AT ONSET

	Number of Participants	Percentage of Participants
Manual stimulation	287	92.0
Rubbing aginst bed/towel/ carpet	19	6.0
Inserting penis	6	2.0

TABLE 40
CURRENT SOLITARY MASTURBATION DATA
(within month preceding interview)

	Number of Participants	Percentage of Participants
None	34	11.0
Less than once per week	19	6.0
1 time weekly	34	11.0
2 times weekly	92	29.5
3 times weekly	99	31.6
Daily	25	8.0
More than 1 time daily	9	2.9

tion is being used widely by sex therapists to correct many problems in sexual functioning. Many of the younger men also recall the highly negative attitude, especially of parents or religious sources, about masturbation. Some talk about how they fought against it, making promises to God not to do it again.

"It felt good but I knew it must be bad. My father tried to tell me about it. He talked about touching myself 'down there' and that I wouldn't be able to have a normal sex life later if I did it."

"I caught my brother playing with himself once. Up till then I thought I was the only one who did it."

"I went to confession so often that I guessed everyone knew. The priest would always tell me to pray to the Blessed Virgin and to say my rosary. I made promise after promise to Mary that I'd stop. The guilt finally went away when I was about twenty-five."

At the time of our interviews virtually all of the participants, at least intellectually, have accepted masturbation. Many are ambivalent about accepting it as completely "normal" but state that they are not as negatively inclined as they had been in the past. Some individuals, however, admit that they continue to feel guilty about their own masturbation, especially because they have a willing sex partner available most of the time. Solitary masturbation still seems to be one of the most private areas for the men in this study.

"I shouldn't need to when Ted's always around and eager to go."

"I know all the books say it's OK but I still feel funny talking about it like this. Some voice in the back of my head tells me it is wrong."

"It's one of the great joys of my life. Without it I'm sure I would have gone stark raving mad at times. I love to take a long time to masturbate."

Although we do not specifically ask questions about changes in masturbation over time, the point is raised frequently enough to deserve comment here. Some men began masturbation at twelve, thirteen, or fourteen and stopped for long periods of time in their late teens or early twenties, usually because they were trying to overcome the "habit." Others indicate that having frequent sexual encounters with others drastically reduced their own desire to masturbate. A bit less than one-fifth of the men report periods in their lives when they were masturbating many times daily, using it sometimes as pleasure, sometimes as tension release, and sometimes simply as a manifestation of their anxiety over some issue. Several men tell us that they used masturbation as a reward to follow the accomplishment of some particularly distasteful task.

An interesting variation on the reasons for attempting to stop masturbation among these men is the fact that the majority of them employed homoerotic fantasies for their masturbation. Many report thinking that if they stopped masturbating the homesexual thoughts and feelings would subside or disappear. In fact some did substitute heterosexual fantasies with varying degrees of success.

"In my early twenties, when I was still in college, I hated to masturbate because I would always fantasize about other guys, roommates, friends, etc. It was awful."

"I tried thinking about girls when I'd jerk off. *Playboy* was always around, but I'd find myself looking for pictures of guys instead."

Age of First Homosexual Experience

(Table 41)

By their sixteenth birthdays, almost three-quarters of the men had had their first homosexual experience. By the end of their twenty-second year nearly all had their first experience. The remaining few had been introduced to homosexual activity by the end of their thirtieth year. The largest clustering is between ages twelve and fifteen. The range of activities in these first homosexual experiences once again runs the

TABLE 41
AGE OF FIRST HOMOSEXUAL EXPERIENCE

Age	Number of Participants	Percentage of Participants
11	12	3.8
12	38	12.2
13	61	19.6
14	79	25.3
15	42	13.5
16	18	5.8
17	12	3.8
18	17	5.5
19	3	1.0
20	6	1.9
21	4	1.3
22	7	2.2
23	3	1.0
24	1	0.3
25	2	0.6
26	1	0.3
27	3	1.0
28	1	0.3
29	1	0.3
30	1	0.3

Number of participants = 312

gamut from looking, touching, and masturbating together, to mutual fellatio and anal intercourse for a few.

Most of the experiences that occurred before age sixteen were not seen by the individuals concerned as homosexual. The person looked upon the activity as pleasant, fun, and sexual, but not specifically homosexual. Many men report that the object of their first homosexual encounter has long since married and had children. In 21 percent of our sample, the first homosexual experience was an isolated or infrequent event that was limited to a few times with a lapse of many years before subsequent encounters. For a far larger portion, the first experiences were followed almost from the beginning by a long series of encounters with other boys and men.

Some participants were distressed enough by their early homosexual activity that they sought counseling or medical help. Some fled into heterosexual expression and marriage before returning to homosexual partners.

Sixteen men whose first experience occurred prior to sixteen had their first experience with a person five or more years older than themselves. In almost every case the older person was a close friend or relative.

Several of the participants remember their first experiences with vivid details reminiscent of a pornographic story. These men had enthusiastic responses to their earliest experiences, and frequently never looked back but only forward to more frequent and longer sexual experiences with same-sex partners.

Age of First Heterosexual Experience

(Table 42)

Approximately one-quarter of the men have had no postpubertal heterosexual experience. Nearly three-quarters have had at least one such experience after puberty. Forty-seven men were married, and another fifty-one lived with female lovers for three or more months at some time in their lives. Of those 225 men who had heterosexual experiences, 62 percent had done so by the end of their eighteenth year, with the largest cluster in years sixteen to eighteen. Another 28 percent had heterosexual contact before age twenty-five, and the final 9 percent were between ages twenty-six and forty-two when they had their first sexual contact with a woman.

When asked about sex with women, many of the eighty-seven respondents with no sexual contact with women seem surprised and amused, and a few are even disgusted. These latter are in the minority, but there are a few. More commonly, we are told that they had considered it and might not refuse if the opportunity arose. They did not indicate that they actively sought out a woman for sex, however.

Men who had their first heterosexual experiences before age nineteen are the largest group. Some of these men proceeded along conventional heterosexual lines and married, even though they had had occasional or even frequent homosexual contacts. Men in this

TABLE 42
AGE OF FIRST HETEROSEXUAL EXPERIENCE

Age	Number of Participants	Percentage of Participants
11	2	0.9
12	5	2.2
13	8	3.6
14	15	6.7
15	19	8.4
16	27	12.0
17	31	13.8
18	32	14.2
19	11	4.9
20	8	3.6
21	13	5.8
22	6	2.7
23	7	3.1
24	6	2.7
25	14	6.2
26	2	0.9
27	3	1.3
28	1	0.4
29	2	0.9
30	5	2.2
32	2	6.9
35	3	1.3
39	1	0.4
42	2	0.9

Number of participants = 225

group commonly explain that they had hoped that if they married their homosexual interest would disappear. Some of the unmarried had sexual experiences with women because of peer pressure to conform. High-school or college buddies insisted or, for some in the military, visiting prostitutes was de rigueur. Some of the men in this group continued intermittent sexual contact with women before their first homosexual experience. Although they generally found sex with women enjoyable, or at least acceptable, their first homosexual experience rang their bells as never before. The intensity of their sexual and emotional connection with a same-sex person overshadowed all of their prior opposite-sex experience.

"When I had my first gay sex, I just *knew* I was home! I've been doing it ever since."

As explained in chapter 11, some of the men who married or lived with women as lovers did so because of family pressure. Others did so because they wanted to have children. Some found that social life and companionship with women was better than with men until they found their current partners.

The men who were twenty-five or older before experiencing sex with a woman did so for a variety of reasons. Some wanted the experience and had a female friend who knew of their homosexuality. Some had casual sexual liaisons with women friends at different times. A few had sexual experiences with lesbians because both wanted to try it. Generally speaking, our participants talk positively about their sexual experiences with women. The large majority, however, found them unsatisfying in the long run and emotionally unfulfilling. Added to this is their strong attraction to men. We do not find that men in our study simply choose homosexuality over heterosexuality as a preference. Most feel that although they have functioned well sexually with women, their emotional, sexual, and affectional attraction is to males.

Some men found that they simply could not have erections with women, although they got sexual pleasure from touching and fondling. Some felt badly because they were not aroused and as a consequence have not attempted such contact again. We do not have numerical data on the numbers who have experienced "performance failure" with women, but it is relatively high by our best estimates.

Kinsey Scale Self-Ratings

(Table 43)

The participants are asked to rate themselves on the Kinsey 0–6 scale of sexual behavior and fantasy for the year preceding the interview.[2] The Kinsey scale rates a person's sexual activities with 0 representing the exclusive heterosexual and 6 representing the exclusive homosexual. No man in the study rates himself below a Kinsey 4 either in his behavior or in his fantasy life during the preceding year. Not surprisingly, the highest percentage rate themselves Kinsey 6 in both behav-

TABLE 43
SELF-RATING ON THE KINSEY SCALE
(in the year preceding the interview)

	0	1	2	3	4	5	6
Behavior					22 (7.0%)	34 (11.0%)	256 (82.0%)
Fantasy					27 (8.5%)	50 (16.0%)	235 (75.5%)

0 = Exclusively heterosexual with no homosexual
1 = Predominantly heterosexual with only incidentally homosexual
2 = Predominantly heterosexual with more than incidentally homosexual
3 = Equally heterosexual and homosexual
4 = Predominantly homosexual but with more than incidentally heterosexual
5 = Predominantly homosexual but incidentally heterosexual
6 = Exclusively homosexual

ior (82.0 percent) and fantasy (75.5 percent). However, 18.0 percent rate themselves as 4s or 5s in behavior over the previous year. This means that fifty-six of the men had one or more sexual experiences with a woman during that time. A slightly higher percentage report themselves as 4s or 5s in their sexual fantasy life.

Some amount of sexual contact with women is not a surprising finding considering how common opposite-sex friendships are among our participants.

Patterns of Sexual Development

Each partner's sexual development affects the couple's sex life together, so it is useful to look at these men's prior homosexual experiences. We have been able to identify five general patterns of sexual development among the men in our sample. Many of the men fit only marginally into one pattern, while others represent a mixture of patterns. Nonetheless, the following patterns of development describe the majority of our participants.

Pattern One

This man usually had his first sexual experience at around age five or six, most commonly with a boy, and from then on had a clear awareness of his attraction to males. Although he had many experiences with both boys and girls in childhood and even into adolescence, he knew his primary erotic attraction was for males, and he acted upon that. He sometimes had negative feelings about his homosexuality but for the most part has always been interested in other men. He may or may not have been in a relationship prior to the present one, but he has had numerous brief gay relationships and has been sexually active with males all the time. He has been to bars and baths and has participated in group sex. He is proud to be gay and is far out of the closet.

Pattern Two

This person tried to be heterosexual. He often had his first same-sex experience at around thirteen or fourteen, then consciously avoided such experiences, putting all his energy into school and scholastic attainment. He dated girls in high school. While in college he began furtive and clandestine homosexual contacts in public toilets or parks. Also while in college, he met the woman he married. After getting married he continued his occasional homosexual contacts in baths or while away on business. He had children but continued to feel unsatisfied. The gradual deterioration of his marriage increased his homosexual liaisons. After the divorce his emotional and sexual partners were exclusively men. He admits that his suppressed homosexuality, not his wife, was the reason the marriage ended. He had many sexual experiences before meeting his present partner.

Pattern Three

Although this person had one or two same-sex contacts in early adolescence, he denied that part of himself for many years. He usually was a devoutly religious man. He was a leader, well-liked by peers and adults. He always had his eye out for the attractive athlete or the handsome man but adamantly denied that to himself and to the world. In high school and college he focused his energy on being well-liked by both men and women. He dated women but never became seriously involved. His masturbatory fantasies were usually about roommates or classmates, and he hated himself for it. In his early twenties he finally gave in and began having occasional homosexual experiences. His gradual self-acceptance and growing positive feelings about homosexuality allowed him to try living with another man whom he loved. He may have had one or two such relationships before the one in this study.

Pattern Four

This person may not have been sexually active at an early age but acquired some of the stereotypic feminine interests, gestures, and behaviors that caused others to label him a "sissy" in early childhood. Some overcame a large portion of these stylized mannerisms. Others carried them into adult life. The typical man in this pattern may have been approached by other boys in adolescence but usually in a provocative and assaultive fashion rather than in the interest of mutual sexual play. He saw himself as the stereotypical "faggot" and behaved accordingly. He offered his anus for penetration and his mouth for insertion by as many men as he could summon, seduce, or command. He recalls his behavior at the time as extremely hostile. He had few satisfying emotional relationships while growing up but finally began to find himself and accept his maleness and his homosexuality. Although he continues to use campy language and the feminine pronoun when talking about some men and to crossdress for special occasions and parties, he has found a new acceptance and love with his current partner. He talks about continuing to grow and change.

Pattern Five

This person came from a family where sex was especially taboo. Correct dress, behavior, and demeanor were the main rules of his parents, who wanted him to be the "best little boy in the world." He wore proper suits and ties and frequently was sent away to boarding school where he had his first introduction to the mysteries of sex with other boys. He played at sports because his father thought it was proper. He learned about masturbation by himself and was excessively clean and furtive about it. During high school he found sex in the sleazy, off-beat places where older men would fellate him. His academic performance was topflight, and he progressed to other good schools. His sexual life was clandestine and, in his eyes, progressively dirtier. He rarely, if ever, dated. He continues to see sex as a disdainful animal instinct, but with equal passion he sought it out in public toilets and with hustlers as he grew older. Now in middle life he has a partner whom he loves and respects; however, he continues to have negative feelings about his own sexuality.

There are many variations on these five themes. Sexuality and its expression have presented problems for everyone at some time in their lives. Some of these men have had minimal difficulty with it. Some have scars from their homosexuality. Some are still floundering because of their own homophobia or self-oppression that has influenced their development. These negative influences have prevented them from connecting sex with love.

Sexual Expression in the Relationship

(Tables 44, 45 and 46)

Contrary to the old popular belief, men in this study do not assume male or female roles in their sex with each other. As there is a fluid interchangeability of functions in their everyday lives, a similar degree of versatility was found in their sexual expression. This information agrees with what other researchers have found (Bell and Weinberg,[3] Saghir and Robins,[4] Harry and DeVall[5]).

The general trend is toward decreasing frequency as years in the relationship increase. Most participants are having sexual contact with their partners at the time of our interviews, but this has not always been the case with every couple. Some tell us that they have had periods of sexual abstinence lasting a year or more.

Of the many sexual behaviors listed for us by the men in this study, only two are engaged in by 100 percent of our sample: kissing with hugging and body rubbing (including fondling of the penis). Tongue kissing (French kissing) is practiced by almost the entire sample, and 95 percent have been fellated by their partners during the year. For some couples the principal method of sexual expression is oral–genital contact. In more than 90 percent of those who use fellatio, the activity is reciprocal. Many couples employ a wide variety of techniques with each sexual encounter, while others have a repertoire of one or two techniques at each encounter. Some describe long sex sessions together lasting from one to several hours.

TABLE 44
TYPE OF SEXUAL BEHAVIOR
(in descending order of frequency in the year prior to interview)

	Number of Participants	Percentage of Sample
Kissing and hugging	312	100.0
Body rubbing and kissing	312	100.0
Tongue kissing	308	98.7
Fellatio	298	95.5
Being fellated	297	95.2
Mutual masturbation	290	92.9
Masturbation together	286	91.7
Mutual fellatio (69)	286	91.7
Being penetrated anally	220	71.0
Penetrating anally	220	71.0
Analingus (doing)	131	42.0
Analingus (receiving)	131	42.0
Other (S & M, bondage, watersports)	22	7.1

Number of participants = 312

All of the participants fondle their partners' penises, and 93 percent use mutual masturbatory techniques with each other. Many couples use intracrural penile containment (between the legs) at some time or other, and may even identify it as mutual masturbation. A high percentage of these men practice masturbation together almost as

TABLE 45
FREQUENCY OF SEXUAL CONTACT BETWEEN PARTNERS

Length of Time in Relationship	More Than 4 Times Weekly	2–3 Times Weekly	1 Time Per Week	2–3 Times Per Month
Years	(%)	(%)	(%)	(%)
1–3	86	14		
3–5	72	23	5	
5–10	51	32	17	
10–15	22	35	35	8
15–20	9	27	51	13
20 plus	0	12	46	42

TABLE 46
LEVEL OF SEXUAL SATISFACTION WITH PARTNER

(a) Current level of Satisfaction

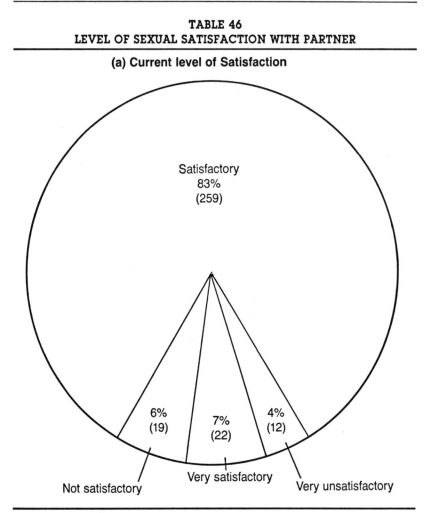

often as mutual masturbation. This may occur simultaneously, or the partners may watch each other for increased erotic stimulation.

Mutual, simultaneous fellatio (69, *soixante-neuf*) is practiced by more than 90 percent of the couples. This technique may or may not include ejaculation and orgasm for both partners.

Seventy-one percent participate in anal intercourse. It is used by some couples as their most frequent sexual behavior. In a few cases one partner is always the inserter and the other always the recipient. These couples explain that each prefers being the doer or receiver

TABLE 46, cont.
LEVEL OF SEXUAL SATISFACTION WITH PARTNER

(b) Change in Level of Satisfaction Since Beginning of Relationship

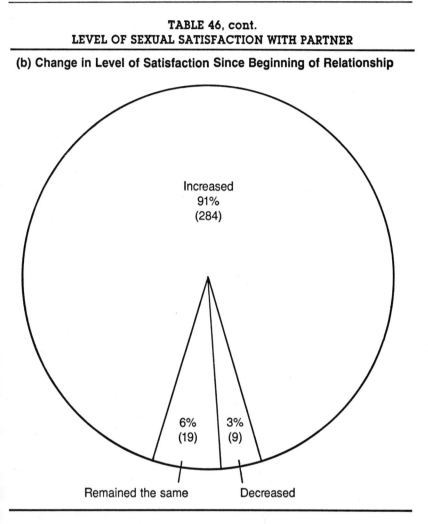

Increased
91%
(284)

6%   3%
(19)   (9)

Remained the same   Decreased

without any thought to roles. More commonly, each partner functions in either position, whether during the same sexual encounter or at different times. In our sample the incidence of reciprocal behavior is high.

Forty-one percent of our respondents have participated in some oral–anal sex play in the preceding year. Analingus was preferred by far fewer participants than anal intercourse.[6] There is, however, a high level of anal eroticism among these couples.

Many couples, while they do not engage in other sexual activities, express some interest in experimenting with their partners. Many men with sadomasochistic interests not shared by their partners seek such experiences outside the relationship. Most couples limit their behaviors together to those described above, reserving their other behaviors for expression with other partners similarly interested. We did interview a few couples who have extensive sadomasochistic lovemaking rituals with each other that include bondage, mild whipping, humiliations of various sorts, urolagnia (interest in urine and urination), and various forms of submission. One couple talks briefly of "fisting," which has become widely publicized in the gay community in recent years.[7]

Ejaculation and orgasm occur in well over 95 percent of the sexual encounters reported by our participants. Some, especially the older ones, agree that they have experienced a marked reduction in their own personal pressure to have orgasm with each and every sexual contact.

In describing their general approach to lovemaking our couples talk about the good feelings they experience with each other in being sexual. At times affectionate interchange is an important part of their sex, and at other times it is sex for sex alone. As with most gay men our participants do not use the term *foreplay*. Rather, they put all behaviors under the rubric of *lovemaking* or simply *sex*.

Sexual Enhancers

The widespread use of drugs that have the reputation of increasing sexual enjoyment is well known by the majority of participants. Many have tried or regularly use marijuana and alcohol. The use of the nitrites, both amyl and butyl, has become common over the past decade. The ready availability of butyl nitrite as a legal, over-the-counter "incense" or "room deodorizer" has greatly increased its usage.[8] Some couples use it with great regularity, while others never have used it. Some of the younger participants have tried other drugs, such as methaqualone (quaaludes or ludes), which has the reputation of being a potent aphrodisiac. Among all drugs, alcohol is far and away the most commonly used substance.

Other than drugs there is a wide assortment of sex toys available, including artificial penises or dildos and rings made from metal, leather, plastic, or rubber. When these rings are applied to the base of the penis and the underside of the scrotum close against the pelvis they have a tourniquet-like action that purportedly prolongs erection. Vibrators, leather and plastic adornments that attach to the penis, scrotum, or nipples; and objects for anal insertion also are available but much less frequently used. Leather harnesses, hoods and masks, slings, and paddles, along with many other imaginative items, are used for enhancing sex play.

Various lubricants for anal penetration are used frequently, including commercially available ones such as K-Y jelly, Surgi-lube, Crisco, and a variety of others specifically marketed for sexual use.

Many couples have a wide assortment of homoerotic pornography. Some collect magazines and pictures, others collect novels, and still others have movies and videotapes they enjoy together or with friends.

Sexual Dysfunction

(Table 47)

We include problems of sexual desire, arousal, and orgasm. Most persons have experienced sexual dysfunction in these categories at some time in their lives. We are interested in the sexual problems that couples report causing upset in their sexual lives. One-quarter of the men tell us they had experienced or are experiencing some form of sexual dysfunction, either with their partners or with others.

Thirty-five men have experienced or are experiencing difficulties with erection at the time of the interview. For several the ability to maintain an erection during sex play has been a problem from early adulthood onward.

"I always can get an erection, especially before we take our clothes off, but then I lose it pretty fast. It may or may not come back. I guess it depends on how much concern I have about it."

Some develop erective problems later in life. Some experience no difficulty with their partners but always have difficulty with others. None of these men has organic problems by history. All claim to have

TABLE 47
SEX DYSFUNCTIONS

	Number of Participants	Percentage of Participants
Erective failure	35	43.0
Premature ejaculation	9	12.0
Retarded ejaculation	15	18.0
Decreased desire	22	27.0
Lack of interest	8	9.9
Aversion to		
anal intercourse	11	13.5
fellatio	2	2.4
mutual masturbation	1	1.2
Number of participants = 81		

had erections at other times, either by self-stimulation or on early morning awakening.

A few men have had their worst difficulties with failures at the beginning of the relationship. In three cases many months went by before the individual felt relaxed and accepted enough by his partner for the natural processes of sexual arousal to take over. Several men report problems they say stemmed from their negative feelings about being homosexual.

Premature ejaculation is seen less commonly among gay men than among heterosexual men.[9] In this sample twelve men had experienced difficulty. Five of them were married or living with women when it happened. The remaining seven have experienced the problem with men. Usually they experienced high arousal very early in the sexual contact. The least touch or brief manipulation rapidly brought them to ejaculation. In a few, rapid ejaculation occurs if they are fellated or penetrate their partners anally.

Retarded ejaculation is seen more frequently among gay men than in nongay men.[10] The men with this dysfunction are able to obtain and maintain erections with no difficulty. Most often they are not able to reach orgasm with their partner. They feel frustrated and often angry and then disappointed with themselves for being unable to reach a climax.

Inhibition of sexual desire is lack of interest in sex or aversion to some or all sexual behavior. Eight of the men have had significant periods when they had no desire to be sexual. These periods are not associated with circumstances such as serious illnesses, depressions, or periods of mourning. The men usually describe these times by saying, "I was totally turned off. If somebody initiated the sex and I got into it, there was no problem with functioning. I just wasn't ever interested enough to seek it out or initiate it with my partner."

We do not find any men with aversion to all sexual activities, but rather only to specific behaviors that cause problems for them personally or for their partners. Aversion to anal intercourse is the most common. Although more men have aversion to being penetrated, several report equally strong aversion to penetrating. Aversions to fellatio and mutual masturbation are less frequent.

Evidence exists that sexual dysfunctions occur less often among homosexual men than among heterosexual men (Haeberle,[11] Masters and Johnson,[12] McWhirter and Mattison[13]). Nevertheless, the anguish that occurs as a consequence is as devastating. Perhaps, however, the major difference between heterosexual and homosexual persons is that sexual activity with another man is less goal-directed and more focused on generalized sensuality and pleasure, as has been noted by Masters and Johnson.[14]

CHAPTER 15

SUMMARY OF THE FINDINGS

To the researchers, so familiar with the data, too much seems to deserve highlighting in the summary. However, when confronting each other with the question, "What are the dozen most useful findings," it was less difficult than we expected to agree on the following twelve discoveries and conclusions.

1. A relationship has an existence of its own. It is a combination of two, but it is more than the sum of the two. We began to see relationships as having a life of their own.

2. As separate entities, the relationships established by the men in our study pass through a series of stages, each stage having balancing characteristics to keep the relationship together.

3. The single most important factor keeping these men together for the first decade is finding compatibility, especially through complementarity. In the second decade it is lack of possessiveness.

4. The majority of couples in our study, and all of the couples together for longer than five years, were not continuously sexually exclusive with each other. Although many had long periods of sexual exclusivity, it was not the ongoing expectation for most. We found that gay men *expect* mutual emotional dependability with their partners and that relationship fidelity transcends concerns about sexuality and exclusivity.

5. By finding these 156 couples, with close to a third of the sample living together longer than ten years, we did dispel the old myth that gay male relationships do not last. Also, in the past few years we have met additional male couples who have been together for forty and fifty years. Male couples in ongoing and long-term relationships are not as unusual a phenomenon as was formerly believed.

6. All of these couples have devised their own special ways of making their relationships satisfying. Their styles of relationship were developed without the aid of visible role models available to heterosexual couples.

7. Couples with greatest relationship longevity have the largest differences in ages. All of the couples in our study who were together for longer than 30 years (8 couples) have an age difference of between five and sixteen years.

8. Male couples have some unique features that distinguish them from heterosexual and lesbian couples. Their relationship *equality* is different. Similarities in *social scripting* make male couples different. And often they have an *economic* advantage because of their joint male incomes.

9. Antihomosexual attitudes influence their relationships and their lives. These attitudes include ignorance about homosexuality, prejudice against themselves or other homosexual people, homophobia itself, self-oppression, and oppression by others.

10. These couples form family units just as stable, dependable, and contributing to the commonwealth as any traditional nuclear family. Many participate actively in civic, church, neighborhood, and political life, most often alongside their nongay neighbors and friends, who accept and embrace them as the individuals and couples they are.

11. One of the more surprising findings was among couples together beyond twenty years. Almost as if the twentieth year is some kind of a watershed, men together beyond that time more often than not report a renewal in the pleasure, companionship, and excitement of their togetherness.

12 One of our more obvious discoveries, which seems clearly evident with hindsight, is the simple idea that the reasons why couples stay together in the first year are very different from the reasons they are together in the fifth, tenth, or thirtieth year. We started out with some naive notion that we would find that love or affection was the binding force in the partnerships. We did find a lot of love, but that it is not by love alone that these relationships thrive.

These are the twelve most salient findings in this investigation. It is our hope that this project will plant seeds, questions, and ideas. As we wrote in the introduction, we think this study demands a reevaluation of male couples.

CHAPTER 16

FUTURE RESEARCH, SPECULATIONS, AND RECOMMENDATIONS

Now that this study is told, what might we ask or say about the future for gay people and their relationships? We will take our authors' privilege and speculate about the near and distant future. Finally, we have a few suggestions and recommendations.

Topics for Future Research

Dozens of new research questions have jumped at us and there are more to come. We can list only a few.

1. A similar study of female couples and opposite-sex couples is clearly necessary so that *their* stages can be compared and contrasted with these. Our stages need thorough investigation, including a more careful look at Stages Five and Six and even beyond. We believe stages will change dramatically as couples starting out in the gay-enriched social climate of the 1970s and 1980s reach these latter stages as compared with our Stage Five and Six participants who were the products of a more repressive, antihomosexual era.

2. Additional research is needed to further examine the characteristics of each stage, which would tell us more about the stages and would increase our knowledge of how they work.

3. The idea that male bonding in childhood is absent or diminished among gay men in relationships and our findings of variations in social scripting both deserve objective evaluation in the near future.

4. In our findings, establishing compatibility is one of the outstanding features for relationship survival and longevity. An important component is complementarity. A more careful

look at the development of complementarity in gay couples and in other combinations of persons in intimate relationships could offer a wealth of information, deepening our understanding of relationships and giving us more clinical tools for helping all couples in distress.

5. We would like to see studies about the formation of the extended families these men are creating. Besides having biological families, these couples and others like them are thoughtfully and carefully selecting those they want to identify as family for long-term, supportive relationships for what some are calling their "gay family."

6. Many of the couples together the longest and some who reported the most satisfaction have wide age differences. These spring-autumn relationships need to be studied. What are the attractions? Indeed, Charles Silverstein's work about gay men's having fantasies and longings for liaisons with their fathers may prove accurate for some.[1] What keeps these couples together with such contentment?

7. There needs to be more research done on couples whose relationships end, either by choice or with the death of a mate. In addition to our explanations, such as the loss of limerence or difficulties with the reappearance of the individual, what are other factors that contribute to terminating relationships? When a couple chooses to end their relationship, how can they do so with increased understanding and minimal distress? How can a man who loses his lover by death be assisted in his grief and loss? Surviving alone may be the final stage of all relationships.

8. Gay fathers in our study had fifty-two children. Miller has begun studies on gay fathers.[2] Now we think the *children* of gay fathers should be studied, just as Kirkpatrick, Roy, and Smith have studied the children of lesbian mothers.[3]

Speculations

1. The fact that relationships pass through developmental stages is an exciting new way to understand and examine relationships. We believe the concept should and will be applied to all relationships, especially those of heterosexual couples.

2. Lacking the traditional models and expectations of being a couple, gay men have had the freedom to experiment with relationship formations and functions. As more research examines these experiments, new benefits will be derived for all relationships.

3. Gay couples increasingly will be more visible in the future. With high visibility will come more integration and respectability within society. As in Holland and the Scandinavian countries, legislation will help recognize and protect their relationships. Already in California the State Commission on Personal Privacy has made specific recommendations along these lines to the legislature and to the California congressional delegations.[4]

4. Contrary to our findings indicating lack of sexual exclusivity among male couples, we believe there is a trend toward more sexual exclusivity in the future. Currently it is being propelled by the fear of Acquired Immune Deficiency Syndrome (AIDS) and the attendant opportunistic diseases, but we believe there is a more conservative undercurrent flowing, and more and more individuals are expressing the desire for sexual exclusivity with one other man.

5. Our research indicates an increase in the political involvement of gay men. Since the data were collected, we have witnessed rapid increases in the political influence of gay people. We speculate that this will continue with even greater influence in the future, following the ebb and flow of liberal versus conservative conflicts.

6. There will be more and more integration of gay men of all age ranges, as has generally been the case with lesbians. Young men will seek out the company and experience of older men, and older men will be more tolerant and accepting of younger men. There will be an easier mixing of the generations among gay men. We have witnessed a movement away from the former preoccupations with youth. We speculate that this trend will continue and gain momentum. Older gay men will be increasingly more valued for their wisdom and experience, especially those men who have proudly moved through the history of the mid-twentieth century as openly gay.

Recommendations

1. More recognition and support systems for gay couples need to be developed. New organizations and activities within the gay community centered on couples would encourage and actively support the ongoing development of their relationships.

2. Continued efforts must be made to recognize gay couples as the developing family units they are. These generally include extended family members, and sometimes children from a former marriage and foster or adopted children.

3. Diverse models of gay family life must be made visible and available to others, especially young gay persons, through movies, books, television shows, plays, poetry, and other media.

4. Retreat communities need to be built—attractive places where older gay persons can go for retreat and retirement and where younger gays also go for retreat and rejuvenation.

We offer these recommendations with a sense of completion of this project, but also with a strong internal yearning to begin anew because so much needs doing.

CHAPTER 17

A PERSONAL COMMENT

This study began as a search for information that would help to answer the questions asked by male couples in our clinical work. In recent decades researchers have opened the doors of their closet to admit personal motivation and personal change resulting from a professional undertaking.

Of course, we went in search of answers because we too hoped to catch glimpses of what the future might hold for human relationships. It was not the primary motivation but it was there—simple human curiosity. The curiosity was rewarded. And there were additional gifts along the way.

Professional Insights

Using the construct of stages of relationship has been spectacularly rewarding. When consulted by a couple now, the stages concept permits us to see separately (1) the personal troubles of each of the two individuals, (2) troubles in the relationship, and (3) troubles resulting from the struggles of each and both partners interacting with each other and with the relationship, which has become a third partner.

Experienced clinicians certainly have glimpsed this truth before in work with couples, but we are now permitted more than those glimpses. We work in a well-lit field that eases unnecessary tension for the therapist as well as the couple. We can see, for instance, when the two partners are in pain because one is left behind in Stage Two as the other has rushed into Stage Three. We can see when the couple is anguished by struggling against the relationship itself, which has grown from their sweet baby into an unruly adolescent, bringing havoc into a once peaceful home. They can work together as a team to help tame and guide their troubled adolescent relationship.

We have experienced remarkably less temptation to become referees to furnish answers, and to rush to fix the reported ailment. The wealth of information offered us in this study and the use of the stages concept have brought increasing understanding that sometimes looks like increased patience as we work with the individuals and the couple to locate trouble spots and undo knots that are often less complex than the pain would have suggested. For this professional gain, we are grateful beyond words.

The Couples

Every time we interviewed a male couple, something happened right in front of us that was difficult to capture in our notes. We sat listening to them tell us about their lives together. We saw them listen to each other and find hints of their future in their past. Our wanting to know all about them, good and bad, joys and sorrows, the exciting and the ordinary, what they liked about the relationship and what they did not like, opened them to self-examination in a new way. As each chronicled his own story, the full range of emotions was relived. A tear in an eye as one remembered a tender memory, the flash of jealous feeling as an old story was recounted, or the shared laugh at a very old, very private joke moved them along the trajectory of reexamination. Couples told us later that they were touched in a way they had not anticipated. "It was like taking inventory and being surprised at finding how much was really there," one man says.

Ourselves

Work on this project continued for eight years. During that time our own relationship passed from late Stage Two and the beginning of Stage Three well into Stage Four. But both of us agree that writing this book has lengthened our stay in Stage Four, although many Stage Five characteristics are starting to appear.

When the interviews started we had no idea how profoundly we would be affected personally by the undertaking. After almost every interview, although we did not talk about it often, each of us measured our relationship against those of our participants. Being permitted to spend so many hundreds of hours with gay men in relationships taught us a great deal that we have been able to apply to ourselves.

We listened as 312 men told us the intimate individual stories of their lives and of how their 156 relationships have grown. The experience for us was like moving through the past, the present, and the future of our own relationship. We felt a connection, a similarity, an identification, a déjà vu. When we were with those couples who had been together less time than ourselves, we remembered what it was like for us then, identifying similar issues we had dealt with, empathizing with them and the ways in which they talked about what was happening, wishing we could reassure them of the normality of what they were experiencing, understanding all too well their joys and sorrows, confidences and doubts.

With couples in our own stage we marveled at the commonly shared sameness of their issues and ours. As we interviewed more and more couples in our own stage, step by step, we let go of our internal belief that we were unique. It was not just all those other couples who shared similarities and could be grouped or talked about in some collective sense. Conversely, we realized the marvelous uniqueness of each of the other couples in our own stage. Each and every one was as different as we were all the same. It was with these couples that we realized that the concept of staging is rooted in truth. And with these couples we witnessed adaptability of the individual and each relationship.

With those couples together longer than us, we felt so privileged to see glimpses of how we might be in the future as individuals and as a couple. We were assured and comforted while being challenged and made watchful. We learned that there is more to come for us, as a couple and individually. We appreciate the privilege to have been permitted a peek at the issues and changes that lie ahead.

And we learned that most important lesson once again. There is such fear that as the individual lets his partner go the relationship will no longer exist. But only then can it continue to exist. It must be tended as a parent tends a child. The relationship needs to be nurtured as if it were a separate entity. The nurturing comes from each man. Each of us must continue to grow and change willingly. We continue to develop, encouraged and assisted by the nurturing we give to one another and the shelter of the relationship we tend. As we let the other go, we grow, and we keep the gift of our relationship alive.

NOTES

Introduction

1. Anderson, S., Working relationships: A new study looks at alternate ways of making relationships wash. *The Advocate*, February 7, 1980.
2. McWhirter, D. P., & Mattison, A. M., Psychotherapy for gay male couples. *Journal of Homosexuality* 7, 79–91, 1981–1982.

Chapter One

1. Lorenz, K., *On aggression.* New York: Harcourt, Brace and World, Inc., 1966.
2. Bayer, R., *Homosexuality and American psychiatry: The politics of diagnosis.* New York: Basic Books, Inc., 1981.

Chapter Two

1. Spock, B., *The common sense book of baby and child care.* New York: Duell, Sloan and Pearce, 1945.
2. Gessell, A., *The first five years of life.* New York: Harper, 1940.
3. Piaget, J., *The language and thought of the child.* (3rd ed.) London: Routledge and Kegan Paul, 1959.
4. Freud, S., *The standard edition of the complete psychological works.* J. Strachey (Ed. and Trans.). London: Hogarth Press, 1953, Vol. 7, 125–243.
5. Levinson, D. J., *The seasons of a man's life.* New York: Alfred A. Knopf, 1978.
6. Gould, R., The phases of adult life: A study in developmental psychology. *American Journal of Psychiatry, 129*(5), 521–531, 1972.
7. Sheehy, G., *Passages: Predictable crises of adult life.* New York: E. P. Dutton & Company, 1976.
8. Vailland, G. E., & Milofsky, E. Natural history of male psychological health: IX Empirical evidence of Erickson's model of the life cycle. *American Journal of Psychiatry, 137*(11), 1348–1359, 1980.
9. Etzkowitz, H., & Stein, P., The life spiral: Human needs and adult roles. *Alternate Lifestyles, 1*(4), 434–446, 1978.
10. Campbell, S. M., *The couple's journey: Intimacy as a path to wholeness.* San Luis Obispo, CA: Impact Publishers, 1980.
11. McKusick, L. H., *Towards a theory of gay male relationship counseling.* Unpublished master's thesis, California State University, Hayward, 1978.

Chapter Three

1. Tennov, D., *Love and limerence: The experience of being in love*. New York: Stein and Day Publishers, 1979.
2. Bell, A. P., & Weinberg, M. S., *Homosexualities: A study of diversity among men and women*. New York: Simon & Schuster, 1978.

Chapter Four

1. Tripp, C. A., *The homosexual matrix*. New York: McGraw-Hill Book Company, 1975.
2. Saghir, M. T. & Robins, E., *Male and female homosexuality: A comprehensive investigation*. Baltimore: Williams and Wilkins Co., 1973 (p. 57, table 4.13).
3. Bell, A. P., & Weinberg, M. S., *Homosexualities*.

Chapter Five

1. Saghir, M. T., & Robins, E., *Male and female homosexuality*.
2. Bell, A. P. & Weinberg, M. S., *Homosexualities*.
3. Clark, D., *Living gay*. Millbrae, CA: Celestial Arts, 1979.

Chapter Six

1. Tripp, C. A., Personal communication, April 1980.

Chapter Nine

1. Gagnon, J., & Simon, W., *Sexual conduct: The social sources of human sexuality*. Chicago: Aldine Publishing Company, 1973.
2. Singer, J., *Androgyny*. Garden City, NY: Anchor Press/Doubleday, 1976.
3. Bems, S., The measurement of psychological androgyny. *Journal of Consulting and Clinical Psychology*, 42, 155–162, 1974.
4. Farrell, W., *The liberated man, beyond masculinity: Freeing men and their relationships with women*. New York: Random House, 1974.
5. Nichols, J., *Men's liberation: A new definition of masculinity*. Middlesex, England: Penguin, 1975.
6. Tennov, D., *Love and limerence*.
7. Tripp, C. A., *The homosexual matrix*.
8. Brain, R., *Friends and lovers*. New York: Basic Books, Inc. Publishers, 1976.
9. Tripp, C. A., *The homosexual matrix*.
10. Green, R., *Sexual identity conflicts in children and adults*. Baltimore: Penguin Books, 1974.

11. Money, J., & Ehrhardt, A. A., *Man and woman, boy and girl.* Baltimore: Johns Hopkins Press, 1972.

12. Freud, S., *The standard edition of the complete psychological works.*

13. Sherfy, M. J., *The nature and evolution of female sexuality.* New York: Random House, 1972.

14. Humphreys, L., *Tearoom trade: impersonal sex in public places.* Chicago: Aldine Publishing Company, 1970.

15. Kinsey, A., et al., *Sexual behavior in the human male.* Philadelphia: W. B. Saunders Company, 1948 (p. 623).

16. Fasteau, M. F., *The male machine.* New York: McGraw-Hill Book Company, 1974 (p. 15).

17. Weinberg, G., *Society and the healthy homosexual.* New York: St. Martin's Press, 1972.

18. Foucault, M., *The history of sexuality, Vol. I: An introduction* (Hurley, R., Trans.). New York: Vintage Books, 1980. (Originally published in France as *La volente de savoir.* Editions Gaillimard, 1976.)

19. Weinberg, G., *Society and the healthy homosexual.*

20. Kessler, D. R., American Academy of Psychoanalysis Annual Meeting. San Francisco: May 1980.

21. Warren, C. A. B., *Identity and community in the gay world.* New York: John Wiley & Sons, 1974.

22. Cass, V. C., Homosexual identity formation: A theoretical model. *Journal of Homosexuality, 4,* 219–235, 1979.

23. Coleman, E., Developmental stages of the coming out process. *Journal of Homosexuality, 7*(2–3), 1982.

24. Dank, B. M., Coming out in the gay world. *Psychiatry, 34,* 180–197, 1971.

Chapter Ten

1. Haeberle, E. J., *The sex atlas: A new illustrated guide.* New York: Seabury Press, 1978 (p. 253).

2. Steakley, J. D., *The homosexual emancipation movement in Germany,* from the Arno Press collection: *Homosexuality: Lesbians and gay men in society, history, and literature.* New York: Arno Press, 1975 (p. 8).

3. Ibid. (pp. 10–12).

4. Ibid.

5. Boswell, J., *Christianity, social tolerance, and homosexuality: Gay people in western Europe from the beginning of the christian era to the fourteenth century.* Chicago: University of Chicago Press, 1980.

6. Marmor, J. (Ed.), *Homosexual behavior: A modern reappraisal.* New York: Basic Books, 1980 (p. 5).

7. Kinsey, A., et al., *Sexual behavior in the human male.*

8. Bell, A. P., & Weinberg, M. S., *Homosexualities.*

9. Ibid. (p. 91).

10. Jay, K., & Young, A., *The gay report: Lesbians and gay men speak out about sexual experiences and lifestyles.* New York: Summit Books, 1977 (pp. 339–340).

11. Spada, J., *The Spada report: The newest survey of gay male sexuality.* New York: Signet, 1979 (p. 176).

12. Bell, A. P., & Weinberg, M. S., *Homosexualities* (p. 35).

13. Saghir, M. T., & Robins, E., *Male and female homosexuality* (p. 11).

14. Ibid. (p. 127).

15. Bell, A. P., & Weinberg, M. S., *Homosexualities* (p. 277).

16. Harry, J., & DeVall, W. B., *The social organization of gay males.* New York: Praeger Special Studies, Praeger Publishers, 1978 (p. 26).

17. Kinsey, A., et al., *Sexual behavior in the human male* (pp. 16–62).

18. McWhirter, D. P., & Mattison, A. M., The treatment of sexual dysfunction in gay male couples. *Journal of Sex and Marital Therapy, 4,* 213–218, 1978.

Chapter Eleven

1. Levinson, D. J., *The seasons of a man's life.*

2. Gould, R., The phases of adult life.

3. Harry, J., & DeVall, W. B., *The social organization of gay males* (pp. 31–61).

4. Slater, E., Birth order and maternal age of homosexuals. London: *Lancet, 1,* 69–71, 1962.

5. Bieber, I., et al., *Homosexuality: A psychoanalytic study.* New York: Basic Books, 1962.

6. Saghir, M. T., & Robins, E., *Male and female homosexuality.*

7. Our participants have a total of 566 siblings; 350 brothers and 216 sisters, giving a female-to-male ratio of 0.62. Saghir and Robins (*Male and female homosexuality*) reported a sister to brother ratio of 0.76. Saghir and Robins' heterosexual control group had a ratio of 1.58 sisters to brothers. These data open the doors for a number of speculations related to questions of development and etiology that have been offered by the other researchers. We believe, although our data compare favorably to the Saghir and Robins' data, that in itself it is too inconclusive for further commentary.

Chapter Twelve

1. Saghir, M. T., & Robins, E., *Male and female homosexuality.*

2. Bell, A. P., & Weinberg, M. S., *Homosexualities.*

Chapter Thirteen

1. Cory, D. W., *The Homosexual in America: A subjective approach*. New York: Greenburg Publisher, 1951.

2. Cory, D. W., & Le Roy, J. P., *The homosexual and his society: A view from within*. New York: Citadel Press, 1963.

3. Bergler, E., *Homosexuality: Disease or way of life?* New York: Hill and Wang Inc., 1956.

4. Bieber, I., *Homosexuality: A psychoanalytic study*.

5. Ellis, A., *Homosexuality: Its causes and cure*. New York: Lyle Stuart Inc., 1965.

6. Voeller, B., Society and the gay movement. In J. Marmor (Ed.), *Homosexual behavior: A modern reappraisal*. New York: Basic Books, Inc., Publishers, 1980 (pp. 232–252).

7. Having dealt with the problem of coming out to families for a number of years, we have seen mothers and fathers distraught after learning of a son's or daughter's same-sex orientation. Indeed, the characteristic first response in parents is to deny that their child is homosexual. Once they have passed beyond the denial stage they become overwhelmed with guilt about their contribution to their child's deviance. Two useful books on this subject have been published in recent years: *A Family Matter*, by New York psychologist Charles Silverstein, Ph.D., and *Now That You Know*, by Betty Fairchild and Nancy Hayward. Each discusses parent and gay child relationships in great depth. *Loving Someone Gay*, by Don Clark, Ph.D., is the largest-selling book on the subject and is the most valuable for both gay and nongay people. *Consenting Adult*, by Laura Hobson, was the first novel written from the parents' point of view about learning of a son's gayness. In 1976 an organization called Parents and Friends of Gays was established. It now has many chapters that assist parents and other family members—as well as the gay persons themselves—to come to grips with homosexuality in their lives. Other books have appeared since, indicating the importance of the relationships between gay people and their families.

8. Green, R., Sexual identity of 37 children raised by homosexual or transsexual parents. *American Journal of Psychiatry*, *135*(6), 692–697, 1978.

9. Kirkpatrick, M. R., Roy, R., & Smith, K., A new look at lesbian mothers. *Human Behavior*, August, 1976, 60–61.

10. Miller, B., Unpromised paternity: The life style of gay fathers. In *Gay men: The sociology of male homosexuality*. New York: Harper and Row Publishers, 1979.

11. Ellis, A., *Homosexuality: Its causes and cure*.

12. Nahas, R., & Turley, M., *The new couple: Women and gay men*. New York: Seaview Books, 1979.

13. Kris, Ernst, The psychology of caricature. In *Psychoanalytic exploration in art*, New York: International Universities Press, 1952. Ernst Kris was one of the founders of ego

psychology and introduced the term "regression in the service of the ego" in the afore-mentioned paper in 1934. It refers to the healthy use of childlike activities, hence the use of the term "regression," meaning a "going back to" playful activities of childhood to assist with the personality protections of the ego itself.

Chapter Fourteen

1. Bell, A. P., & Weinberg, M. S., *Homosexualities* (p. 231).

2. Kinsey, A., et al., *Sexual behavior in the human male* (pp. 636–656).

3. Bell, A. P., & Weinberg, M. S., *Homosexualities*.

4. Saghir, M., & Robins, E., *Male and female homosexuality*.

5. Harry, J., & DeVall, W. B., *The social organization of gay males*.

6. *Analingus* refers to oral–anal contact, sometimes called rimming.

7. *Fisting* refers to the insertion of a closed and lubricated fist and sometimes forearm as far as the elbow into the rectum and up the sigmoid colon. Jack Morin makes a brief reference to this practice in his book *Anal Pleasure and Health*. Burlingame, CA: Down There Press, 1981.

8. Butyl nitrite is packaged under many different trade names with slightly differing formulas.

9. McWhirter, D. P., & Mattison, A. M., Treatment of sexual dysfunctions in homosexual male couples. In S. R. Leiblum & L. A. Pervin (Eds.), *Principles and practices of sex therapy*, New York: Guildford Press, 1980.

10. McWhirter, D. P., & Mattison, A. M., Treatment of sexual dysfunction (1978), Treatment of sexual dysfunctions (1980).

11. Haeberle, E. J., *The sex atlas* (p. 253).

12. Masters, W. H., & Johnson, V. E., *Homosexuality in perspective*. Boston: Little, Brown and Company, 1979 (p. 406).

13. McWhirter, D. P., & Mattison, A. M., Treatment of sexual dysfunction (1978), Treatment of sexual dysfunctions (1980).

14. Masters, W. H., & Johnson, V. E., *Homosexuality in perspective* (p. 406).

Chapter Sixteen

1. Silverstein, C., *Man to man: Gay couples in America*. New York: William Morrow and Company, Inc., 1981.

2. Miller, B., Unpromised paternity: The life style of gay fathers.

3. Kirkpatrick, M., et al., A new look at lesbian mothers.

4. *Report of the commission on personal privacy*. State of California, 1982, Pines, B., Chairperson, Coleman, T. F., Executive Director.

BIBLIOGRAPHY

Allen, C., When homosexuals marry. *Sexology*, February 1957, pp. 416–420.

Anderson, S., Working relationships: A new study looks at alternate ways of making relationships wash. *The Advocate*, February 7, 1980.

Bass-Hass, R., The lesbian dyad. *The Journal of Sex Research*, 4(2), 1099–1126, May 1968.

Bell, A. P., & Weinberg, M. S., *Homosexualities: A study of diversities among men and women*. New York: Simon & Schuster, 1978.

Bell, A. P., Weinberg, M. S., & Hammersmith, S. K., *Sexual preference: Its development in men and women*. Bloomington: Indiana University Press, 1981.

Bems, S., The measurement of psychological androgyny. *Journal of Consulting and Clinical Psychology*, 42, 155–162, 1974.

Bennett, P. H., The structure of gay male relationships. *Blueboy*, August 1978, p. 68.

Bergler, E., *Homosexuality: Disease or way of life?* New York: Hill and Wang, Inc., 1956.

Berzon, B., & Leighton, R., Achieving success as a gay couple. In B. Berzon, & R. Leighton (Eds.), *Positively Gay*. Millbrae, CA.: Celestial Arts, 1979.

Berzon, B., & Leighton, R., *Positively Gay*. Millbrae, CA.: Celestial Arts, 1979.

Bieber, I., Dain, H. J., Dince, P. R., Drellich, M. G., Grand, H. G., Kremer, M. W., Rifkin, A. H., Wilbur, C. B., & Bieber, T. B., *Homosexuality: A psychoanalytic study*. New York: Basic Books, Inc., Publishers, 1962.

Bieber, I., Clinical aspects of male homosexuality. In J. Marmor (Ed.). *Sexual Inversions*. New York: Basic Books, Inc., Publishers, 1965, (pp. 254–255).

Biernacki, P., & Waldorf, D., Snowball sampling: Problems and techniques of chain referral sampling. Paper prepared for presentation at the annual meeting of the American Sociological Association, Boston, August 1979.

Blaine, W. L., & Bishop, J., *Practical guide for the unmarried couple.* New York: Sun River Press, 1976.

Blair, R., Gay couple counseling: Introductory perspectives for counseling in paramarital relationships among homosexuals. Conference proceedings, *The Homosexual Counseling Journal,* 1(3), 88–91, July 1974.

Boswell, J., *Christianity, social tolerance, and homosexuality: Gay people in Western Europe from the beginning of the Christian era to the fourteenth century.* Chicago and London: The University of Chicago Press, 1980.

Brain, R., *Friends and lovers.* New York: Basic Books, Inc., Publishers, 1976.

Brown, H., *Familiar faces, hidden lives: The story of homosexual men in America today.* New York: Harcourt, Brace and Jovanovich, 1976.

Buskirk, J. V., An exploration of gay argot and its effects on group maintenance. Paper for linguistics 155, University of California, Berkeley, December 8, 1976.

Bozett, F., Gay fathers: Evolution of gay-father identity. *American Journal of Orthopsychiatry, 51,* 552–559, 1981.

Bozett, F., Gay fathers: How and why they disclose their homosexuality to their children. *Family Relations, 29,* 173–179, 1980.

Bullough, V. L., *Homosexuality: A history.* New York: New American Library, 1979.

Bullough, V. L., *Sexual variance in society and history.* Chicago and London: The University of Chicago Press, 1976.

California Commission on Personal Privacy. *Final Report.* by Thomas F. Coleman, Executive Director. Sacramento, December 1982.

Campbell, S. M., *The couple's journey: Intimacy as a path to wholeness.* San Luis Obispo: Impact Publishers, 1980.

Carpenter, C. R., Sexual behavior of free ranging rhesus monkeys (Macaca mulatta) II. Periodicity of estrus, homosexual, autoerotic and nonconformist behavior. *Journal of Comparative Psychology, 33,* 143–162, 1942.

Cass, V. C., Homosexual identity formation: A theoretical model. *Journal of Homosexuality, 4,* 219–235, 1979.

Chafetz, J. S., *Masculine-feminine or human?: An overview of the sociology of sex roles.* Itasca, IL: F. E. Peacock Publishers, 1978.

Chang, J., & Block, J. A., A study of identification in male homosexuals. *Journal of Consulting Psychology, 24*(4), 307–310, 1960.

Chevalier-Skolnikoff, S., Male–female, female–female, and male–male sexual behavior in the stumptail monkey, with special attention to female orgasm. *Archives of Sexual Behavior, 3,* 95–116, 1974.

Chevalier-Skolnikoff, S., Homosexual behavior in a laboratory group of stumptail monkeys (Macaca arctoides): Forms, contexts, and possible social functions. *Archives of Sexual Behavior*, 5, 511–527, 1976.

Churchill, W., *Homosexual behavior among males: A cross-cultural and cross species investigation*. Englewood Cliffs, NJ: Prentice-Hall, Inc., 1967.

Clark, D., *Loving someone gay*. Millbrae, CA: Celestial Arts, 1977.

Clark, D., *Living gay*. Millbrae, CA: Celestial Arts, 1979.

Clarke, L., & Nichols, J., *I have more fun with you than anybody*. New York: St. Martin's Press, 1972.

Clarke, L., & Nichols, J., *Roommates can't always be lovers: An intimate guide to male–male relationships*. London: St. James Press, 1974.

Coleman, E., Developmental stages of the coming out process. *Journal of Homosexuality*, 7(2–3), 1982.

Committee on Cooperation With Governmental Agencies of the Group for the Advancement of Psychiatry. Report on homosexuality, with particular emphasis on this problem in governmental agencies. (Report No. 30, p. 7.) January 1955.

Cory, D. W., *The homosexual in America: A subjective approach*. New York: Greenburg Publisher, 1951.

Cory, D. W., & LeRoy, J. P., *The homosexual and his society—a view from within*. New York: The Citadel Press, 1963.

Cotton, W., Role playing substitutions among male homosexuals. *Journal of Sex Research*, 8, 310–323, 1972.

Curry, H., & Clifford, D., *A legal guide for gay and lesbian couples*. Reading, MA: Addison-Wesley, 1980.

Dailey, D., Adjustment of heterosexual and homosexual couples in pairing relationships: An exploratory study. *Journal of Sex Research*, 15(2), 143–157, 1979.

Dank, B. M., Coming out in the gay world. *Psychiatry*, 34, 180–197, 1971.

DeCecco, J. P., & Freedman, M., A study of interpersonal conflict in homosexual relations. *Homosexual Counseling Journal*, 2(4), 147–149, October 1975.

Denneny, M., *Lovers: The story of two men*. New York: Avon Books, 1979.

Dickey, B. A., Attitudes towards sex roles and feelings of adequacy in homosexual males. *Journal of Consulting Psychology*, 25(2), 116–122, 1961.

Dover, K. J., *Greek homosexuality*. Cambridge, MA: Harvard University Press, 1978.

Ellis, A., *Homosexuality: Its causes and cure*. New York: Lyle Stuart Inc., 1965.

Ellis, H. *Sexual inversion* Vol. II *Studies in the psychology of sex.* Philadelphia: F. A. Davis Company, Publishers, 1915.

Erikson, E. H., *Childhood and Society.* New York: W. W. Norton & Company, Inc., 1963.

Erwin, J., & Maple, T., Ambisexual behavior with male–male anal penetration in male rhesus monkeys. *Archives of Sexual Behavior, 5,* 1976.

Etzkowitz, H., & Stein, P., The life spiral: Human needs and adult roles. *Alternative Lifestyles, 1*(4), 434–446, 1978.

Evans, R. B., Childhood parental relationships of homosexual men. *Journal of Consulting and Clinical Psychology, 33,* 129–135, 1969.

Evans, R. B., Parental relationships and homosexuality. *Medical Aspects of Human Sexuality,* April, 1971, p. 164.

Fairchild, B., & Hayward, N., *Now that you know: What every parent should know about homosexuality.* New York: Harcourt, Brace, Jovanovich, 1979.

Farrell, W., *The liberated man. Beyond masculinity: Freeing men and their relationships with women.* New York: Random House, 1974.

Fasteau, M. F., *The male machine.* New York: McGraw-Hill Book Company, 1974.

Ford, C. S., & Beach, F. A., *Patterns of sexual behavior.* New York: Harper and Row, Publishers, Inc., 1951.

Foucault, M., *The history of sexuality, An introduction* (R. Hurley, Trans.) New York: Vintage Books, 1980.

Freedman, M., Homophobia. *Blueboy,* April, 1976.

Freud, S. Three essays on sexuality. *The standard edition of the complete psychological works* (J. Strachey, Ed. and Trans.). London: The Hogarth Press, Ltd., Vol. VII, 125–243, 1953.

Friday, N., *Men in love.* New York: Delacorte Press, 1980.

Gagnon, J., *Human sexualities.* Glenview, IL.: Scott, Foresman and Company, 1977.

Gagnon, J., & Simon, W., *Sexual conduct: The social sources of human sexuality.* Chicago: Aldine Publishing Company, 1973.

Gebhard, P., & Johnson, A., *The Kinsey data: Marginal tabulations of the 1938–1963 interviews conducted by the Institute for Sex Research.* Phildelphia: W. B. Saunders, 1979.

Gebhard, P., Memorandum on the incidence of homosexuals in the United States. In a letter to the National Gay Task Force from the Institute for Sex Research, University of Indiana, Bloomington, 1977.

Gessell, A., *The first five years of life.* New York: Harper, 1940.

Goodall, J., *In the shadow of man.* New York: Dell Publishing Co., Inc., 1971.

Goode, E., & Troiden, R. R., Heterosexual and homosexual activity among gay males. *Deviant Behavior, 1,* 37–55, 1979.

Gould, R. L., The phases of adult life: A study in developmental psychology. *American Journal of Psychiatry. 129*(5), 521–531, 1972.

Gould, R. L., *Transformations: Growth and change in adult life.* New York: Simon and Schuster, 1978.

Gonsiorek, J. (Ed.), *Homosexuality and psychotherapy: A practitioner's handbook of affirmative models.* (No. 4 of the Book series, Research on Homosexuality.) New York: The Haworth Press, 1982.

Green, R., *Sexual identity conflict in children and adults.* New York: Penguin Books, 1975.

Green, R., One hundred ten feminine and masculine boys. *Archives of Sexual Behavior, 5,* 425–426, 1976.

Haeberle, E. J., *The sex atlas—a new illustrated guide.* New York: The Seabury Press, 1978.

Haist, M., & Hewitt, J., The butch–fem dichotomy in male homosexual behavior. *Journal of Sex Research, 10,* 68–75, 1974.

Harry, J., Decision making and age differences among gay couples. *Journal of Homosexuality. 8*(2), Winter 1982.

Harry, J., The marital liaisons of gay men. *Family Coordinator, 28,* 622–629, 1979.

Harry, J., & DeVall, W. B., *The social organization of gay males.* New York: Praeger Publishers, 1978.

Harry, J., Gay male and lesbian relationships. In E. Macklin, & R. Rubin (Eds.), *Contemporary families and alternative lifestyles.* Beverly Hills: Sage Publications, 1983.

Harry, J., & Lovely, R., Gay marriages and communities of sexual orientation. *Alternate Lifestyles. 2,* 177–200, 1979.

Hart, H. (Chairperson), Families & children of gays. *Final report of the task force on sexual preference.* State of Oregon, Department of Human Resources, 1978.

Hatley, S., Panel III: Panel of male couples. *The homosexual counseling journal, 1*(3), 110–125, July, 1974.

Hite, S., *The Hite report on male sexuality.* New York: Alfred A. Knopf, 1981.

Hobson, L., *Consenting adults.* Garden City, NY: Doubleday, 1975.

Hoffman, M., Homosexuality. *Today's education: NEA Journal*, 46–48, November 1970.

Hoffman, M., *The gay world: male homosexuality and the social creation of evil.* New York: Basic Books, Inc., 1968.

Hooker, E. A., The adjustment of the male overt homosexual. *Journal of Projective Techniques, 21,* 17–31, 1957.

Hooker, E. A., The homosexual community. In J. Gagnan, & W. Simon (Eds.), *Sexual Deviance.* New York: Harper and Row, 1967.

Hooker, E., Parental relations and male homosexuality in patient and nonpatient samples. *Journal of Consulting and Clinical Psychology, 33(2),* 140–142, 1969.

Humphreys, L., *Tearoom trade: Impersonal sex in public places.* Chicago: Aldine Publishing Company, 1970.

Hunt, G. L., Jr., & Hunt, M. W., Female–female pairing in western gulls (Larus occidentalis) in southern California. *Science, 196,* 1466–1467, 1977.

Isaac, S., & Michael, W. B., *Handbook in research and evaluation.* San Diego: Edits Publishers, 1971.

Jay, K., & Young, A., *The gay report : Lesbians and gay men speak out about sexual experiences and lifestyles.* New York: Summit Books, 1979.

Jones, C., *Homosexuality and counseling.* Philadelphia: Fortress Press, 1974.

Jones, R. W., & Bates, J. E., Satisfaction in male homosexual couples. *Journal of Homosexuality, 3(3),* 218–223, Spring 1978.

Jones, R. W., & DeCecco, J. P., The femininity and masculinity of partners in heterosexual and homosexual relationships. *Journal of Homosexuality, 8(2),* Winter 1982.

Kafes, R. (Moderator), Panel II: Therapists' panel on male couples. *The Homosexual Counseling Journal, 1(3),* 100–109, July 1974.

Katz, J., *Gay American history.* New York: Thomas Y. Crowell Company, 1976.

Kimmel, D. C., Psychotherapy and the older gay man. *Psychotherapy: Theory, Research and Practice, 14(4),* 386–393, 1977.

Kinsey, A. C., Pomeroy, W. B., & Martin, C. E., *Sexual behavior in the human male.* Philadelphia: W. B. Saunders Company, 1948.

Kinsey, A. C., Pomeroy, W. B., Martin, C. E., & Gebhard, P. H., *Sexual behavior in the human female.* Philadelphia: W. B. Saunders Company, 1953.

Kirkpatrick, M., Smith, K., & Roy, R., Lesbian mothers and their children: A comparative survey. *American Journal of Orthopsychiatry*, 51, 545–551, 1981.

Kirkpatrick, M., Roy, R., & Smith, K., A new look at lesbian mothers. *Human behavior*, 5, 60–61, August 1976.

Klein, F., *The bisexual option: A concept of one-hundred percent intimacy*. New York: Arbor House Publishing Co., 1978.

Kopkind, A., The gay rights movement: Too many enemies. *Working papers*, July–August, 1978.

Kris, E., The psychology of caricature (1934). In *Psychoanalytic Exploration in Art*. New York: International University Press, 1952.

Laner, M. R., Permanent partner priorities: Gay and straight. *Journal of Homosexuality*, 3(1), 21–39, Fall 1977.

Lasswell, M., & Lobenz, N., *Styles of loving: Why do you love the way you do?* Garden City, NY: Doubleday and Co., 1980.

Lee, J. A., *Colours of love*. Toronto: New Press, 1973.

Lee, J. A., Forbidden colors of love. *Journal of Homosexuality*, 1(4), 401–418, 1976.

Levine, M. P., *Gay men: The sociology of male homosexuality*. New York: Harper and Row, Publishers, 1979.

Levinson, D. J., *The seasons of a man's life*. New York: Alfred A. Knopf, Inc., 1978.

Lewis, R. A., Commitment in lesbian and gay male living-together relationships. Paper presented at the annual meeting of the American Sociological Association, New York City, August 27–31, 1980.

Lewis, R. A. (Ed.), *Men in difficult times: masculinity today and tomorrow*. Englewood Cliffs, NJ: Prentice-Hall, 1981.

Leznoff, M., & Westley, W., The homosexual community. *Social Problems*, 3, 257–263, 1956.

Lorenz, K., *On aggression*. New York: Harcourt, Brace and World, Inc., 1966.

Lumby, M. E., Homophobia: The quest for a valid scale. *Journal of Homosexuality*, 2(1), 39–47, Fall 1976.

MacDonald, A. P., Jr., Homophobia: Its roots and meanings. *Homosexual Counseling Journal*, 3(1), 23–33, January 1976.

McKusick, L. H., *Towards a theory of gay male relationship counseling*. Unpublished master's thesis, Master of Science in Education, California State University, Hayward, 1978.

McNeil, J., *The Church and the homosexual.* Kansas City: Sheed, Andrews & McMeel, Inc., 1976.

McWhirter, D. P., & Mattison, A. M., The treatment of sexual dysfunction in gay male couples. *Journal of Sex and Marital Therapy,* (4), 213–218, 1978.

McWhirter, D. P., & Mattison, A. M., Treatment of sexual dysfunction in homosexual male couples. In S. R. Leiblum, & L. A. Pervin (Eds.), *Principles and practice of sex therapy.* New York: Guildford Press, 1980.

McWhirter, D. P., & Mattison, A. M., Psychotherapy for gay male couples. In J. C. Gonsioreck (Ed.), *Homosexuality and psychotherapy: A practitioner's handbook of affirmative models.* Number 4 of the Book Series, Research on Homosexuality, 1982. Also appeared in *Journal of Homosexuality,* 7(2–3), 79–91, Winter/Spring 1981–1982.

Macklin, E., & Rubin, R. (Eds.), *Contemporary families and alternative lifestyles: Handbook on research and theory.* Beverly Hills: Sage Publications, 1983.

Maracek, J., Finn, S. E., & Cardell, M., Gender roles in the relationships of lesbians and gay men. *Journal of Homosexuality,* 8(2), Winter 1982.

Marmor, J. (Ed.), *Sexual inversion: The multiple roots of homosexuality.* New York: Basic Books, Inc., 1965.

Marmor, J. (Ed.), *Homosexual behavior: A modern reappraisal.* New York: Basic Books, Inc., 1980.

Martin, D., & Lyon, P., *Lesbian/Woman.* San Francisco: Glide Publications, 1972.

Masters, W. H., & Johnson, V. E., *Homosexuality in perspective.* Boston: Little, Brown and Company, 1979.

May, R., *Sex and fantasy: Patterns of male and female development.* New York: W. W. Norton and Co., 1980.

Mead, S., *Men loving men: A phenomenological exploration of committed gay relationships.* Unpublished Ph.D dissertation, California School of Professional Psychology, San Diego, 1979.

Mendola, M., *The Mendola report: A new look at gay couples in America.* New York: Crown Publishers, 1980.

Michels, B., *Social scenes of the male gay community of San Diego.* Unpublished Master's Thesis for the School of Social Work, California State University, San Diego, 1974.

Mickley, R., *Sharing and growing: Enriching a committed relationship.* Published Ph.D. dissertation for International College, Los Angeles, CA, 1980.

Miller, B., Gay fathers and their children. *Family Coordinator*, 28(4), 12–20, October, 1979.

Miller, B., Unpromised paternity: The life style of gay fathers. In M. P. Levine (Ed.), *Gay men.* New York: Harper and Row Publishers, 1979.

Money, J., & Ehrhardt, A. A., *Man and woman—boy and girl.* Baltimore: The Johns Hopkins University Press, 1977.

Morin, J., *Anal pleasure and health: A guide for men and women.* Burlingame, CA: Down There Press, 1981.

Morin, S. F., Heterosexual bias in psychological research on lesbianism and male homosexuality. *American Psychologist*, 32(8), 629–637, August 1977.

Morin, S. F., & Garfinkle, E. M., Male homophobia. *Journal of Social Issues*, 34(1), 29–47, 1978.

Morrow, J. E., A possible explanation of the excessive brother-to-sister ratios reported in siblings of male homosexuals. *Journal of Nervous and Mental Disease*, 140, 305–306, 1965.

Moses, A., & Hawkins, R., Jr., *Counseling lesbian and gay men: A life issues approach.* St. Louis: The C. V. Mosby Co., 1982.

Nahas, R., & Turley, M., *The new couple: Women and gay men.* New York: Seaview Books, 1980.

Nichols, J., *Men's liberation: A new definition of masculinity.* Middlesex, England: Penguin, 1975.

National Institute of Mental Health. *U.S. Task Force on Homosexuality: Final report and background papers* (E. Hooker, Chairperson) Rockville, Maryland: National Institute of Mental Health, 1972.

Norsic, D., Celebrating lovers. *Blueboy*, April 1978, pp. 68–72.

O'Neill, N., & O'Neill, G., *Open marriage.* New York: Avon Books, 1972.

Ovesey, L., Pseudohomosexuality and homosexuality in men: Psychodynamics as a guide to treatment. In J. Marmor (Ed.), *Sexual Inversion: the multiple roots of homosexuality.* New York: Basic Books, Inc., 1965 (pp. 211–233).

Paul, W., Weinrich, J. D., Gonsiorek, J. C., & Hotvedt, M. (Eds.), *Homosexuality: Social, psychological, and biological issues.* Beverly Hills: Sage Publications, 1982.

Peplau, L. A., What homosexuals want in relationships. *Psychology Today*, 15, 1981.

Peplau, L. A., & Cochran, S., Value orientations in the intimate relationships of gay men. *Journal of Homosexuality*, 6, 1–19, 1981.

Peplau, L. A., Research on homosexual couples: An overview. *Journal of Homosexuality*, 8(2), Winter 1982.

Piaget, J., *The language and thought of the child* (3rd ed.). London: Routledge and Kegan Paul, 1959.

Pleck, J. H., & Sawyer, J. (Eds.), *Men and masculinity*. Englewood Cliffs, NJ: Prentice-Hall, Inc., 1974.

Reese, R. Coping with couplehood. *The Advocate*. October 19, 1977. Reprinted in M. P. Levine, *Gay men: The sociology of male homosexuality*. New York: Harper and Row, 1979.

Roberts-Hill, W., *Homosexual marriages*. Las Vegas, NV: M-T Publishers, 1969 (out of print).

Robinson, B., Skeen, P., Hobson, C. & Herrman, M., Gay men's and women's perceptions of their relationships with parents. *Family Relations, 31*, 79–83, 1982.

Rogers, C., *Becoming partners: Marriage and its alternatives*. New York: Delacorte Press, 1972.

Ruitenbeek, H. M. (Ed.), *The problem of homosexuality in modern society*. New York: E. P. Dutton and Co., Inc., 1963.

Ruitenbeek, H. M. (Ed.), *Homosexuality: A changing picture*. London: Souvenir, 1973.

Saghir, M. T., & Robins, E., *Male and female homosexuality—a comprehensive investigation*. Baltimore: The Williams and Wilkins Company, 1973.

Sheehy, G., *Passages: Predictable crises of adult life*. New York: E. P. Dutton & Company, Inc., 1976.

Sherfy, M. J., *The nature and evolution of female sexuality*. New York: Random House, Inc., 1972.

Silverstein, C., *A family matter: a parent's guide to homosexuality*. New York: McGraw-Hill Book Company, 1977.

Silverstein, C., *Man to man—gay couples in America*. New York: William Morrow and Company, Inc., 1981.

Silverstein, C., & White, E., *The joy of gay sex: An intimate guide for gay men to the pleasure of a gay lifestyle*. New York: Crown Publishers, 1977.

Simon, W., & Gangon, J., The lesbian: A preliminary overview. In J. Gagnon, W. Simon, (Eds.), *Sexual deviance*. New York: Harper and Row, 1976.

Singer, J., *Androgyny*. Garden City, New York: Anchor Press/Doubleday, 1976.

Slater, E., Birth order and maternal age of homosexuals. *Lancet 1*, 69–71, 1962.

Slater, E., The sibs and children of homosexuals. In D. R. Smith, & W. A. Davidson (Eds.), *Symposium on nuclear sex*, New York: Interscience Publishers, 1958.

Smith, J., *Beyond monogamy*. Baltimore: The Johns Hopkins University Press, 1974.

Socarides, C. W., *The overt homosexual*. New York: Grune and Stratton, Inc., 1968.

Sonenschein, D., The ethnography of male homosexual relationships. *Journal of Sex Research*, 4(2), 69–83, May 1968.

Spada, J., *The Spada report: The newest survey of gay male sexuality*. New York: Signet Books, 1979.

Spock, B., *Baby and child care*. New York: Pocket Books, 1946.

Steakley, J. D., *The homosexual emancipation movement in Germany*. From the Arno Press collection: *Homosexuality: Lesbians and gay men in society, history and literature*. New York: Arno Press, 1975.

Stein, P., & Etzkowitz, H., *Life spiral or life cycle: A new conceptualization of life stages*. Paper presented at Society for the Study of Social Problems, annual meeting in Chicago, September 4, 1977.

Stoller, R., *Sex and gender: On the development of masculinity and femininity*. New York: Science House, 1968.

Tennov, D., *Love and limerence: The experience of being in love*. New York: Stein and Day, 1979.

Terry, M., *Couplings and groupings*. New York: Avon Books, 1972.

Tessina, T., & Smith, R., *How to be a couple and still be free*. North Hollywood, CA: Newcastle Publishing Co., 1980.

Tripp, C. A., *The homosexual matrix*. New York: McGraw-Hill Book Company, 1975.

Trumbach, R., London's sodomites: Homosexual behavior and western culture in the 18th century. *Journal of Social History*, 1977.

Tuller, N. R., Couples: The hidden segment of the gay world. *Journal of Homosexuality*, 3(4), 331–343, Summer 1978.

Vaillant, G. E., & Milofsky, E., Natural history of male psychological health: IX empirical evidence of Erikson's model of the life cycle. *American Journal of Psychiatry*, 137(11), 1980.

Voeller, B., & Walters, J., Gay fathers. *Family Coordinator*, 27:149–157, 1978.

Voeller, B., Society and the gay movement. In J. Marmor (Ed.), *Homosexual behavior: A modern reappraisal.* New York: Basic Books, Inc., 1980.

Walker, M., *Men loving men: A gay sex guide and consciousness book.* San Francisco: Gay Sunshine Press, 1977.

Warren, C. A. B., *Identity and community in the gay world.* New York: John Wiley & Sons, 1974.

Weinberg, G., Society and the healthy homosexual. New York: St. Martin's Press, 1972.

Weinberg, L. E., & Millham, J., Attitudinal homophobia and support of traditional sex roles. *Journal of Homosexuality, 4*(3), 237–245, Spring 1979.

Weinberg, M. S., & Bell, A. P., *Homosexuality: An annotated bibliography.* New York: Harper and Row, Publishers, 1972.

Weinberg, M. S., & Williams, C. J., *Male homosexuals: Their problems and adaptations.* New York: Oxford University Press, Inc., 1974.

Weinrich, J. D., Human Sociobiology: Pair-bonding and resource predictability (Effects of social class and race). *Behavioral Ecology and Sociobiology, 2,* 91–118, 1977.

Weinrich, J. D., Homosexual behavior in animals: A new review of observations from the wild and their relationship to human sexuality. In R. Forleo & W. Pasini (Eds.), *Medical sexology: The third international congress.* Littleton, MA: PSG Publishing Company, Inc., 1980.

Williams, C. J., & Weinberg, M. S., *Homosexuals and the military: A study of less than honorable discharge.* New York: Harper and Row Publishers, 1971.

West, D. *Homosexuality.* London: Gerald Duckworth and Co., 1955.

Westermoreland, C., *A study of long-term relationships among male homosexuals.* Unpublished Ph.D. dissertation for United States International University, San Diego, CA, 1975.

Westwood, G., *A minority.* London: Longmans, 1960.

Winkelpleck, J. M., & Westfield, J. S., Counseling considerations with gay couples. *The Personnel and Guidance Journal,* 294–296, January, 1982.

Winch, R. F., *Mate selection: A study in complementary needs.* New York: Harper and Row, 1958.

Woodman, N., & Lenna, H., *Counseling with gay men and women.* San Francisco: Jossey-Bass Publishers, 1980.

APPENDIX

INTERVIEW FORMAT

These are the questions we asked in the interviews.

1. Age _____
2. Date of birth _____
3. Occupation _____
4. Self-employed?   a) yes b) no
5. Annual income (individual)
   a. 0 to 5000
   b. 5000 to 10,000
   c. 10,000 to 15,000
   d. 15,000 to 20,000
   e. 20,000 to 25,000
   f. Over 25,000
6. Religion while growing up
   a. Roman Catholic
   b. Jewish Orthodox
   c. Jewish Conservative
   d. Jewish Reformed
   e. Protestant
   f. Protestant fundamentalist
   g. non–Judeo–Christian (explain)
   h. None
7. Current religion _____
8. Education (Indicate highest level completed)
   a. grades 1–12
   b. college 1 2 3 4
   c. graduate school
      1) Master's
      2) Ph.D.
      3) M.D.
      4) J.D.
      5) Other

d. Technical training _____ (explain)

9. Are you currently a student? yes no
   If yes indicate:
   a. high school
   b. college 1 2 3 4
   c. graduate school
      master's
      doctorate
      Other
   d. technical school (explain)

10. Military service? yes no
    If yes:
    a. Army
    b. Navy
    c. Air Force
    d. Coast Guard

11. Officer _____ Enlisted _____

12. Number of years _____

13. Rank at discharge _____

14. Type of discharge:
    a. honorable
    b. general
    c. dishonorable

15. Do you live in a:
    a. house
    b. condominium
    c. apartment

16. Do you own your own residence? a) yes b) no

17. Does your partner own your residence? a) yes b) no

18. Place of birth: city _____ state _____ country _____ population _____

19. Were you reared in a rural community? a) yes b) no

20. Were you reared in a suburban community? a) yes b) no

21. Were you reared in an urban community? a) yes b) no

22. Siblings? a) yes b) no

23. If yes how many? a) sisters _____ b) brothers _____

24. In order, which are you? _____

The following questions pertain to your father:
25. Is he living: a) yes b) no
26. Is he separated from your mother? a) yes b) no
27. If yes, how old were you when they separated? _____
28. Is he divorced? a) yes b) no
29. If yes how old were you when they were divorced? _____
30. Is he remarried? a) yes b) no
31. If yes how old were you when he remarried? _____
32. Is he retired? a) yes b) no
33. If yes what was his occupation? _____
34. If no what is his occupation? _____
The following questions pertain to your mother:
35. Is she living? a) yes b) no
36. Is she separated from your father? a) yes b) no
37. If yes how old were you when they separated? _____
38. Is she divorced? a) yes b) no
39. If yes how old were you when they were divorced? _____
40. Is she remarried? a) yes b) no
41. If yes how old when she remarried? _____
42. Is she retired? a) yes b) no
43. If yes what was her occupation? _____
44. If no what is her occupation? _____r
45. Would you describe your childhood as:
    a. happy
    b. unhappy
    c. chaotic
    d. harmonious
    e. mixed
    f. other _____
46. While growing up was religion important? a) yes b) no
47. Practiced religion?
    a. Roman Catholic
    b. Jewish Orthodox

c. Jewish Conservative
d. Jewish Reformed
e. Protestant
f. Protestant fundamentalist
g. non-Judeo–Christian (explain)
h. none

48. How did you learn about sex?

   a. parents
   b. siblings
   c. friends (peers)
   d. older person
   e. written material
   f. other

49. At what age did you begin to masturbate? _____

50. At what age did you have your first sexual contact to orgasm with another person? _____

51. At what age did you have your first same-sex contact to orgasm? _____

52. At what age did you have your first opposite-sex contact to orgasm? _____

53. During adolescence, did you date girls? a) yes b) no
   Explain _____

54. Did your parents know of your same-sex orientation? a) yes b) no

55. At what age did your parents learn of your same-sex orientation?

   a. 13–15
   b. 16–19
   c. 20–24
   d. 25 or over
   e. never

56. Are other members of your immediate family gay? a) yes b) no

57. If yes:

   a. brother
   b. sister
   c. mother
   d. father

58. Have you ever received psychological counseling or medical treatment for your same-sex orientation? a) yes b) no

59. If yes at what age? _____

60. If yes who was responsible for getting you to the professional?

    a. parents
    b. authorities (including civil)
    c. friends
    d. self
    e. other

61. If yes, whom did you see?

    a. psychologist
    b. family physician
    c. clergy
    d. psychiatrist
    e. other

62. If yes, was it:

    a. very helpful
    b. somewhat helpful
    c. of no help
    d. detrimental

63. What are your own feelings about the origins of homosexuality?

    a. genetic and biological predisposition
    b. learned from early childhood
    c. psychological predisposition
    d. combination of above
    e. other

64. Do you consider homosexuality an illness or aberration? a) yes b) no

65. As a child (before adolescence), were playmates predominantly boys, or girls?

    a. boys
    b. girls

66. As a child or adolescent, were you ever called "sissy" or some other pejorative equivalent? a) yes b) no

67. Was nudity acceptable in your family? a) yes b) no

68. Did you have physical contact with your father during preadolescence? a) yes b) no

69. If yes, contact included:

    a. hugging and kissing
    b. lap sitting and holding
    c. wrestling and jostling
    d. spanking

    e. other physical punishment
    f. other

70. Did you have physical contact with your father during adolescence? a) yes b) no

71. If yes, contact included

    a. hugging and kissing
    b. holding (embracing)
    c. wrestling and jostling
    d. contact sports
    e. spanking
    f. other physical punishment
    g. other

72. Did you have physical contact with your mother during preadolescence? a) yes b) no

73. If yes, contact included:

    a. hugging and kissing
    b. lap sitting and holding
    c. wrestling and jostling
    d. spanking
    e. other physical punishment
    f. other

74. Did you have physical contact with your mother during adolescence? a) yes b) no

75. If yes, contact included:

    a. hugging and kissing
    b. holding (embracing)
    c. wrestling and jostling
    d. contact sports
    e. spanking
    f. other physical punishment
    g. other

76. Did you have childhood hobbies? a) yes b) no

77. If yes, what hobbies? _____

78. Did you have hobbies as an adolescent? a) yes b) no

79. If yes, what hobbies? _____

80. As a preadolescent did you participate in sports? a) yes b) no

81. If yes, which category?

    a. team sports contact

   b. individual sports contact
   c. team sports noncontact
   d. individual sports noncontact

82. As an adolescent did you participate in sports? a) yes b) no

83. If yes, which category?

   a. team sports contact
   b. individual sports contact
   c. team sports noncontact
   d. individual sports noncontact

84. Describe your academic performance in elementary school:

   a. below average
   b. average
   c. above average
   d. outstanding

85. Describe your academic performance in high school:

   a. below average
   b. average
   c. above average
   d. outstanding

86. Describe your academic performance in college or university:

   a. below average
   b. average
   c. above average
   d. outstanding

87. Describe your academic performance in graduate school:

   a. below average
   b. average
   c. above average
   d. outstanding

88. Were you a leader in school? a) yes b) no

89. If yes, when in school?

   a. elementary
   b. high school
   c. college
   d. graduate school

90. Generally speaking, in high school or college what type of activity were you engaged in?

   a. political

b. academic
c. social
d. athletic
e. other
f. none

91. Were you a follower in school? a) yes b) no
92. If yes, when in school?

a. elementary school
b. high school
c. college
d. graduate school

93. Have you had any encounters with the law as a consequence of your sexual behavior? a) yes b) no
94. If yes, what type?

a. arrest
b. citation
c. verbal warning
d. other

95. Were you ever convicted? a) yes b) no
96. For what? _____
97. Have you had any chronic medical illness (e.g., diabetes, cancer, heart disease)? a) yes b) no
98. If yes, what? _____t_____
99. Do you have any current medical problems? a) yes b) no
100. If yes, what? _____t_____
101. To which of the following have you come out?

a. parents
b. family other than parents
c. employer
d. straight friends
e. work colleagues
f. none of the above

102. How do you spend your leisure time at home? Choose three that consume the major part of that time.

a. reading
b. watching television
c. entertaining
d. doing hobbies
e. gardening
f. working on home
g. having sex
h. lounging
i. cooking
j. participating in athletics

103. How do you spend your leisure time away from home? Choose three that consume the major part of that time.

    a. entertainment such as movies, plays, museums, etc.
    b. sports or other physical activities such as jogging, surfing, bicycle riding, etc.
    c. going to bars, discos
    d. going to baths and cruising (parks, beaches, etc.)
    e. going to the beach
    f. traveling
    g. visiting friends
    h. having dinner parties, brunches, etc.

104. Do you own a pet? a) yes b) no

105. If yes, what kind?

    a. dog
    b. cat
    c. bird
    d. other

106. Which of the following have you been to (check all of the appropriate ones):

    a. gay bars or discos
    b. gay baths
    c. gay cruising areas
    d. gay organizations
    e. gay bookstores
    f. gay beaches
    g. gay dances
    h. gay movies
    i. gay church or related place
    j. none of the above

107. Which of the following have you been to more than twice in the last two months?

    a. gay bar or disco
    b. gay bath
    c. gay cruising areas
    d. gay organizations
    e. gay bookstore
    f. gay beach
    g. gay dance
    h. gay movies
    i. gay church or other related place

108. I consider myself to be politically:

    a. conservative
    b. moderate
    c. liberal
    d. radical
    e. apathetic

109. Prior to your present relationship, had you lived together in a relationship with a partner of the opposite sex? a) yes b) no

110. If yes, with how many partners? _____

111. If yes, for how long with each? _____

112. Prior to your present relationship, had you lived together in a relationship with a partner of the same sex? a) yes b) no

113. If yes, with how many partners? _____

114. If yes, for how long with each? _____

115. What is the term you use to describe your current primary relationship?

    a. lover
    b. partner
    c. companion
    d. spouse
    e. roommate
    f. friend
    g. other

116. Do you share the same bedroom and bed with your partner? a) yes b) no

117. Do you share the same bedroom with your partner but have separate beds? a) yes b) no

118. Do you sleep in separate rooms? a) yes b) no

119. Do you masturbate? a) yes b) no

120. If yes, estimate frequency of masturbation per week. _____

121. Choose one of the following responses that best suits you:

    a. I do not have sex with anyone other than my partner
    b. I have a few scarce sexual encounters with others but they do not threaten my relationship
    c. I may sleep with anyone I choose and may establish an affair simultaneously
    d. I may have many sexual encounters with others, but they do not threaten me or my relationship

122. If you consider your relationship monandrous, how do you deal with your and your partner's outside sexual contacts?

    a. talk about them
    b. don't talk about them
    c. have hurt feelings
    d. become angry
    e. other _____

123. Estimate the number of outside sexual encounters in the past year.

    a. male _____
    b. female _____

124. Have you and your partner shared sex with one or more other individuals (threesome, etc.)? a) yes b) no

125. If yes, how many times? _____

126. With a person of the same sex, or of the opposite sex?

    a. same
    b. opposite

127. Do you spend:

    a. almost all of your free time socializing with gay people
    b. most of your free time socializing with gay people
    c. half of your free time socializing with gay people and half with straight people
    d. more than half of your free time socializing with straight people

128. Do you spend:

    a. almost all your free time with your lover
    b. most of your free time with your lover
    c. half of your free time with your lover and half independently
    d. over half of your free time independently

129. On the Kinsey scale how would you rate yourself?

    a. Fantasy 0 1 2 3 4 5 6
    b. Actually 0 1 2 3 4 5 6

130. Age of partner: _____

131. Length of relationship _____

132. How did you meet?

    a. through mutual friends
    b. at a gay meeting place
    c. it was love at first sight
    d. you approached him or he approached you
    e. other

133. Where did you meet?

    a. at a bath, bar, or disco
    b. at a friend's house
    c. at a party
    d. through work or school
    e. at a tearoom or cruising area
    f. other

134. How long was it before you and your partner were aware of the beginning of a relationship? _____

135. Did you have sexual contact with your partner at the beginning of the relationship? a) yes b) no

136. Was the attraction to your partner primarily sexual? a) yes b) no

137. How long after you met did you start living together? _____

138. How are the everyday chores of living handled between you?

    a. they are shared equally
    b. each has specific responsibility
    c. they are negotiated
    d. they are disputed
    e. all is done by one person

139. How do you and your partner communicate your differences, especially when something he does bugs you?

    a. tell him immediately
    b. wait to discuss it later
    c. give nonverbal clues
    d. withdraw and become silent
    e. other

140. How many social friends are not "yours" or "his," but are friends that you have in common?

    a. almost all
    b. over half
    c. about half
    d. under half
    e. few or none

141. My social life:

    a. is totally independent of my partner
    b. includes my lover sometimes
    c. includes my lover usually
    d. almost always includes my lover

142. My political attitudes and my lover's political attitudes may be called:
     a. extremely different
     b. mostly different
     c. mixed
     d. rather similar
     e. mostly similar
     f. extremely similar

143. My hobbies and outside interests and my lover's may be called:
     a. extremely different
     b. mostly different
     c. mixed
     d. rather similar
     e. mostly similar
     f. extremely similar

144. Are you and/or your partner interested in the gay activist movement? a) yes b) no

145. If yes, to what extent?
     a. financial donations
     b. political action
     c. active participation in openly gay organization
     d. other

146. Do you regularly read a gay paper or magazine? a) yes b) no

147. If yes, which? _____

148. How are the household finances handled between you and your partner?
     a. all bills equally divided
     b. all bills paid by one person
     c. careful records maintained on all expenses
     d. other

149. Do you have joint bank accounts? a) yes b) no

150. Do you own property? a) yes b) no

151. If yes, is it owned jointly? a) yes b) no

152. Are household items owned and purchased jointly? a) yes b) no

153. Do you have a will? a) yes b) no

154. If yes, does it include your partner? a) yes b) no

155. Do you and your partner go on vacations together? a) yes b) no

156. At the beginning of your relationship, did you make a formal commitment to each other? a) yes b) no

157. If yes, which of the following comes closest to describing the commitment:
     a. verbal contract
     b. formal ceremony
     c. written agreement
     d. time-limited agreement

158. Later in your relationship did you make a commitment to each other? a) yes b) no

159. If yes, which of the following comes closest to describing the commitment:
     a. verbal contract (private)
     b. formal ceremony
     c. public contract (in presence of friends)

160. Do you feel there are romantic elements in your relationship? a) yes b) no

161. If yes, which of the following are included:
     a. surprise gift-giving
     b. candlelight dinner
     c. watching the sunset
     d. returns to old favorite places
     e. sharing a song
     f. other

162. I think:
     a. my relationship will last forever
     b. my relationship will last a very long time
     c. my relationship will last for a while
     d. gay relationships never last

163. Which of the following are the most common causes of friction:
     a. household chores
     b. finances
     c. friends
     d. outside relationships
     e. social life
     f. sexual differences
     g. role distinctions
     h. other

164. Is the sexual part of your relationship with your partner:
     a. always important
     b. sometimes important
     c. never important

165. Do you and your partner make long-range plans? a) yes b) no

166. If yes, do plans include (check all that are appropriate):

    a. purchasing things
    b. estate planning
    c. trips together
    d. retirement
    e. others _____

167. Have your and your partner ever been separated for more than one month? a) yes b) no

168. If yes, was the separation:

    a. planned
    b. a result of misunderstanding
    c. for business or family reasons
    d. other

169. Was the separation useful for your relationship? a) yes b) no

170. Have you ever been in a heterosexual marriage? a) yes b) no

171. If yes, for how long? _____ years

172. Do you have children: a) yes b) no

173. If, yes, how many male children? _____

174. If yes, how many female children? _____

175. Are your children aware of your sexual orientation? a) yes b) no

176. Over the past year, estimate the weekly sexual contact with your partner:

    a. none
    b. less than once a week
    c. one time weekly
    d. two to three times weekly
    e. more than four times weekly

177. Given a choice about sexual contact, would you prefer this frequency to:

    a. increase
    b. decrease
    c. remain the same

178. Since the beginning of your relationship, has the frequency of sexual contact:

    a. increased
    b. decreased
    c. remained the same

179. Since the beginning of your relationship has the quality of your sexual relationship:

    a. increased
    b. decreased
    c. remained the same

180. Rate the current quality of your sexual relationship with your partner.

    a. very satisfactory
    b. satisfactory
    c. not satisfactory
    d. very unsatisfactory

The following two questions should be answered using the list below by circling the appropriate number

a. mutual masturbation	1 2 3 4
b. masturbation together	1 2 3 4
c. body rubbing/friction	1 2 3 4
d. fellating	1 2 3 4
e. being fellated	1 2 3 4
f. mutual fellation (69)	1 2 3 4
g. rimming	1 2 3 4
h. being rimmed	1 2 3 4
i. anal intercourse (penetrating)	1 2 3 4
j. anal intercourse (being penetrated)	1 2 3 4
k. other (S&M, bondage, water sports, etc.)	1 2 3 4

181. Answering for yourself over the past year, which of the above sexual behaviors have you engaged in with your partner?

    1. more frequently
    2. less frequently
    3. occasionally
    4. never

182. Rate each according to your preference and fantasy about each.

    1. more frequently
    2. less frequently
    3. occasionally
    4. never

183. Are you currently or have you ever experienced a situational or permanent sexual dysfunction with your partner and/or others? a) yes b) no

184. If yes, which of the following dysfunctions:
   a. difficulty with erection
   b. ejaculating too rapidly
   c. difficulty with ejaculation
   d. lack of interest in sex
185. What percentage of the time do/did you have the problem?
   a. under 10%
   b. under 50%
   c. over 50%
   d. all the time

Additional Questions on Questionnaire

1. What is special about your relationship?
2. What are the things you like most about your partner?
3. What are the things you like least about your partner?
4. What kinds of things about your partner would you like to see him change?
5. What kinds of things do you think your partner likes most about you?
6. What kinds of things do you think your partner likes least about you?
7. What kinds of things would you like to change about yourself?
8. What are some examples of issues in the relationship that you are currently dealing with? (Give examples if pause or look of unclearness)
9. Describe how you both go about dealing with these issues.
10. How would you describe the quality of your relationship?
11. In what ways are you and your partner alike?
12. In what ways are you and your partner different?
13. Describe the ways in which you deal with conflict over issues.
14. Do you experience any difficulties with others as a result of your being in an ongoing homosexual relationship?
15. If so, from whom?
16. If so, what are the difficulties?
17. How do you and your partner deal with them?
18. What effects, if any, do they have on the relationship?

19. In what ways, if any, do you believe your relationship to be similar to a heterosexual relationship?

20. In what ways, if any, do you believe your relationship to be different from a heterosexual relationship?

21. What are the things most important to you in your relationship?

22. What do you think are the things most important to your partner in the relationship?

23. What are the things that are least important to you in the relationship?

24. What are the things that you think are least important to your partner in the relationship?

25. What plans, if any, in any area have you and your partner made for the future?

26. Describe your friends and friendships (gay/straight; men/women).

27. Do you experience any forms of influences outside the relationship that tend to lend support in maintaining the relationship?

28. If so, describe them and their effects.

29. Do you experience any forms of influences outside the relationship that tend to influence the dissolution of the relationship?

30. If so, describe them and their effects.

31. If you have children, do they know of your homosexuality and of your relationship?

32. If yes, describe the process and manner of your disclosure and their understanding.

33. To those people who know of your homosexuality, describe the process of your disclosure or their knowing, and also their understanding.

34. Who knows of your relationship with your partner and who doesn't?

35. In general, how do you go about deciding to whom to disclose your homosexuality?

36. Describe the importance of sexual expression as part of the relationship.

37. If sexual contacts outside the primary relationship are experienced, describe the ground rules/agreements/unspoken understandings with regard to:
    a. with whom
    b. when
    c. under what circumstances
    d. range of sexual activity
    e. communicated or not communicated back to partner
    f. if so, how and when

38. What influences, if any, do outside sexual contacts have on the primary relationship?

39. Describe any distinctions between more desirable and less desirable out side sexual contacts for yourself.

40. Describe distinctions, if any, between more and less acceptable outside sexual contacts of your partner.

41. What problems arise, if any, with outside sexual experiences?

42. If you have outside sexual contacts, describe the reasons for them.

43. If you have outside sexual contacts, describe any pattern, such as whom you seek out, where, with what frequency.

44. If you have outside sexual contacts, describe the degree of interpersonal involvement you have with those sex partners (e.g. anonymous in the baths, park, or sex in the context of an ongoing relationship.)

45. If your relationship is monandrous, how was that decision arrived at?

46. If the relationship is monandrous, do you have outside sexual contacts? If yes:
    • why?
    • under what circumstances?
    • describe the degree of interpersonal involvement
    • how is this communicated or not communicated back to partner?
    • what influences, if any, do outside sexual contacts have on the primary relationship?
    • what problems, if any, arise with outside sexual contacts?

47. If the answer to #46 is no, describe your satisfaction with the arrangement.

48. How are the following household chores accomplished?
    • housekeeping
    • cleaning
    • cooking
    • doing dishes
    • shopping
    • making repairs
    • bill-paying

49. Has it always been this way? If not, describe the changes.

50. Do you have household help?

51. How do your jobs affect the relationship? Differences/similarities, aids/interferences?

52. What are your common interests (e.g. hobbies, studies, friends, leisure)?

53. What are your different interests?

54. In what ways, if any, do these common and/or different interests affect your relationship?

55. How is money handled (e.g. all goes together, everything kept separate, etc.)?

56. How did this method of handling money evolve in the relationship?

57. What changes have you experienced in the relationship over time?

58. Do you have advice for other male homosexual couples?

59. In what way, if any, has gay liberation affected you and your partner and the relationship? Describe.

60. What might you have done differently in the relationship?

61. What plans, if any, do you have for retirement?

62. Is there much competition between you and your partner?

63. If yes, describe the type, and ways in which it manifests itself.

INDEX